Following her family split, Valerie McKee decided to pursue a dream of volunteering in a third world country. Once she took retirement from her prestigious job in a renowned public Cambridge school, she gained a place with Voluntary Services Overseas as a teaching advisor in northern Ethiopia.

This candid autobiography records the highs and the many lows of that extraordinary year, during which, she aimed not just to survive but to be an effective volunteer.

To my fabulous children, and all who have supported me, boosting my confidence to complete my one-year volunteering.

Valerie McKee

THIRTEEN MONTHS OF SUNSHINE

AUSTIN MACAULEY PUBLISHERS™

LONDON * CAMBRIDGE * NEW YORK * SHARJAH

A CIP catalogue record for this title is available from the British Library.

ISBN 9781398408470 (Paperback)
ISBN 9781398408487 (ePub e-book)

www.austinmacauley.com

First Published 2022
Austin Macauley Publishers Ltd®
1 Canada Square
Canary Wharf
London
E14 5AA

Many thanks to everyone at VSO, for their training and support, as well as the education offices I dealt with in the country, and the lovely Ethiopians I met along the way.

Introduction

Thirteen Months of Sunshine is a book based on the detailed diaries I kept while placed in northern Ethiopia by the Voluntary Service Overseas. My time there covered a year spanning 2012 and 2013. The Education Department where I was based really appreciates the support given by VSO. Ethiopians realise that in order to progress as a nation they need to educate their population, and developing a modern, national education system is a massive undertaking. Although VSO does an amazing job preparing volunteers for such work, in reality, I left England knowing very little about Ethiopia, so this is a record of much of my year of my learning and if I am honest, my survival!

First Month

Coffee ceremony with snacks & scattered herbs.

Homelife was shattered: my husband leaving us. I'm just another statistic I tell myself in the hope that I will feel better. In the end, I pack in my job as deputy headteacher of a thriving private school in Cambridge to follow my need to volunteer. To actually 'do' something. Voluntary Service Overseas has always been in my head; so, seizing the opportunity to try to gain a place on their training course and then be lucky enough to be employed in some new country as yet unknown to me... Well, here goes. And thus, my story really begins *before* I set out for Ethiopia.

After jumping over plenty of VSO hurdles, I was nearly there; my education experience and qualifications put me in a good position for placement. I'd had a pretty picture of the Thai-Burmese border in my head but that wasn't to happen; another volunteer wasn't needed there, and a definite 'no', I'd rather not work in Lagos, Nigeria. I will be travelling on my own and anyway I value my life! Two posts came up at either end of Ethiopia, one in the southern mountains near the difficult Kenyan border – plenty of uphill school visits and challenges; the other in the Tigray region just far enough from the dangers of war-torn Eritrea. Then 'yes', I was accepted in the Tigray Mekelle Education Office as a teacher support trainer.

My divorce process already begun; the family home placed in the hands of an agent for rent and my things packed into storage. It has been a tremendous hassle, not least sorting my finances to cover regular needs in a distant land, but to stash a little away to have something extra when I am out there as the wages for an Ethiopian teacher aren't great. I'm not normally a teary person but there have been times! But eventually, all valuables and jewellery are locked away for safekeeping. I'm wearing no rings or my usual necklaces and silver earrings, just basic studs and a cheap watch – even that could be valuable to an African who has nothing I suppose.

Finally, I'm ready to go.

My predictable life into which I usually cram 101 per cent has to go otherwise I risk going insane pretty quickly. I don't want to just survive but get what I can out of the next year, and I do appreciate I simply have to keep my wits about me. I know very little about either being a volunteer or about Ethiopia! So, I wave goodbye to my friends and children and fly from England's green and pleasant land, realising I have to be alert for absolutely anything my new life can chuck at me.

Addis Ababa, February 2012

On the flights, the travelling group of volunteers slowly became apparent; perhaps we recognised it in ourselves – that back-packer style as we take matching connecting flights via Frankfurt.

As we are beginning to hook up, the group compare notes on such things as baggage allowances; be impressed, I have a mere 25 kg for my whole year! Included in that are a few little gifts to open later and a couple of essentials like my special comforting 'Mrs Beeton' pottery mug from home. With about 15 new volunteers landing here on the starter 10 days, there seems quite a variety to mix and chat with.

VSO has linked our bunch together with either medical or educational projects and after these introduction days each of us will be sent all over this country; none together necessarily but many of us will meet up with other volunteers, which should be good from a supportive point of view at least. Sharing a tiny room with a young midwife means we're pretty organised with our suitcases and various bits brought for survival, but it is fun. There are showers and a loo, but the water supply is intermittent, so it's a bit of a lottery. I learn quickly that the jug for toilet flushing will be a regular feature. Actually, getting to sleep in our little beds is interesting as the crickets are *extra* loud but also the dog population comes alive in the cooler evenings. Outside the compound appears to be a constant mass dogfight going on. (Goodness I hope it isn't widespread!) I don't think they are strays necessarily – I have noticed sleeping dogs by shops or houses just lazing about during the day: Heinz mix, 'nothing-breeds'… I would never go near one. They seem only interested in the latest poor bitch on heat anyway and then they trot about purposefully in local gangs.

Everything so far here has been an event and all good learning curves. I don't want to brag but the weather is good, clear and hot but fresh and breezy by day, cooler by night. Addis Ababa is 2,400 metres above sea level, apparently making it the third-highest capital in the world. There appear to be few creepy insects here with it being so high which is handy, there is no need to use mosquito mixtures just yet which is such a relief, plus we don't have to start our malarial medication…no doubt that could change when I move on. However, I have seen one lizard, a vulture and lots of different small birds so far; they all look so exotic to me. Beautiful metallic shiny African starlings are really dazzling.

But this dust isn't good, something to get used to I suppose, and the poverty, which is obvious. Urban areas, so far, seem a mix of small corrugated slum shacks squashed together, building sites where 60s style blocks of flats are going up, or just a few very modern twentieth-century glass-fronted buildings dotted about between open dry spaces. The heavily gated barbed-wired compound surrounds the functional brick building where I am at the moment and is owned by the Red Cross – the Ethiopian VSO office have hired the place for our induction – barbed wire is widespread. Most residents employ guards to patrol the compounds and buildings for unwanted animals and burglars or worse. I may have to have one myself when I get posted, which will be weird having a servant.

Roads are a combination of dust and patchy tarmac. There *are* cars and in Addis, these range from smart up-market jeeps only a foreigner could afford to the battered makes from long ago. Taxis here are old bangers smartened up regularly by the standard blue paint over the bumps and rust and the buses look similar: blue vans fitted with bench seats but called 'line' taxis. These form queues at key points in the city and have a route – or line – which they follow. Already we have been told they are useful but to be wary: never to go in one unless we know the price, have the right money ready so there's no debate or sign of a hidden purse, and then only get on if it has other passengers of a mixed type in there already to avoid kidnap. Great.

Abyssinia is the old name for Ethiopia, often mentioned in the Bible. Addis Ababa ('New Flower') hasn't been the modern capital very long but in 1887, Emperor Menelik II decided to connect up the states and move his capital from further north to this more central location. And it is still growing. Houses which are single-roomed hovels generally made with tin or stone and topped by its corrugated tin roof fight for space between high rise places, some of which are hotels while others are proud offices. Whatever the poverty here, there seems no shortage of satellite dishes on every roof space! There are a few shopping malls, if you can call them that, but they are not big, only having small units in them targeted really for the tourists who I feel Ethiopians think 'need' these spaces. A security guard bag search and frisk on entry to any of these collections of stores is quite the norm. There are plenty of small one-roomed shops lining the dusty streets. Occasionally, these can be entered for browsing and buying, but more often the buildings themselves are for storage or a bed, and the items for sale – particularly the food stuff – are arranged on a sackcloth on the street. The clothes shops look funny with their western worn-out mannequins out the front – white-skinned, very dated – usually tied by the neck to the shack behind. I've seen sports gear, especially shorts displayed on half bodies swinging in the wind over the pathway beneath! Whichever style or product on sale, shops are absolutely rammed or piled high with stuff. I wouldn't say these people have much to spend and proprietors can sit on their tiny stools or a rock outside for ages just meeting people and calling out, occasionally flicking a duster over their stock. Some are open seven days a week but others actually close on Sundays and definitely for religious holidays, as the orthodox Christian faith here is really important. With a constant stream of dusty feet, the shoe-shine boys do a fair trade for those who have shoes. Perched high on their raised seating, and the boy squatting in front working so hard by using minimal polish and plenty of elbow-grease.

Ethiopian times and clocks are an experience! Days run from dawn till dusk then dusk till dawn, simple! Therefore, the Ethiopian times are 0 to 12 in daylight (our 6 am till 6 pm) and again 0 to 12 for those hours of darkness, (6 pm till 6 am) Obvious! Another snag is that there are no clocks around, no calendars, no diaries. I did see the odd clock all glittery and gold as an ornament in churches, but without batteries, just pretty things on display. Somehow planes seem to run perfectly and other time-led operations generally use daylight clues but I have learned to make absolutely sure when booking appointments which clock they are using: "Is that *my time* or *Ethio* time?" They usually enjoy the joke.

I haven't found out yet why but their millennium is seven years, three months behind ours so the dates for my calendar are 'wrong'.

Adding to all this, their calendar is wildly different; being spread over thirteen months beginning the new year in what is actually my September. This is after the long Ethiopian rains when their spring returns again and they kick it all off with great New Year celebrations. That starts off the first set of months each having a neat 30 days, then the leftover few days are put into the thirteenth short month at the year's end.

As with much of Africa, there were many tribes which were not always fixed in one place: movement with livestock, weather or geographical problems was constant. Tribes had their own languages and customs so Ethiopia has quite a number of main languages, Amharic being the one spoken in this Addis area. It isn't easy to learn their guttural sounds – we are having intensive lessons regularly – I suppose I will pick it up when I have to use it more. The beautiful unique Ge'ez script is also another learning curve but luckily out and about they are keen to use English. These people want to make progress in the modern world.

We really are a mixed bunch with ages that range from probably mid-20s to 60+ destined to go to all corners of Ethiopia. As the days go by, we need to talk together to discuss personal issues and we learn more about each other. I know I will miss my family: Ruth and Ella in England I am hoping to meet somehow over the year but Tom in Canada… I will have to rely on Skype. I bought a new laptop for this trip, loaded with the latest programs but I made it quite clear to the poor guy in the store in Cambridge that if anything went wrong, I would simply cry buckets and possibly chuck in my trip! There is a family with two young children coming over relying on their mother's doctoring expertise – gosh, I hope they stay fit and well; another young woman is a librarian and is a returning volunteer. One very lively loud girl in her early twenties is from America. Although she has Ethiopian parents, she wears the latest western clothes and makeup, and is preparing to work on the Addis Empowerment of Women programme. She is really funny, used to the very hot chilli or garlic extras regularly on offer with our food and it is good to hear tips from her, but even she is not keen to go out in the dusk or evening. Another completely different older volunteer is intending to share a flat with her and clearly already in this introductory phase, they don't get on. Doesn't bode well.

The Entoto hills surround the city; we had an organised trip up there. As with much of Africa, it suffers from deforestation, so eucalyptus trees were introduced to make impressive forests up in the mountains, supplying wood for building and fuel amongst other things. It was great to see the mountains. However, the church on the top with its spooky overgrown graveyard wasn't so good; we weren't able to go into the church and were really hassled by children and beggars. Some graves had rough wooden or metal crosses, some were covered in a lot of barbed wire, others piled with massive rocks to avoid them being dug up by anything after dark, plus there was a lot of rubbish around – rags, toilet paper, yuck! I will remember that huge vulture sat on one grave making a weird honking sound. Most odd.

On the return trip, we stopped at the National Museum. I have my ticket which reads: 'Federal Democratic Republic of Ethiopia Ministry of Culture and Tourism Authority for Research & Conservation of Cultural Heritage'. We had to wait for ages for it to open on our request then it cost just about 50p each to get in. I was keen to see the ancient 'Lucy' skeleton. I had heard the archaeologist discovered the relic – aged about 3.5 million years old, marking one of the earliest humanoid finds in Danakil in the North East of the country – about the time of the popular Beatles song 'Lucy in the Sky with Diamonds', hence he named this oldest ever female skeleton 'Lucy'. How stunning this trip should have been for me but anyone really could have handled those prehistoric bones lying unceremoniously on their rough table display, and I would have preferred not to have had the annoying kid leaping about wanting to sell us information. It was a bit of a let-down, to say the least, and I should have been amazed but was more bothered by the understatement and sadness of the exhibits. They have mind-blowing artefacts here but perhaps Ethiopia has more important priorities than ancient dead relics.

The VSO organisers themselves are very worried about letting us loose in town as of yet, knowing the dangers and culture 'stuff', they think we wouldn't be able to cope I suppose. There are a few large markets but those hold way too many hazards for us naïve visitors I think. One here is the largest open-air in Africa, the Merkato, covering a few square miles so I would need a map for it no matter where it was in the world.

Coffee: it was invented here!

Apparently, an Ethiopian farmer accidentally discovered that roasted coffee beans, indigenous to East Africa, made an excellent drink when ground into boiling water. After that, coffee plants were grown a bit further over in the Middle East, followed by the more distant lands around the globe, and the rest is history. I had noticed 'Kaldis' coffee shops with their logo so like 'Starbucks' in Addis… I wonder who thought of the symbol first? Anyway, Ethiopians don't really know instant coffee at all. Coffee has a ceremony of its own and we were to learn this at the Red Cross. It begins with fresh green beans roasted over the charcoal fire which are smelled by the gathered guests in turn before the beans are taken away to be ground in a pestle and mortar. A small clay spouted jug designed for the purpose holds the grounds and boiling water over the fire for the first 'stewing'. That first shared pot, poured into (thankfully) tiny china bowls or cups, is incredibly strong. There are nibbles offered alongside, usually of fresh cooked popcorn and pieces of bread or fruit. The clay jug is topped up and boiled repeatedly so that traditionally the guests should enjoy three cups of strong coffee; by the end, you are well wired and heady, believe me!

Another ongoing learning thing for me is Ethiopian music. It really is unique and not what I would call 'African'. There are modern artists who play in an Ethio jazzy style – Teddy Afro is their favourite. Constant background rhythms of beating drums, flutes, strange twangy individual instruments combine to make their music are around everywhere, especially on their TV programmes. Talking of TVs, they tend to have a huge old fashioned boxy one in offices, shops – everywhere really – running constant news on a loop or dancing with a desert or countryside backdrop. They will be covered by a cloth because of the dust problem and most huts have a receiver disc somewhere on the tin roof. It all looks so bizarre. In fact, if you don't have a TV, you are not considered up to date! Dancing in Ethiopia is another different thing too. Further south there is the jumping dance element which I have seen before by neighbouring Kenyans but everywhere here the shoulder nudging with the jumping is extremely important. Some of this shoulder touching could be called 'bashing' as it is quite rough! On one cultural evening at the Red Cross, we had lessons in dancing. We all found it hard to coordinate the elements but it was energetic, exhausting and pretty aggressive actually. The manic laugh that goes with it was through pain and effort on our part.

I have met the British Ambassador! As is the usual practice, we were invited to a 'tasty nibbles and pat-on-the-back' sort of do at the British Embassy which was fun. Set within well-guarded walls and barriers, the building stood out as very British; shutters, old colonial style, and inside, heavy furniture, china and for a change, a posh, 'normal' functioning loo! Everyone is keen for us all to be happy and safe and the VSO are held in high regard for all their hard work in the country. I made sure I talked to as many different new people as possible including the ambassador and his wife, there is such a lot I really don't know (plus it made me wonder how people get jobs like that – who-knows-who network I suppose, because I felt there is a lot they do not know either). The hardened guests in our group made sure they ate and drank their fill; I haven't got to that stage yet but no doubt it will come over me after a time of abstinence. On the way back we stopped at the edge of a market to buy traditional scarves with our female office ladies, although men do wear these too. They helped us barter for lovely large twinkly Addis woven scarves which can be worn around the waist as a belt, loosely around the neck, over the head in the dust and at special times, or by women and girls to tie a baby high on the back…very useful things.

The food here is mixed and not all hot curry flavours: some meat, some fish and lots of vegetable dishes. The fruit is lovely and I enjoy oranges, mangoes and melons. I am definitely not eating salads yet until I know I have washed *my* leaves in safe water. The water is on and off which isn't great but unusually for this country, bottled water is available for teeth brushing so that's okay. Amongst other lessons, we have had water filter lessons. The containers we are given are Indian apparently and work on the rock filtration method. A large steel urn sits over another with the rocks (the size of a large church candle) fixed in the middle. Water already boiled for a good three minutes fills the top drum and it very slowly (a few hours) filters through to the lower tank with its tap. The whole contraption has to sit on a chair or stool so the tap can be used underneath. I am struggling to keep well at the moment so feel a bit limited with pure clean water and food and trying to keep hands spotless.

Internet connections are all owned by this (nervous-of-new-technology) government. They're still debating if Skype is a communist undercover system that should be banned, but so far, they've not decided. Result: I won a basic Nokia phone in a raffle from a previous volunteer so all I have to do is register it. The others have to go and buy an Ethiopian phone and charger. Once you have bought your computer dongle from a government-approved shop or market stall in Addis Ababa (we had to be accompanied as still too naïve to venture out alone), we all had to be taken to the head offices to sit about for half a day in queues with our ID pictures, then complete duplicate forms for computer access numbers.

Queues here are orderly in offices. There are usually rows of chairs or benches (as they all feel they should always sit) so it is a regular shifting of position from seat to seat then finally to the front desk where the methodical civil servant does his methodical job. After that is another office, complete with the regulation frisk and bomb detector swipe on entry for firearms as we wait again in order to hand over our ID pictures and forms. But signing up for the dongle for laptops? Not the right office: the correct one is two miles, 'over there'. Another dodgy line taxi again, more waiting shuffling forwards in long queues of very patient people to triple-sign for that. It's all very tedious but part of the learning curve as we wind down from the manic London life we may be used to I suppose. There is a guy in the Red Cross set up who fixes it all onto our laptops and mine seemed to be sorted pretty quickly, phew.

Emails are coming through at odd times. The storage of my stuff at home and the rental side don't seem problematic, thank goodness. But my family, who already think I am bonkers, have not been able to get through until now so they are pretty worried, and besides, I just need to make contact for my own sanity too. There is a computer room and today I amazingly found the time, the access and the connection to actually Skype Tom. I was so happy, I can't describe it.

But now I am properly ill. My medic roommate, who has been to Africa before and is pretty clued up, but even she arrived with a sickness while others here have gone down with something too, so it was only a matter of time before I had it…bugger. We have been drilled to wash hands and disinfect always and I do. There is a salad on offer at times but no, we should avoid that unless we washed it ourselves correctly. I don't eat fruit skins; I avoid additional chillies which are regularly on offer besides all pretty well-spiced dishes. The omelettes have to be rubber-hard and eggs solid boiled, no soft-boiled eggs loaded with bugs for a year: okay. I *am* doing all of these things. There is a lot to do and remember and I desperately don't want to be ill so struggle on and collapse in the evenings. I wasn't too bothered about missing the cultural evening – dancing and spicy traditional food – just not well enough, but then I missed a shopping trip for essential supplies and had to ask another to get my bedsheets for me. Double bugger: the ones they bought for me were nasty static nylon and defiantly not my choice!

The volunteer I am to work with in Mekelle will be somewhere in Addis for meetings tomorrow apparently and my Programme Manager was giving a lecture today elsewhere so nobody has come here to talk directly to me about my placement. I watch and keep my fingers crossed while the rest have been teamed up to meet and debrief. Doesn't fill me with confidence but they have reasons I'm telling myself. I think I will be flown up to my placement on Sunday. It is getting very close; I am beginning to feel nervous again.

To date, we have been carted about in accompanied small groups and have been gently taught about our work, how to live and keep healthy, other safety issues, plus the back-up plans in case of a coup or similar. Women do not go out after dark – 6.45 at the latest – and anyway, in the day, stick with a group to be safe. While on one outing some kid nearly nicked my bag; it is always strapped to my front, well zipped up. He was trying to sell me a packet of tissues from his tray with one hand, whilst this artful dodger used his other to frisk my bag. Have to admire the skill really!

The gender talks are interesting but logic to me. The main gift in our rooms and at tables seem to be condoms, since HIV aids is rife (as I expected), and everywhere there are adverts for condoms and safe sex. Women appear 'invisible', voiceless, quiet here, and for me basically, I have to be firm when someone makes an advance on me, or if a friend is *too* friendly, but I do realise I have to be a hermit after dark. Arranged marriages from birth are normal, brides are such young children.

Saturday, 11th February

It's my birthday! I brought a couple of things from Ruth and Ella to open today which made me 'sad-happy'. I wish I felt better: exhausted, struggling around, taking part in talks and lectures, water supply on/off in turns and getting used to different foods. Today we had language sessions with a city scavenger hunt thrown in. All had shawls at the ready to use for masks or a headcover for the hot dusty city. Ruth managed to ring me on my new phone while Dan was having his shoes polished, so I had a proper chat which was great. Back at the Red Cross, they were really sweet and had organised a cake for me all big and expensive, loaded with buttery cream, white chocolate and some strawberries. I did make an effort to show enjoyment but it was a shame my stomach wouldn't let me eat much of it.

Now, my pans and cutlery are all bought – some by myself, others by another volunteer following my requests as I am too ill to move now but I am looking forward to cooking for myself. In Addis, we are given an extra trunk – it's a cardboard coffin-sized box – for transporting all the additional things: water filter system, the kerosene cooker, my attractive flowery nylon sheets, fluorescent green loo brush!!! On arrival in Mekelle, I will buy a PO box and open a bank account for my meagre wage too. I should be well set up in no time.

Sunday, 12th February

Bye to the Red Cross!

For some reason, I am one of the last to be moved to my placement and I have to stay in a hotel for an extra few days. I can't complain plus learning to be patient is important here. The hotel is a little way down a dirt track but off a nice enough main road with cafes, and the area is fairly clean. Here they are looking at me as if I am an alien, and clearly didn't believe me when I said I have no laptop to hand over to the receptionist for 'safekeeping'! I am locking my suitcase and have my padlock I am using on a cupboard in the room so I will just have to hope. The big box of household things is being stored at the VSO office – perhaps I should have put more in that…not sure. Another volunteer forgot to lock her stuff and lots had disappeared. I haven't anything I would call valuable apart from the laptop, but to people who literally have nothing, absolutely anything is worth nicking. This hotel is pretty busy with evening revellers…

I'm meeting a volunteer working near here at about four o'clock to have what will be a quick tea along the main road and getting back well before dark to hole up and read/write/rest up. It's all a bit boring now. I want to get going.

Wednesday, 15th February

The stomach bug has nearly run its course. Papaya juice is supposed to help so I have been trying that. Yesterday's midnight tummy gurgling after my 'treat', chewy steak sandwich, kept me well awake, so I'd heard the late hotel revellers stumbling back after two to their room opposite, clearly having a row – I wouldn't mind so much but I can't translate what they were shouting about. (Still not sure if this is really a brothel.)

Today, managed banana and bread, was picked up with my crazy local baggage allowance box by the VSO driver for the airport and dropped off just through the car park gate pretty much on time, which is amazing for around here. Next bit was comedy. The regulation VSO massive packing box just about sat on the trolley sideways, it swung up the slope to departure entrance nearly wiping out others on the path, but refused to go through the doors. Nobody helped. There was a lot of staring at this struggling foolish forengi. I figured if I undid the bolted door, it would fit. I have never seen someone move so fast. The angry uniformed conveyor-belt woman jumped into action and was furious with me for unlocking the extra door, yelling in Amharic, but it was pretty plain what she was on about. I pretended not to understand – 'forengi' and all that. She was not amused, probably as I was also pretending not to understand but was being super-nice. She gave me a hard time checking in at every point after that. Grrr.

Finally, I got rid of all baggage, always moved along by security guys indicating with rifles through various scanners (shoes and belts on-off-on-off…but you just don't question it…) to go as directed to Gate 9 per the ticket and TV. Silly me. I thought it looked a bit abandoned – Gate 11 as I guessed, of course! Eventually, departure was prompt as the plane was full, why wait?

It wasn't significantly hotter but was SO windy at Mekelle. Not sure what might be different, planes and airports are the same, right? 'Baggage collection at carousel 1' – there is only one. Through the Perspex doors, I could see dotted family members and thankfully, the current mentor VSO and her husband, Barbara and John, on hand to pick me up. I was whisked to a standard battered blue taxi; the fee was negotiated and they offloaded me at the flat, taking a picture of me with my luggage on arrival to record this historical moment.

Finally, a foot-note:

Mekelle, *or Mekele, Mek'ele, Makale* – **Tigray, Ethiopia**	
General:	
History:	Mekelle is one of the oldest towns in Ethiopia but came to the fore in the late 19th century when Emperor Yohannes IV made it Ethiopia's capital. It has expanded rapidly over the last 20 years and is now one of the second largest cities in Ethiopia, population approximately 200,000. It has a university spread over four campuses and is currently expanding to six, which makes Mekelle a lively and attractive town for the young. The people are friendly and welcoming.
Location: *geographical, environment, population size*	Mekelle is located in the Northern part of Ethiopia at approximately 2,100 meters above sea level. It is the capital of the Tigray region, the northern-most region of Ethiopia.
	It is 780 km north of Addis, reached by a tarmac road, which continues north to Adigrat, close to the Eritrean border. Mekelle is situated in a bowl surrounded by highlands. The highlands have sparse vegetation due to much tree clearance and low rainfall.
	It is bounded to the north by Eritrea, to the west, Sudan and to the east and south by the Afar & Amhara regions of Ethiopia. It covers a little more than 80,000 square kilometres of mostly highland terrain between 1500-2000 metres above sea level. In some places, the mountains reach about 3500 metres. The state has a population of around 3.5 million inhabitants

Climate and clothing	Mekelle has a very agreeable climate. Generally, the air is fresh and clear, and during the dry season, the sky is vividly blue and clear. There is no risk of malaria and for most of the year, there are very few mosquitoes. During the rainy season, there are more, but they are not malarial.
	Most days the maximum temperature is between 25°C–30°C, so it is hot around mid-day and early afternoon. From November to February it is slightly cooler, but rarely a maximum of less than 22°C. The evenings are cooler, and a light jumper would be needed, as is typical of high-altitude places, but it is not cold. In November – February, a warm fleece would be required if out after sunset, especially if windy, overnight temperature might drop to 10°C. The sun rises around 6.00 am throughout the year and sets around 6 pm.
	Mekelle has two rainy seasons – the main rains start around early July and continue until mid-September. During this time, it rains heavily on most days, but not all day and the temperatures are lower than other months. Travel on unmade roads is more difficult at this time, but movement around Mekelle is not affected. Small rains usually occur around late March-April. They are not too significant, short heavy showers and getting around the town is not affected by them. It can be windy at any time of the year, and in exposed areas, especially where there are earth roads can be dusty.
	Clothing for good days in a UK, spring, summer and autumn is suitable. An umbrella can be handy for protecting from the sun during the day and during the rainy season. Most local Ethiopians don't have a raincoat, but a thin rain jacket would be worth bringing. Women: Although it is warm, shorts and short skirts are not generally worn out, cut-offs covering the knee are fine. Shoulders are usually covered; anything goes for necklines. Men: again, shorts are not generally worn, but cut-offs are fine. Light trousers are a suitable weight during the day and jeans in the evening.
	Footwear – uneven pavements and un-made roads mean that robust footwear will survive better. Given the climate, sandals are fine throughout the year, but continuous wear of sandals can result in cracked skin, so some closed in footwear might be worth including.

Local/National language	The local language is Tigrinya and the National language is Amharic. Both are widely spoken and, along with English, taught from primary school. The dominant working language in offices depends on the number of people from outside Tigray working there. If the majority of people are local from Tigray, Tigrinya will dominate. If quite a number come from elsewhere in Ethiopia, Amharic will be more widely spoken.
Socio-economic groups:	
Ethnic groups	The vast majority of people in Mekelle come from Tigray. Within Tigray, there are areas with other ethnic groups which also have their own language e.g. Irob. Mekelle has a mixed Ethiopian population drawn by the universities.
Economic activities	The town itself has several industries including a large cement works and engineering works. Outside the town agriculture, cattle raising and grain production, is the occupation of the majority, and in the more remote areas, subsistence farming predominates. Further afield in Tigray there is some gold mining.
Religion	The different religions co-exist amicably in the region and religion is important to the people. Saints' days and religious festivals are significant in their culture. As well as numerous Ethiopian Orthodox Christian churches there are also several Islamic mosques, a Roman Catholic Church, an Ethiopian Evangelical Church of Mekaneyesus (Protestants) and other missionaries. Ethiopian Orthodox Christianity represents 95.6% of the people, Muslims 4%, Catholic 0.4% and Protestant 1%.

Second Month

'Arches' market Mekelle
with chicken seller: fresh = live tied on the pole,
So customers can check size & meatiness!

The guard let us into the condominium block where I am going to live after a debate. He is very serious; actually sleeps across the main block's doorway. My little flat is up the stairs on the third floor, and the taxi driver managed to carry the giant coffin of a box and my case up easily enough, keen to carry anything on their heads or shoulders it seems. Just forget the wheels on the suitcase, plus there appear to be no lifts anywhere so that's not an option. This new home that used to belong to Barbara and John, is very basic but just right for me. Handy too as they know where to find me. They showed me quirky stuff like the tiny shop opposite, temperamental TV, hoped I like the plastic table cloths and stretchy mad flowery suite covers disguising whatever nasty stuff was underneath and my massive blue plastic water storage barrel. Clearly saving water is key.

I feel lucky; Mekelle is such a nice place, it's cleaner for starters. There is one week before the actual work begins.

Wide streets are tree-lined and wide, (tall date palms or shorter flowering trees); some are tarmac and the smaller side streets are cobbled too. There are teams of ladies in overalls and wide-brimmed hats sweeping streets in parts of the town. Useful corrugated iron is still obvious here for roofs and walls but mainly around the building sites, as all the little tiny cottages I have seen so far are dry stone-walled and occasionally, wattle and daub. The wooden door frames tend to be brightly painted which adds character while the more modern buildings are pastel colours – no point in using Mediterranean white by the looks of it. Beggars and the poverty are evident here as well, but already I feel more confident away from the hustle of the capital Addis Ababa further south.

One of the few places that apparently is 'okay' to eat at is the Axum Hotel and is just down the road from my place. There is so much to learn. That is a particularly safe hotel and many tourists use it as well as business people. Mekelle is the stop-off before heading for the rock churches or the northern historic sites. This spot is airy and has a lovely shady courtyard garden with tables and waiter service. I didn't want to unpack but instead get some fresh air, so I coped with an egg sandwich before heading for the market area to buy basic food and essential water-conserving washing up bowl.

My flat actually has three rooms which are fine. In the lounge sits an empty shelving unit, a cronky corner table topped by the little TV, a long table with a couple of upright chairs which is great for working at but it does take up a bit of space. There are two two-seaters that I haven't investigated properly yet – crazy brown flowery nylon stretch covers over the lot I'm assured serve a purpose, plus there is a low bright Formica coffee table and a wardrobe. The bedroom has just enough space for a basic large classic wooden framed bed and mattress, a chair and a tiny bedside table. Next is a bathroom with its permanent drainy smell which I can't seem to get rid of, but it has a sink, mirror and shelf, and a hole in the floor for the shower drainage. Tacked on the end is the kitchen which is a corridor sort of thing with a high metal sink unit at one end complete with its cold tap beside that massive blue barrel for storing water. A small plastic cloth-covered table for my kettle and electric ring opposite a large wobbly cupboard take up part of the kitchen, my huge water filter unit is already set up on another chair. I am filled with dread by the paraffin burner which I would have to put together to use on the balcony so I haven't got that out of its box! One of my town shop purchases was a cockroach spray which I fired into the cupboard straight away. I have already caught a few of these small scuttling creatures chucking them over the tiny balcony – they are a smaller variety but still yucky and annoying.

I said 'balcony' although it is more like a shelf –it will be handy for my washing and discretely watching the world go by, which can be very interesting. I already feel I know the crippled old man with his two cows and goats who passes twice a day from his hovel to the hillside pasture and back again. There are horses and carts, donkeys and herds of cattle at different times mixed in with the occasional car or lorry. A bean tree grows near the road with lovely fist-sized vivid reddish tulip-shaped flowers attracting bees which is great to look down on over the balcony.

Those pigeons have to go. The kitchen window is propped open at a good nesting-angle which has accommodated a pair of cooing pigeons. Barbara and John had enjoyed their 'pets' but I'm not a fan. Apart from the noise, there are droppings below in the sink area which can't be healthy surely. I'm going to struggle with germ-avoidance as it is! Plus, I have the road below me. It is a busy route anyway with a bit of motorised traffic but cattle, donkeys, hand carts and the like, plus the dog fights and pack-rape out there kept me awake, so deadening that row by closing the window was a better idea.

Then I thought I had a *pair* of sheets. Wrong. I had only one in the set with a pillowcase for the solid VSO issue pillow, so had to make do with the spikey itchy wool regulation blanket which stayed on top some of the night.

2 am: I've literally ripped open the pillow and halved the contents of the solid sponge in there and folded it till I could sew it up so at least it is a bit better than it was. Will find the sewing kit in the morning.

Today I walked about loads. Haggled as best I could for two more sheets but the ones I managed to buy, I discovered, are worse static nylon and *so* thin, they'd better last me the year. Brown flowers, how lovely. I decided I would rotate the three sheets I now possess each time I wash and as I will be pummelling them myself in the sink, I think one each change will be enough! The main Commercial Bank is central so that's a bonus. Once I got into it after being frisked by a female guard who swopped my camera for a raffle ticket, I joined a massive queue that shuffled along the zig-zagged benches ever closer and managed to open a bank account. They appear to like us forengies as we are more likely to have actual money. Later, I emailed my bank details to VSO but since I couldn't find the post office, I'm unable to send my postal box address yet. Nobody does post or personal letters here really, therefore, there are no roadside post boxes anywhere or places to leave mail at houses so the only way to receive mail is to rent a tiny postal box at the city Office wherever that may be – hopefully tomorrow's discovery.

I'm walking everywhere as I don't yet trust the three-wheeler taxis – those little Indian style blue things are called a bajaj here, tuk-tuks in other countries. Some have doors, there are no lights, and if there are any mirrors, are they to aid the driver!

To calm my stomach, I cooked a plain rice-based tea with fresh local avocado and some nuts before watching a film in bed. (Made a mental note: must put some homey pictures up too.)

The language we were taught in Addis Ababa is NOT what they speak here. Ethiopia having a lot of tribal languages means the one spoken here it is Tigrinya, so I am having to rethink how I go about talking to locals. Luckily, they recognise that English is the tongue of the western world and they try so hard to learn so it is good that I could try to use both. So far, I can say a few basic foods and count to five (three is 'seleste', which I can remember easily as there were three holy spirits. And five is 'hamsa', for me it sounds like 'handful' = five!). Shops here are just random even tinier sheds or stone huts with a few things in so it isn't difficult at the moment and there is a lot of pointing, which is easy.

Electric bill confusion erupts between me and the guard. I had to pay the previous two months bills, then he gave me a bit back…derr! Our conversation was really stilted and lots of shrugging shoulders, looking at a grubby Tygringa notebook and basically going through my skimpy purse for some cash. Better check with Barbara how it all works.

All local shops and even street sellers have phone and laptop credit scratch strips. However, the Ethiopian system is loaded with viruses and everyone seems to want to get hold of modern technology – even though they don't know how to, or simply can't use it. This evening I had trouble with my firewall… I bought the strongest to be sure before I left the UK but it is struggling: I must be careful. Also, I'm hiding this laptop under my mattress at the moment when I go out and my squished empty-looking work bag shows it is clearly empty of anything worth stealing! I'm getting into the habit too of having my laptop propped up in bed with a film or reading a book in the evening which means I am earlier to bed. They stick to the dawn-till-dusk thing here, so if I have to be up about six o'clock, I had better get on with it. My bedroom arrangement has to change, I decided too. There is one plug point and that is on the wrong side and the door keeps bashing the side of the bed. Keen to get organised, I emptied the room, removed the mattress before struggling with the wobbly heavy wooden four-foot, locally made box frame, finally happy I could plonk the mattress back on top. I reposition a chair and small container table thing for the plug. Scrubbing the bit of the concrete floor now exposed to make the colour match and finally putting up a few photos of my children by the bed finished the job. It feels so much better.

On the Friday, as we walked around my local area, Barbara showed me the office where I will be based but today it is empty, all at a conference somewhere else apparently, all week.

Oh.

They never came to the programme office in Addis to meet me either as they were too busy. I will have to get used to sudden change of plans like this or things simply happening without warning. Anyway, at least it's quite easy to get to from mine, taking about ten minutes' walk through the town and down a dirt track. The office looks like a long scout hut with the usual tin roof and worn ill-fitting metal and glass windows. The wooden board 'Mekelle City Education' is swinging badly by a nail by the track – all faded, but at least there is a sign. Remembering landmarks as I go and having to learn where places are is novel as there are no maps and very few signs. Barbara did show me another good place for a coffee, which although the coffee is quite good, is recommended entirely around the toilet facilities. Basically, toilets with a door is a good call, then if there is a vat of water and jug for sluicing afterwards, it's a bonus. Loo roll is actually translated as 'soft' in Ethiopian, how handy is that word, but we have to always be prepared for none. They are, however, freaky about handwashing and there is always a jug of water for that.

It's dusty, breezy and hot. I am wearing my longish clothes (skirt or linen trousers to cover up) and my Addis long glittery scarf over my head or shoulders as I feel the need to keep the sun off or dust out of my face. At least this wind keeps the insect life down to the walking kind so I ought to be grateful, but my place has a serious cockroach problem. These smaller shiny brown speedy little buggers can easily dive into mine via the huge gap under the door along with all the sand and dust around, so it is a never-ending job of sweeping and mopping the concrete floor.

Another result: I booked my post box in the general town post office too. The box itself is literally about the size of a small shoebox. If anything large arrives, then I'm told a note is posted saying it is waiting for collection at the main desk. That costs more money and the rate seems pretty haphazard plus it entails queuing, waiting while the package is located which may be at yet another desk, signing in a couple of ledgers… Whatever it takes though, now I can keep in contact with the outside world and my children which will be great knowing the internet connection is all over the place and unreliable.

I have been introduced to two young doctor volunteers working at the Mekelle hospital: a paediatrician, Tsitsi and a gynaecologist, Sarah. I really don't envy them. Goodness, they have some harrowing stories about girls' medical and childbirth problems. Medic volunteers usually only stay for a few months – six is a very long time – mainly because of the horrendous stuff they have to deal with. Although of *African* heritage but not *Ethiopian,* Tsitsi has to manage a fair amount of racism directed at her and her own country which must add to her exhaustion.

The learning curve I am on is related to this country's place in the continent. Ethiopians seem very cautious of other nationalities and make assumptions about their character. Ethiopian's problems with Italy, in particular, came to a head when Britain, who didn't want the French to have a stronghold over any part of the River Nile, or Egypt to have the entire river, helped Ethiopia attack Sudan in the late eighteen hundreds. This was the beginning of the Ethio European struggles and as a consequence, Eritrea was portioned off, Ethiopia's Emperor Yohannas IV died in one of many battles with Italy and Ethiopia lost its coast and port on that side of the continent. Although Italy never conquered Ethiopia, there is still an influence that is evident in the style of these buildings, streets and some foods available here in the north. Some pizza restaurants are amazing in Ethiopia, and we all met in one early evening this month. It was literally hours before we were served. Unfortunately, Barbara and John arrived even later – just as the electricity went off. There was no other option prepared on the limited menu so they had to simply sit and watch us finish our food!

I don't know Barbara that well yet but she seems preoccupied. Their new house is gorgeous having a cool courtyard with mixed trees (including an avocado that actually drops fruit too often so a safety net hangs above the seating area to avoid getting 'bombed'). There are outside rooms and washrooms, plus a self-contained guard's accommodation (okay, still the tiniest room, but it is his).

However, now I understand.

They moved out of my flat without a problem and prepared to take on their new place. But the guard at their new place got murdered.

Actually strangled. There. On the day of the move.

It seems he was about thirty, was paid a good cash wage by the previous landlord and since he didn't need all that money he stashed it away in the hut somewhere, probably boasted about it, and got killed in the compound by his 'friend' he had let in that evening. Nobody is admitting to anything and nobody saw a thing. The murderer is keeping his head down and is still out there doing what he does in his normal life!

On reflection, my arrival adding to their work-load can't be helping.

They shared a bajaj taxi back via mine so I wouldn't be alone in one, and I scurried in to read, tucked up in bed but not a great sleep, too much buzzing around my head.

This weekend I took a different route to town, feeling good. Fewer shops this way, but so many busy pool rooms tucked behind any bars or shop fronts, all click-clacking in the back. It is lively today as well, lots of reasons to celebrate I am told, with a Government feast day and fasting starting tomorrow. Animals are being dragged or carried about, whiskey drinking and chewing chat is going on too outside these places. They simply pull up a rock to sit on when they run out of their tiny woven-leather-topped stools. An occasional goat is tied to a tree handily to take home after! Not a lot of cigarette smoking goes on – tobacco is a luxury that isn't generally affordable here.

Some foods are sold by travelling vendors. The shouting chicken sellers amaze me. Live birds (no fridges so freshly killed live meat is the best plan), about ten or so birds with their feet tied and the pole threaded through their claws to be carried across the sellers' shoulders. Customers come out to squeeze the bird's breasts to assess how meaty they are – not a lot of meat on anything in Ethiopia let alone chickens! The vendor lays them all on the path to extract the chosen one which is then carried upside down by its claws, still clucking down to a back yard somewhere until needed. Actually, I am finding chicken dishes are the most expensive and realise probably because they are so thin it takes a few to create a meal. Food shops vary but generally, they are in little huts or what is really the front room of a tiny house separated by a rough sacking curtain. Each has a particular special stock so it takes a while to buy things – like the eggs I get in one tiny hut which are sold singly into my hand. Others may sell drinks, piles of the latest harvested vegetables, great sacks of pulses on the floor, herbs and so on. I have tried some 'shiro' powder which is an Ethiopian mix of spices, and although I don't really do spicy foods at the best of times, shiro changes the flavour of the staple diet of lentils to add some variety. Other straight chillies are really powerful, Ethiopians love adding these to everything. The vendors' sacks bother me a bit as they are open to the dust or children's hands and are just topped up when new supplies arrive. I am already used to being a bit picky about where I get my pulses and then wash these thoroughly to remove the extra tiny stick or gravel!

'Supermarkets'? There must be a handful of these here; bigger rooms with shelves to hold a little more variety of stock in them. One actually has Dutch cheese triangles 'Vache Qui Rie', which I find I have to use as there is a lack of actual cheese. Here they believe the cow's milk is for feeding their young not for other things. Local honey is everywhere, often sold ladled into pots. I have discovered my egg lady has Ethiopian red wine for sale – which isn't *too* nasty, plus I can get local gin as well. I have a bottle of gin now to have with '7up' which I discovered in another shop too, but without a fridge; it's amazing what you can tolerate when needs must. Struggle on!

Late lunch at Barbara and John's. Their landlord Ephraim was there without his 'sick' wife (she's pregnant but they don't divulge that), but he had with him, his two boys – lovely but lively and cheeky. They got a proper clip round the ear for having a serious game with John's cigarette lighter! He is a great VSO supporter and knows the staff in my office as well which can be handy. My walk to and from theirs isn't fantastic as I have to go past the bus station which is a really sleazy area. The best plan for me is to scarf up, walk fast and keep looking ahead, ignoring all shouts and comments. In a place where nothing is wasted, there are stacks of vehicle parts around the bus station especially, and so many different tyres of all states of wear actually down to the fabric inside. I have to negotiate these rickety piles too as I dash past. Apparently, there is a sort of MOT on vehicles, but they sub in and out wheels and other parts so they look good for the test, then revert back to the worn afterwards. And worn is incredibly threadbare: various states of cloth with bits of rubber on them all fetch their price!

Back at mine: Wow, my shower is brilliant! It has a full force downward and if I remember to switch the electricity on half an hour before I need it – twice a day at the moment – I can have a lukewarm blast! I feel lucky I have more than a hose shower for my year here…the bathroom is one wet space so I'll have to keep everything on the stool outside the door. Sorted.

Skyped Ella!!! I couldn't see her but she could see me so I showed her my flat. Made my day!

Typical: there are two letters back at the now Addis office which I will have to wait for, either till someone goes down there or we get a visitor up to my region to bring them.

On returning to the flat, I find the cockroaches have had a fun time in my absence and I have to kill a few – carefully so not to crush and spread the eggs (!), but the one that got away in my bedroom stays on my mind.

I may be wishing I packed more books with this hermit existence.

The first working week when I actually got going went something like this:

Day 1

My excitement is huge. Work has been a long time coming.

I arrive at 8:15 to meet the guy I am working with. I am shown into an open plan office, a bit like an old schoolroom with large rectangular tables around the perimeter. One area is separated to take what looks like a larger boardroom table and chairs together with an important-looking table at one end, there the desk 'Office Manager' sign is in evidence. My chap, Gamunzudik, is smiley and tried to talk to me but is clearly busy and distracted. There are a couple of large old-style computers I can see under bits of cloth, a huge old-fashioned TV, the tables which seem to be allocated to each of the office personnel, and every available space is loaded with piles of paper documents – some tied in brown paper bundles with string, some wrapped in buff card folders. I am given a CD ROM to use and read from; I haven't taken my laptop in as after VSO induction I'm scared it will be either stolen from me as I walk or pick up the viruses which abound here. There isn't a computer to take a CD here apparently, so I sit somewhere in the middle staring about me for just over an hour, smiling if looked at. There are a couple of women at tables too, I think one is the secretary as she is spoken to often and seems to have a useable computer and printer. Metal chairs are placed at both sides of each table for visitors and meetings. The proverbial huge old TV is on by the main door showing Ethiopian dancing on a loop. I am finding that TVs in Ethiopia are status symbols. There's a telephone I notice too, locked to a stand, but most here seem to have their old-style mobiles. Bits of cloth or bags are draped hiding some tall things – I assume they may be old PCs and rusty filing cabinets. A lot of the metal-framed glass windows have tatty bits of fabric hanging somehow or very old tourist posters and the like taped to them – probably to keep out the sun as much as stop people looking in. Dust is inside as well as outside! Where there are windows or doors, they are standing open or don't close properly and it is so windy here dust is bound to happen.

Ethiopians have a gentle manner and all is quiet here but pleasant enough. Having made my excuses to leave for a break to whiz back to mine plus there isn't a toilet here for me, I returned to the office for another sitting around session. Next, I was introduced to the manager who is really pleased I am there – I think they need some magic wand or other, that will be interesting!

In between my office visits, I found tinned tuna in one shop which was a good surprise. I have figured that at the moment a tin of baked beans or this tuna is equal to a day's wage for me so it will be a treat but am loving all the fresh fruits and vegetables, which is just as well as I have to shop daily pretty much. Here there seems a fair variety – just have to be flexible and work around what has been brought into the market that day.

And what I miss? Well, soft boiled eggs, (they have to be cooked thoroughly here as the chickens are not inoculated or tested for anything!); oh, and being able to go out for a stroll in an evening just for pleasure.

Back in my new 'home', I read up on anything educational I could get hold of at the office, but not much is around to enlighten me.

Result: I have invented a method of cooking Welsh Cakes in a flat pan on the electric ring. Although they got a bit burnt, I feel so proud! Hopefully, I will get better at this style of cooking. The paraffin stove remains firmly in its box but Barbara has given me their extra electric ring so now I have two…luxury.

Day 2

Curriculum guy, Ato (Mr) Mulu, also thinks I am the magical replacement for the previous volunteer. Apparently, I have my own office which is in the process of being cleaned and not ready yet – it was carefully locked up.

Mental note: I must be more appreciative tomorrow. Sat about half-hour then Ato Mulu took me around the corner to see two schools: Primary = Elementary,

Secondary = Preparatory. I try to look calm but am really excited. All are very friendly, spoke good English and I booked to see a couple of lessons in English. I will make observation sheets ready so I have a focus which will be hard as it is likely to be very different. Since they believe English is *the* key to success in their rise in the western world, children are taught it from five years of age. Mulu took me to a hidden local café for a lemon juice tea – yum. He is direct and open. Apart from him quizzing me intently about my family and marital status, we talked about professional development and my role in the Education department.

As far as they are concerned here, I am happily married: I wear no wedding ring and no jewellery of any value so I don't get robbed. In my bag, I carry a jolly picture of us all taken at a friend's wedding just two years ago which helps my cause. And yes, my husband isn't here but we'll be meeting up over this year, i.e. hands-off thanks!

I actually can go out if I am with a group so I am trying to get the numbers of a few taxis I can use safely after dark but I am still not keen. In the day, I walk everywhere which can be quite a distance. My office and basic shops luckily are a few minutes away which is just as well as wherever I am, I have to come back here to use the loo. Apart from the ones in the main hotels I could use with a jug and bucket to flush and taking my own paper, others seem to be holes in the ground visible to everyone or simply the gutter. The ladies in the office laughed when I asked them where I could go to the toilet there.

The only annoying thing now is that I am not so keen on being shut away after six as it gets too dark and dodgy…am reading like crazy and have watched two films – tricky though spreading those a bit so I don't run out of stuff to do. I will try to borrow some books because it looks as if I will get through quite a lot!

Day 3

I'm prompt and although I know not how, schools seem to start on time too, so visiting lessons have to be on time. I arrived early at the office, sat around as usual staring about me. The local secondary school, Atse Yohannas, is just around the corner so the office goes there often and are very friendly with the head. I'm really interested in their set up. The office guy and I are called in together to sit towards the back of the bare classroom: double short desks with fixed benches fit three to four students on each, about 50 in the class, mixed. Our lesson was English, some textbooks are around so they can see over to one somewhere but there is a lot of chalk and talk from the front. Uniform is clearly a regulation but so threadbare and poor. I notice that because it is so very worn that the students wear other things underneath that appear equally thin but it adds a layer. They are very respectful and some seem to be trying while others simply shut up. Feedback afterwards was weird. I had my usual three positives and three targets or suggestions as I would do in England, but the office guy had pages and pages of depressing negative comments. The poor teacher, I felt for him. The next lesson was easier to judge as students were not quite so squashed, a few posters were stuck on the walls too which makes such a difference – if not stimulating, it is something to look at when bored. It was a vaguely more active lesson so feedback slightly less painful.

The central dry dusty area of this school compound has piles of stones and logs to sit on and a few trees for shade. The caretaker is a local guy and he appears to know my landlord. He took me to proudly show off the garden near the open football pitch. Students manage the garden in lesson times under his watchful eye: with maize, bananas, some veg and a couple of sad-looking chickens plus the whole thing is well fenced with strong barbed wire – there is no shortage of this stuff – as he doesn't want anyone helping themselves to the produce. I had to have the statutory cup of tea and dry bread roll in the staff room where I was stared at and introduced to a few stressed busy teachers.

Today I read some Ethiopian education documents online but as I have to pay for every second of this internet I am downloading as much as I can then deleting afterwards. Later, I walked to the castle up on the hill over the other side of town and met Barbara and a U.S. Peace Corps education volunteer, Diane. She was very energetic, boisterous and had plenty to say which even I think may be a bit too loud and inappropriate but she's certainly a lively person in the mix here. It's lovely up at the Castle; now converted into a small basic hotel with fantastic all-round views down various steep steps to the road and town beyond. We hugged the shade by the walls drinking more green tea.

Day 4

Gamunzadik, who I am to work alongside is the Continuous Professional Development (CPD) guy. He seems quite old and is so lovely. Nothing is too much trouble. His English is good but he checks phrases with me and pronunciation, as well as making sure I am okay. He obviously gets on well with others and they always ask for his help with stuff. The other one, Ato Solomon Mulu continues to be a bit eager to help *me*. He is very keen to settle me into my little office (they don't have this luxury themselves) All are worried I may forget to lock up or lose the key. It is so dusty in there that after the cleaner had finished, they spotted me wiping over again and sent Akeza, the secretary back to do it yet again. Oh dear, I don't want anyone to get into trouble.

I have decided to keep a hand-written log and detailed observations partly for something actually to do but to remember it all. I will have to keep the writing small as I am learning paper is at a premium. Already I have read a few files in the stash here, seeing what's tucked away. The office lot are very respectful of the VSO boxes of files and old papers and it seems an unwritten rule nobody else is allowed to touch these. I can tell that the first volunteer, Susan was here in 2005 and had pretty much my brief. I can now see how others fared as well; a lot has moved on since then.

Amongst the paperwork, I found a pamphlet about female genital mutilation, very detailed and showing the different types carried out often in this Tigray region. It generally takes place on young girls before puberty by an older 'wise' woman or relative in very unhygienic places. FGM seems to range from a bit of cutting – removal of parts that could give pleasure to a serious tightening of the female opening apart from making peeing and monthly menstruation incredibly painful. The symbol of virginity is obvious. It makes me shiver thinking about the consequences of that plus now I am beginning to understand the wider implications of childbirth. These medics have to deal with the subsequent problems such as overtightened birth canals, where the urethra is combined with the vaginas and not to mention the severe bleeding when torn anywhere for whatever reason. I feel really sick reading about it. God knows how the girls and mothers feel but I am struggling to get my head around it, on the one hand, these people are deeply religious while on the other they perform such heathen acts of violence on their precious girls.

Day 5

More lessons are planned for me to observe. School rooms are grouped in long huts made from stone or tin complete with mainly very bare walls and open high windows spaces. Occasionally, the outside walls facing the compound will have painted diagrams on them or the alphabet in Tigrinya or English. Dust is everywhere as usual. Teachers are in their regulation white lab coats over their clothes and the students are in their threadbare uniform. I have spotted the odd whip or short rubber hose tucked into a lab coat pocket…hmmm. We had talks about that in Addis and it is supposed to be illegal to whip children now, but it still goes on 'to maintain discipline' in the classroom. Knowing this, I do see teachers speedily hide the evidence when I am around, in their pockets or under a pile of papers.

Routinely, classes have about 50 students packed two or three onto Victorian-style benched desks so there is not much room to move, but they are quite attentive while the teacher blurs on and in the English lessons, carries out a comprehension with the whole class. Classes are dust traps around a dry, windy, central field and the rooms I have seen have housed roughly forty to sixty pupils. Both the teaching and the class environment is so very dull – which is what they want me to sort out. It is in the younger classes where there may be more 'exciting' posters or notices pegged up on strings around and across the room, however, there are plenty where there is literally nothing to look at other than old cracked plaster or brick. I have now had to give instant feedback which felt a bit weird but I think I did well enough. We gather together, subject tutor, the office guy and the teacher plus occasionally the principal all concentrating hard on my opinion and ideas, sometimes wanting more negativity than I am prepared to give. When I have observed more, I can make a plan of action and have more meetings and the like to help the teachers deliver better. It is clearly quite a big job but I am excited by it.

To date, I have visited five schools and have watched different ages, from 6 to 14. Today I asked the class of 14-year-olds at the end of their lesson what they thought of their room. Apart from being shocked by me addressing them as adults in this way, the question itself surprised. They are never involved in their education or asked to give an opinion; I began to get the real answers: they thought it was a bit dull. Not counting the regulation enormous blackboard across one wall, theirs was completely bare. I am still not sure if they know what an art lesson is and as far as I can tell at the moment, I have heard of a subject called 'aesthetics' that covers all extra things like music and art. I was really pleased I got an unprompted response; I have *my* ideas but if it isn't what *they* want, then I could be wasting my time.

Next task is to make my proper plan which I have to put to the education office and VSO, it will be fine I am sure. They want me to get the teachers to be more active in the class, improve results and encourage more interested learners.

It all goes together really well but with such large classes and very little resources, it is a challenge! Everyone I have met so far is really supportive and keen to change for the better but they are not sure how to do it or where to begin.

Footnote for this month from my new office – my placement outlines official notes.

Overall placement purpose and specific placement/partner objectives

The final work plan will be subject to agreement between the volunteer, the employer and VSO at the start of the placement:

- To develop the quality of teaching and learning in Grades 5–8
- To support the continued development of teaching and learning in Grades 1–4
- To coordinate and implement CPD (Continuous Professional Development)
- To support schools in their SIPs (School Improvement Plans)

Likely duties and responsibilities of the volunteer

The volunteer's responsibilities may include:

- Supporting the Mekelle City Education Office in the development of methodologies for the delivery of 2nd cycle education (age group 11–15).
- Training second cycle teachers in active learning methodology.
- Working with Cluster Supervisors and Directors to identify school and their own individual needs for development.
- Working with teachers to develop teaching aids and stimulating classrooms.
- Developing lesson planning in line with a more active learning style.
- Training on a variety of areas such as behaviour management and special needs inclusion.
- Undertaking classroom observations and providing formative feedback.
- Actively promoting inclusion (inclusive education) and gender equality.

Third Month

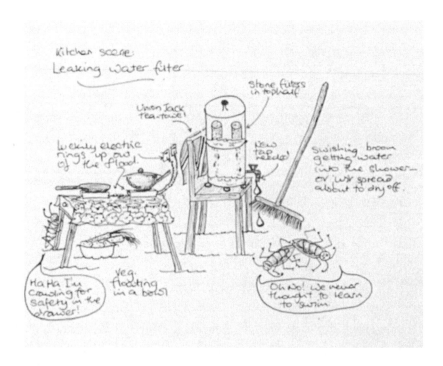

With a shawl around my shoulders, I grab the small ruck-sack which I carry on my front, say 'Shalom' to the cleaner on the stairs and avoid skidding in the latest wet mopped floor, (they try so hard to keep everywhere clean but with the animals and perpetual dust it's a never-ending struggle), then smile at the guard – he grins back showing the few teeth he has left. Waving to the shop keeper outside on his stone stool, I cross the road avoiding a couple of bajaj taxis, horse-drawn carts or donkey trains – no 'look left and look right' routine here really for casual traffic. I don't go down the alley opposite mine as I have seen what goes on down there and anyway, it doesn't look safe. The main roads are bordered by very, very deep storm drain ditches ready for the rainy season floods. In the dry season, as with any back lane, it is a good place for an easy toilet, but it dries quickly and isn't frowned on. The clambering in and out is a bit of a joke though.

Then it's past the dusty waste ground littered with charred ox bones (from the last feast) and into the main street towards town. I always nod to the uniformed guards outside the hotel as they sit in the shade clutching their little bomb detectors, then I check out the progress of the weaver birds nesting above in the beautiful trees there. From here the route is full of little shops and bars or fruit juice cafes busy with men outside sitting on their low stools or rocks, chatting. Busy women may be washing their front pavements, slopping water from vessels made from large old plastic bottles and the shoe-shine boys have a brisk trade along this stretch. Negotiating parts of the path is tricky and I know where to avoid tripping on the wobbly slabs, the open holes to the storm drain, the huge drop down from their very high kerbs where the roads have been made up, plus the sleeping beggars and the pavement sellers. Some of these sell a variety of eucalyptus sticks which are used generally to chew as teeth cleaners: it seems to work. The white sparkle on many Ethiopian's teeth is a surprise to me.

Beggars don't usually hassle as much during the early hours but later on, they will be constant. If I am with Diane, she will stop to remonstrate with them explaining she is a volunteer working for their country earning little money, this winds them up I think and makes matters worse! I don't bother – smiling does wonders. Now, if you can also imagine a school nearby with 1,350 children, *all* walking there in ragged uniforms and flip flops, coming from every direction for the start of their day, carrying the odd book, a canister or old bottle for water and maybe a small item for lunch, some lads kicking along anything round, or four or five girls arm in arm stretched across the street, then that is where I leave them to turn into the rough track to the City Education Office. I may have had a call along the route of 'forenji' ('foreigner'), which I don't mind since as a white person, I admit, I am an oddity, but some school children know me now and call out 'teacher, teacher!' which is really lovely. Progress!

If I need to go to a school, my day usually begins very early just before six o'clock in the morning and I'm still walking everywhere. Some schools maybe 45 – 60 minutes away, and the office car, such as it is, is seldom around or available but I wouldn't presume to be able to ask them for a lift; it is usually at the disposal of the manager. The most impressive thing I see and I try to attend regularly are the flag ceremonies. It is a sort of assembly which lasts about 20 minutes and is held half an hour before daily lessons begin at 8.00. All students must be in the compound lined up in their year groups, military-style, ready for discussions, student readings, HIV/Aids talks and so on and I like to get there just before this so I don't interrupt or cause the forenji distraction. I have been handed the loud hailer without warning a couple of times to address the roughly dressed 1,650 students' eyes fixed on me, the chosen forenji. I can't remember what I said, but once I had to repeat it all word for word – apparently my speech was too short! They do love a microphone. Then, at the end, the Ethiopian flag is raised with precision timing while everyone including the teachers stand to attention, properly spaced in straight lines, hand on heart, singing with great respect their national anthem, occasionally there may be an accompanying instrumental rendition over the tannoy. Stirring stuff. It is just tremendous and starts the day so well.

Schools here are arranged in groups according to regions within Mekelle. Each group or cluster has a supervisor who works closely with the head or principal. The cluster supervisors I have met so far are amazing, work hard and really get involved with their schools and these in turn report to and work with the Education Office. It all seems to work well so no school needs to feel left to muddle along alone. I am usually arranging a series of observations and giving immediate, short, verbal feedback before leaving for my lunch break back at the flat which may include another shower. If I decide to visit the school's libraries, they are usually only open during lunchtimes, I have to fit that in as well. In the afternoons, I generally return to the office, discuss where I have been, the teachers I have seen and I handwrite up my reports. The office is genuinely interested in how I see these characters in schools, possibly it confirms what they are thinking but they can see my point of view as well. We do have a laugh too as I think I am a bit open with my verbal reporting to them! If I have seen a teacher a few times I will give a written feedback to the teacher for their portfolio, and after a few visits, I will compile a full school report to give to the cluster supervisor and the principal. They share these among other schools in their patch to work on their good practice. A lot of my work is handwritten: there is no internet in Government schools or in this old office, the computers are few and nearly always unavailable. Viruses abound therefore my laptop remains under my mattress and hand writing is best for me, scribing a copy for them and one for myself.

As I find different strategies for their active teaching, I do type these but the actual printing is another issue. Paper is precious. Each sheet is sold singly, I have discovered in the few stationery stores in town. If I am allowed to use the (ancient) photocopier and the secretary signs me onto it, I feed in one piece of paper at a time and remove the excess to lock away again in my office. After waiting around, I usually do manage to print off some to give to English coordinators in schools: the teachers are keen to have help with active teaching, and any ground-level support is welcomed. Actually, talking of stationery, I wish I had brought a load of biro pens with me from the U.K. They are like gold dust. There will never be a pen left lying about and even beggars will ask for 'pen' as well as 'money'.

I am wearing my watch which is a source of fascination here – we were warned that batteries would be hard to come by so I have two with me, there is a large clock that should have a battery in it in the office but I was told that that clock was bought by a previous volunteer who had tried to improve timekeeping however when the battery ran out that was that. It is still stuck at 10.15. That particular guy actually hasn't a good reputation here as he also tried to schedule proper meetings with an agenda plus organise minutes for them to refer to on a regular basis so the office could be more organised and aware of what everyone was doing. This was a step too far. Calendars serve no purpose other than to provide colourful pictures on walls for years to come or to provide shade at a window and block the sun. The old mobile phones about the office were useful for timing and schedules when school meetings are called. With dates, here they bumble along and appear to have plenty of time to sit about and talk about things. What's the point of forcing on issues when impromptu unforeseen happenings either make a meeting impossible or mean nobody would turn up. As the year went on, I could see it would be frustrating for a Westerner coming from our busy diarised systems. I would walk miles to attend events or to agreed gatherings only to discover it was never finalised anyway or even cancelled. It would be just my problem, and each time I have to just shrug my shoulders and turn around. I have no idea how they knew when festivals started – maybe the moon was the key. Family celebrations were just 'next week' or 'the day after tomorrow', no need to write that down.

Afterwards, I leave the office between 5.30 – 6.00 in the evening and am always in by 6.30 or earlier so I am indoors well before it gets dark. I tend to go to sleep after writing my log, catching up on emails, watching films or reading at around 9.30. Once a week volunteers tend to meet up for an evening meal somewhere so I am back then by taxi by 9.30 anyway. During the week, we may also meet to talk about work really to clear the air over a cup of coffee. Barbara and I have created a Wednesday meeting afternoon since we are both in education and need to touch base with each other which is a good idea for us. Being introduced to the truly yummiest pizza restaurant in its open courtyard where they cook on a set of proper Italian style open-fired ovens has been a bonus, although that one is really popular so juggling seating together early then waiting absolutely ages for food is the norm.

Saturday = weddings!

When a fasting season is around the corner – which is pretty frequent actually – they have to cram in these celebrations while they can offer a decent meaty meal to their guests. Weddings are seriously big white religious affairs and after the ceremony, the convoys of battered decorated cars spread out right across roads as they cruise from the church all through the streets. Guests hang far out of the windows shouting and clapping while blasting their horns – don't mention health and safety here or what could happen in oncoming traffic. Ethiopian brides stick to the white fizzy, princess frock theme but the cars are borrowed just for each blasting town tour so they switch about between wedding parties and keep on coming around!

Walking about the town on such a festive Saturday can mean a few diversions. There will be an unannounced row of rocks indicating a road closure, then onto the road itself is placed a long marquee/tent for the feasting relatives as well as locals who are always invited to join the queue. Massive pans of various stews are there to share with traditional injera bread, and benches line the tents for everyone. It will be a good hearty meal for them so they all turn out. Although the wedding party have western-style dresses the guests and all the rest wear their beautiful Ethiopian traditional super-clean white embroidered clothes.

Beginning a Saturday differently makes me feel better, more like a weekend. So, using my trusty mop to clean through the flat (with water recycled from my hair wash) is a great start. I do not have a local maid as many others do for their shopping, cleaning and cooking. I probably end up having to pay more for my food as I know I am not nearly as good as a local at haggling for my purchases, but also the flat is so small, she would get under my feet, she may not be as freaky about getting rid of cockroaches as I am…and anyway I wouldn't have much to do at the weekends!

Later in the day, Saturdays for me also is my chance to feel British as I patiently tweak the rubbish areal sitting on the television to get a connection and a picture, so I can get the three o'clock kick-off BBC football which is just fantastic! I feel as if I am watching a disproportionate number of Stoke games on Saturday TV but I enjoy hearing English commentary and with the time difference it is 6 pm, so a good evening's entertainment.

Regular shopping every day of the week is routine now as I can't store fresh foods for more than a day or two either in my wooden cupboard or better still on the stone floor which is vaguely cooler! However, I doubt if I will ever be buying meat. Butcher shops can easily be spotted by the groups of dogs lurking around the door for bones. Then as I get closer it's the smell of death. A carcass is brought in early that day, bits are hacked off and sold, and when it's gone – it's gone. Chickens can't be told to stop laying so at least in fasting times although to share them in a communal meal would be wrong eggs are always available. I buy a couple at a time and carry them home carefully in my bag, first to check if they really are fresh, floating them in a glass of water, then to eat for tea. The Tigrinya for fresh eggs I love: "Oon-khoo-la-leikh" is how I sort of say it and they understand, occasionally impressed!

Not long after I arrived in Mekelle to carry out my VSO work, I had to adjust to the fasting period before Easter. Their Easter is incredibly important and comes a week after ours so is an enormous continuous celebration from Friday to Sunday then back to work on Monday. The fasting, however, begins fifty-five days before the Easter weekend. I haven't quite got my head around why that long; I can appreciate the forty days and nights in the wilderness and maybe add onto that the Holy Week seven, but fifty-five? Anyway, that means strictly no animal products are eaten. I took a potato salad to a 'do' the other week and had to sort out a different dressing as salad cream has eggs and milk in it. I have to keep eating eggs myself but out there it's a definite 'no'.

During this time meat is going to be difficult to come by and I have become accustomed to being what amounts to a vegetarian. Just before the 'fast' began, the huge meat-eating feast took place and was repeated at the end. This meat-eating is so huge another industry profits– the skin and leather producers. On street corners are high piles of fresh pelts dripping with blood, hooves and skull still attached, sellers hovering waiting to be paid by the collector in his cart. The fly population benefits too. During the following month, it seems a case of frugal fare while saving up for the next celebratory feast. Saint George is important here – even the big beer company is 'St George'! In fact, they celebrate him on the 23rd of *every* month but the one in April is seriously big. Uniformed brass bands sometimes practise for feasting at weekends which in their American style outfits are quite entertaining even while rehearsing.

Another spectacle I like to drop by is the camel market on the edge of town. So many different camels all chomping and grunting, they are more useful for long-distance travel since the donkeys are reserved for local transportation of goods. Carting goods such as the salt blocks from the Danakil Depression in the middle of nowhere can only be done very well by camels: perfect for heat, dust, dry conditions and no need for petrol top-ups along the way. Another market is for charcoal – the fuel everyone uses round here. The massive eucalyptus poles left from their uses such as scaffolding are lugged over to this market, piled high for specialist burning into charcoal, then heaped for sale. The donkeys that carry this or the hay around can barely be seen under their loads. Everything and everyone work so hard when they can here.

Sundays = bike races!

In a country where poverty is everywhere, I am amazed by the smart bikes and their riders I see whirring through the town on a Sunday. Occasionally there are races involving road closures and martials but usually, it is groups of cyclists geared up in the latest lycra and go-faster helmets whizzing through. It is the bee-buzz noise that first wakes me up! On race days, there are crowds of over a hundred out there clapping and cheering so I can't get out until they have gone which is awkward if they are there a few hours.

The weather is warmer now although the wind gets up at odd times, which keeps it at a comfortable temperature, but it does blow everything about. We have also had a few thunderstorms in the evenings which are quite dramatic in terms of watching the sparks fly from the wiring between the street lights…and don't worry, I have a good supply of candles at the ready for when the electricity finally gives out! On my tiny protected balcony, my little plants – rocket and two tomatoes – in their make-shift grow bags (broken washing up bowl, large tins, a cut down plastic lemonade bottle) are doing surprisingly well and I hope to have my own salads soon. I am so incredibly proud and anxious it is positively stupid.

Actually, in order to get soil up to my balcony, I have had to scrape small amounts of soil into a small bag from places I pass in the day, a little at a time then carry it up to the balcony. The best place is my office garden as they don't look at me much and already think I'm a bit odd so no questions asked! I think sometimes about greener gardens in Cambridgeshire, warming up for summer planting. As I sit here gazing out, I can see buzzards a plenty whirling about perhaps picking off any pigeons. There are builders balancing on the rough scaffolding over the road, hidden by my brown flowery nylon sheet which is blowing in the breeze on the balcony, and all is sunny and warm, so that won't take long to dry.

The other activity I can see from here is the modest local stadium up the hill from mine and on Sundays, there are organised football coaching sessions. Many children of all ages are there with parents lining the stand. Surprisingly, they play on actual grass, wearing training bibs and using a good ball, all of which is amazing.

Walking about town is a feature of my Sundays. I am now trying to cover different routes spotting the schools and on my return to the flat, draw a map so I can remember the way. I have tried to ask my office manager for directions which is a waste of time. We now have a laugh about it as all he can say to me is, "You simply go round there and over there and there it is."

I joke and enquire about a new school saying: "I am simply going over…" and he gets it. They really do not do mapping or directions. All this walking is making my sandals filthy so I scrub them up on Sundays but they are so comfy I will buy another pair online, then I can get them sent from a helpful friend in England. If they arrive in the post here of course… I can but hope. Thank you, Gail. (Pip managed to order me some more thyroxine in England as VSO weren't quick enough to get the monthly supply sorted but those never reached me. Ooo. It's a lottery.)

Shops are open as usual except offices and banks, and the post office is only open a few hours. The bank is roped off with a guard in place to stop anyone sitting on the steps. Coffee shops and pool rooms are more popular on the weekends. There must be quite a few as the clunk of balls sounds pretty constant to me as I walk down the back streets. Others may have a disco sized speaker outside their coffee shops transmitting the football game showing inside to lure passers-by. There are different markets according to the day of the week and Sunday is no exception. The cattle market on the edge of town I discovered one

Sunday is amazing. I had heard the cattle here have ridiculously huge horns and now I can believe it. Some look more like oxen and are used to pull small wooden ploughs but others are for producing meat. The cattle are herded by skilled bare-backed horse riders on their decorated steeds rushing around like something out of Lawrence of Arabia.

Religion does play an important part in Ethiopian life. The majority of people here are Orthodox Christians while others may be Catholics or Muslims. Around the churches are sellers of icons and scripts with some boys selling orthodox styled hand-carved crosses hanging on black string, ready to wear, and most Ethiopians wear their crosses. Some women have a similar cross tattooed on their foreheads. Another feature is the queues of people all dressed in their Sunday best traditional white clothes kneeling and chanting by the outside church and kissing the walls in supplication. The walls are quite worn and shiny in the lower parts, just a sign to me of their incredible belief and trusting faith. The call to prayer on Fridays booms from the speakers on the top of the mosque but the call to prayer at many other times is the competing Orthodox Christian's own loudspeakers. It is so deafening and happens at all times of the day and night but Sundays are even louder and more frequent.

A typical working week this month.

Monday

The office had a massive meeting about which I knew nothing. They were using my chairs and blocked the entrance, so I received lots of what looks useful hand-outs, before I turned about and had a day's paperwork at the flat. Did some online banking, skyped Ella – her birthday so that was lovely even though I couldn't see her she could see me with my Ethiopian backdrop.

But I still wanted to DO something. I tried to find another school I had heard of but got lost. There is a woman who apparently used to be a good teacher but has now serious mental issues patrols the street where the office is based. She saw me and spent a while shouting abuse at me but worse still throwing serious sizeable rocks at me. Luckily, she's not as good on her feet so I managed to scurry away. The local shoe-shine man I nod to regularly (a cripple who is stuck permanently in a squatting position) thought it was hilarious. Thanks! My mood wasn't great anyway. By chance, I happened on another school and introduced myself. I was looked at for twenty minutes, the deputy head said to come back tomorrow.

After working on my reports so far and saving all of it on my memory stick, I returned to the office later at 5.30 and sixty of them were still there engrossed but I managed to tell my chap about the school. Then I returned to the flat, wrote emails to a few British museums pleading for free posters for school resources, and made a better batch of Welsh cakes this time with dates which were tasty.

Tuesday

The office has arranged for me to visit an entirely different school and I was taken part of the way there but couldn't find it! I returned to the flat via the shops but a call from the office came to tell me to go instead straight away to the one I myself had arranged yesterday.

The head was waiting.

For two hours she talked to me about her philosophy and model school before I saw the classrooms. Every set of about fifty junior age children was poised ready to impress me. Just a handful of students in each class spoke and gave learned phrases in English, number facts, alphabet and so on. The rest sat and tried their best to look attentive. No wonder the head wanted me to turn up and of course, I responded with praise and enthusiasm.

As I was passing the post office on the way to the food market I called in, and hey presto, Jude, my great Uni friend has sent me a cute parcel with tasty treats and rubber gloves! How clever; all this hand scrubbing and cleaning the flat isn't great, so these are perfect.

The office has an older Office Windows so mine won't work on their computer. I will have to beg time on theirs to retype everything if they want it presented that way. At mine, when I write my emails, I am preparing them on Word and managing to past them onto the emails very quickly as internet connection time is so precious and I need to keep in touch with my amazing family and friends.

I have had no water today and electricity is on-and-off so tinned tuna is helpfully washed down by a much-needed 7up and gin! Watched 'Jeeves' episode in bed: relaxing.

Wednesday

An early 7.45 start at school flag ceremony, duly respectful and a good atmosphere. Tick. I saw a younger class lesson and the new teacher was very keen to have ideas and support after my previous visit. I did a bit of alphabet around the room rather than having one-star child spouting and the rest listening. She has taken on some suggestions I made to her at a previous visit and the class looks a bit more child-centred today.

Then, oh dear, I went to another experienced older teacher's lesson which was dire. The woman reminded me of the Gingerbread House witch and I really felt for the couple of boys she belittled because they couldn't read some new words. But then I myself was reprimanded for looking for the keywords in the class to support the reading: how can they learn the words if they have never been told? When I reported to the office, we had a laugh and they knew exactly who I was referring to when I described her as 'scary'!

Barbara and John met up this afternoon with me and with some US peace corps volunteers nearby for our regular 'Wednesday meeting'. The Americans are embarrassingly loud, it is noticeable (Ethiopians are quietly spoken, women more so), but they do have a different take on things and it is good to share experiences. The cafe's avocado juice and lime was lovely. Afterwards, Barbara and John came around to check out the flat as although it is tiny, I have managed to change it a little since they left, I think they approved.

Yes! My car has been sold in England. But the DVLA are hassling me for car tax, I filled in the SORN forms already...so lucky lots of this can be done online but messages are being missed. Oh NO!

Thursday

Visited a small primary school all morning after calling to arrange observations there yesterday. It's confusing; these run a shift system so the teachers alternate between mornings one week and afternoons the next. However, the children attend for the same half-day – their shift – and work at their homes labouring the other half. All children seem to be given homework but books are scarce and I haven't seen many school bags loaded with school things. Only those universal draw-string British football team bags which are owned by a lucky few. The shift system does mean families get their help in the home or on the farms and the child still receives a bit of schooling, but obviously, it is at a pretty low level. The teachers work hard and their cluster supervisor is very helpful. This school has a working field garden which is part of their education and food supply actually for these needy children. In their rough area at the side of the garden, I noticed a few razor blades; I am sure they are just thrown away as worn rubbish but yet another hidden danger. Actually, in Grade 3 (that's young primary age), a textbook there has 'razor blade' on its vocabulary list. I don't know if our children would know what they are now that we have different electric shavers and wonderful contraptions for shaving. Here the blades are very useful for kitchen uses as well as plenty of other things such as sewing and cutting instead of expensive scissors, at least that's my theory.

Passing the post office again, (okay I am fixing walks that way as I am ever hopeful!), I have a note in my box to say there is an oversize parcel for collection after 2.00. Oversize isn't difficult with this small envelope sized box. Can't wait!

Over lunchtime I visited another school's library. It is a secondary school thus it is only open while students have their lunch break and the librarian is a teacher. But…oh dear. This librarian was quite proud he had arranged the vast number of books purely in colour and size order. It is amazingly muddled. Also, as I start poking around some shelves, I discovered shelves doubled deep so the set of books behind were really dirty, one patch had a rat's nest in it so speedily I left that area alone! I am learning that the number of books any school has gives it an edge. Books are usually donated by well-meaning western countries plenty having labels in them such as 'Gifts from the American People'. Unfortunately, some subject matter is really inappropriate for these people: 'My friend's a drug addict', 'Going to the disco', 'Choosing a handbag'…not really for Ethiopian life. Still, if they felt able, they could learn the language. It will take a lot of tact and care to alter things in this library.

Back to the Post Office after 2.00 to wait twenty minutes, fill in a form at one desk which I take to another to pay 5 birr (equal to 25p), where I complete the large ledger and eventually receive an amazing parcel of exciting treats – chocolates, Polo mints, OXO, cheeses…from Pip. I can't describe how excited I am!

The weather is changing with massive overhead thunderstorms. I was stuck in my room in the office for fear of being struck by lightning and couldn't attend a planned school visit – hope they understand. Wrote up more feedback notes ready. I have discovered there is an Education meeting for all volunteers in Addis next Monday and they have missed me off the list. Apparently, Barbara will get onto them and let me know tomorrow, but flights are involved as well as a hotel room booking…watch this space. I offered my office guy a Polo sweet and he took the whole bloody tube – so very excited, grabbing them back was an impossibility!

Friday

Up early today, the call to prayer was full volume as were the dogs in the street plus outside mine a lorry had its loud engine running for five whole minutes. I wrote a lot of emails, some quick-fired over to VSO in Addis. Result! I have my flights now and a hotel bed with the others for the course so I can relax and look forward to that.

Today I had a brainwave. Now that I am familiar with the textbooks that are used in English lessons, I could suggest activities to match the texts as a guide for teachers who struggle with exciting lessons. I am trying with the middle grade just to see if it could work. Working in the office was tricky as they had a coffee ceremony from mid-morning. The secretaries organised it, lit the charcoal fires *on the office floor*, arranged chairs around and off we went. One and a half hours and three coffees later I was well wired and smoked out really so it was difficult trying to get anything else done. The office shut then for the afternoon.

Decided to walk to another school library, cloudy but dry so the long walk wasn't too awful. The Mailiham School principal is sad; they are very poor and he hasn't a big TV in his office, but I say that's a good thing, it is distracting and to me doesn't show wealth or a good school at all. He is very chatty as are the two young librarians who are introduced to me. They are next door to Alene School which is a primary age school with absolutely no resources at all. I was thinking sharing some would be a good idea then when I saw all the baby board books loading shelves in the older student's library, I thought I had it sorted. Between us, we had a laugh and bagged up the books that clearly were not suitable for secondary children and I was set to talk to the principals and cluster supervisors, tact at all times, no rush.

Early evening on the way out to meet up with volunteers I met Solomon from the office. He told me about a meeting tomorrow in the office which I knew nothing about. It's beginning to be a theme! He says all the principals will be there so *surely* I should go too. After a lovely pizza, I got a bajaj back on my own which was a first, but this particular driver is a known safe chap and a devout

Christian so the conversations are very religious-based which I can cope with and respond respectfully which he appreciates.

Saturday

I duly got to the office on time for the meeting, but the OHP wasn't fixed till 10.30 so I did a bit of greeting and catching up with some school heads in between coupled with a quick return to mine for a toilet break. Others saw the delay and disappeared to the nearest coffee shop which I really didn't want to do! It was worth it staying till lunchtime and I know the office like it when I am there supporting them – having a volunteer in the office gives them a certain kudos.

I find that if I wash my sheet and clothes on a Saturday, I hang the sheet on the balcony on the outside like a curtain and hidden below that I hang my underwear... I can't have the local population eyeing up my smalls! It is so hot it all dries quickly. That water is used afterwards for a final floor-wash with sloshing about the puddle from the sadly leaking filter. I packed my bag for Addis, leaving space for the parcels there for me to bring back. The bag is a bit bashed about so I am hoping it lasts the year. Managed to make cauliflower cheese today with cheese triangle sauce and it was just fine plus I cleared out the rest of my fresh food supply ready to go away. Since my water filter is leaking badly right now, I need a spanner from the VSO office to sort it out. Finally, I am ready to go. Getting away is exciting – even if just for a couple of days, so maybe I will do more of this to help me through the year.

Sunday

Mother's Day in England: Ruth rang. I'm so happy, it is lovely to hear her voice and a great start to the day.

Shared a taxi to the airport with Barbara and John, the God-fearing driver chap insisted he could get us up the mountain to the airport in his bajaj and at one point I wasn't sure at all. It took longer than a proper car but luckily, we had time to spare. I can still picture us leaning forwards just willing the bajaj to make it up there. Then our group nearly missed the boarding for our flight as we were talking with other volunteers too much and it had been actually called earlier! Addis taxi haggling was an experience with the driver guy starting at 500 birr, we got it straight down to 400 but finally to 140! Arguing for the best price is such a pain but some actually do enjoy it.

Back in Addis and the hustle and bustle with beggars, shops, slums mixed with modern glass structures, actual traffic and the variety of places to eat is fun. Meeting other volunteers, sharing experiences, talking at a normal speed (you just can't when talking to someone who doesn't speak English as their language); all good.

During the following couple of days, we were together often for updating informative lectures as well as individual debriefings at the head office. I very much appreciate where I am placed. Addis itself is different and perhaps has a nurturing feel to it, but I really have to think for myself and just get on with things as I see fit. True, it is very lonely, but not half as bad as the single volunteers placed out in somewhere like the Afar region which is clearly dangerous, challenging, hot and remote. I don't think I would have coped with that. Having to sleep outside the hut for fresh air, being constantly invaded by local urchin children, cooking over a lit fire or gas…no thanks. Before I left the city (with the filter spanner!), I was able to pick up little bits of different foods including garlic sausage, some proper cheese and Marmite.

The weather is seriously changing. It is called 'the small rains', but somehow means water may be on but electricity off at random times. Practise for 'the big rains' no doubt. Back in Mekelle I felt at 'home', helped greatly by my Post Office diversion as I picked up *four* parcels. Wow! Sian sent different basics so well-chosen in a great Olympics bag; Gail sent my online things I ordered: knickers (!) and more sandals, plus some cute very English tea towels; Jeanne's contained chocolates, as well as DVDs, and my sister posted make-up plus antibiotics – how clever! Every bit was such a delight to receive and made me so grateful for everyone back home. I cried lots of happy tears!

Fourth Month

Lodge in Abi Adi.
Clever use of split sticks
for frame covered in brush
& bamboo : so Hobbit-like!

Ornithologists are often visitors to Ethiopia to catch sight of the different rare birds around here and Barbara's John is a keen bird watcher. There are plenty of walks around Mekelle but it is essential to have a guide, not just to stop us from getting lost in the vast empty countryside or in what are really barren empty mountains, or from being robbed…or worse. An Ethiopian person in the group keeps us safer.

In the wilder parts, it is quite beautiful and unspoilt with eucalyptus trees, the odd massive baobab tree, wandering mountain goats and cattle, isolated farms surrounded by hedges of large cacti plants, the beautiful 'tuckle' homes that are built using local sticks or bamboo, topped with straw found up in the hills here are functional. The ones the tourists stay in, however, are based on these but obviously fitted out with mod-cons for the Western market! And then there are the amazing birds. The bee-eaters and tiny brightly coloured birds are my favourite, flitting about or making crazy ball-like nests. Mad scurrying spotty guineafowl are funny. I have already been excited by the shiny petrol bright colours of the starlings, and have seen hoopies too in the office garden – they're actually much smaller in reality than I thought they would be. It is weird getting walking shoes on in a hot climate but we are rubbish at walking over rough ground, unlike the women who either get on with it in their basic cheap plastic shoes and flip flops or in bare feet as the rest seem to manage. Then, while the farmer happily carries his stick across his shoulders, the women smile and get on with being laden with urns or bales of stuff like hay, just like their donkeys! It really makes me think though when I see how they struggle to grow crops, ploughing such tiny rocky patches with a simple wooden plough tied to a single ox and bashing the solid ground with wooden pick-axes. Between 1974 and 1991 were the worst times for the countryside in recent history for Ethiopians when the armed forces committee, or Derg, took over what was previously the imperial feudal system. Collective land ownership was forced on the people and the weak agriculture declined even more. World recognition of Ethiopia through Band Aid came with the worst famine in living memory in 1985 which followed three years of drought. That famine was not helped by the fighting already taking place in the Tigray region between the army and ordinary people which alone resulted in the deaths of thousands. The west was slow to help because of these initial corrupt struggles and the Derg actually blocked food aid to troublesome Tigray, meaning that one in five people were affected by famine and in the end, one million died.

On odd occasions, we come across camel trains. Not long ago Mekelle was the centre for the salt trade and a special market was held for this. The Danakil Depression is the lowest place on earth and is basically an isolated, hot, dangerous place (physically volcanic danger as well as being bandit country). There is nothing there: no petrol, no supplies, no water. As I have mentioned, camels are the best option for trudging without a drink of water over the empty vast salt plains, but in the Danakil, they plod in long trains for days to sites where the half metre slabs of salt are hacked out skilfully with sharp knives, stacked, loaded up and brought back to a market. Alongside the salt fields are active volcanic craters which attract foreign visitors but scare the Ethiopians. Spitting unexplained fire from God's earth isn't great for them; must be the devil's work.

As volunteers, we are told we are not to go there although I have heard some Europeans who kit out strong four-wheeled-drives with supplies, barrels of water and fuel, to take a chance. These days, rather than bring it all the way into town, the camels carry the salt to accessible outposts where trucks can distribute the salt more efficiently and the Mekelle market sadly is no longer needed.

A late special lunch at Barbara and John's this month figured too. Their maid does most of the cooking so they are supplied with authentic Ethiopian food all the time. That is fine but I still struggle with raw chillies and copious amounts of garlic but often this comes in a separate additional paste so I can opt out. Barbara has given me some avocados from their amazing trees in their garden, collected in the large net fixed to avoid being smashed. They have a great crop so I am really keen to 'help' eat some and I feel set up for a few days! Ephraim, their landlord, was there too, a total VSO supporter and a lovely gentleman. He has been extremely helpful especially with our medication – knowing who to see and what to say whenever anything is needed by a volunteer. So, my thyroxine which never arrived from England – either via post or head office – has been sorted after a visit with him this month to one of the few reputable pharmacies, I would never have felt able to trust anyone for the right drugs at the right price. The place we went into was tucked in a back alley and the thyroxine which usually is only available on prescription in England was bought for quite a small amount of money. In fact, Ephraim introduced me to the pharmacist there and between us agreed I could purchase any more as I wished at a specified price. Such a relief.

My walk to and from Barbara and John's isn't great, passing the sprawling, sleazy, dirty bus station; like many bus stations, the third world over I suppose. As usual, I tighten my scarf over my head and part of my face and concentrate on where I am rushing. Actually, I have decided if I head straight through the biggest crowd they say less – probably a bit shocked! I did have once a chap who tried to walk alongside a silent focussed me and kept asking as they do for specific funding for a relative's eye operation or something, but I was walking *so* fast he was more struck by my speed and we parted pretty quickly.

There are plenty of wheel shops around that do a great trade in used tyres, all stacked up showing their numerous grades of cloth beneath the patchy rubber. The ones that are completely blown or show a large amount of fabric are bought by cart owners and the selection of random wheel sizes on one cart alone always amuses me. I don't suppose it makes a difference to the horses pulling the motley unbalanced collection along. Many cars or taxis don't have lights, have no tread on the wheels and some don't go out in the rain as on a downward hill the brakes wouldn't work. It makes it a bit of a lottery as a passenger paying a three-wheeled taxi to get home safely – 'un-mugged' anyway, but after a few beers maybe my inner bravado dulls any thoughts of: 'do his brakes work?' or 'can he actually see where the road is because I can't'!

When getting ready to be a volunteer, I was quite excited about learning to ride a motorcycle. The volunteers are usually sent out with helmets and the rest of the safety is up to them. However, in Ethiopia, the roads are *so* unsafe that VSO actually forbids us to ride motorbikes here. I can now understand why: the driving itself is terrible even before you add in the quantity of the stimulating drug 'chat' they chew. There is the rare helmet to be seen, worn by a few on motorbikes – those who feel it is worth popping a builder's helmet on as they set off, but even the police prefer to wear their smart peaked cloth caps. I did see a helmet actually in the office once but it was locked in a cupboard as it was too precious. Therefore, it shouldn't have worried me to see a child perched behind his father on a scooter carrying window glass across his knees…no gloves, no helmet, just a few large panels of glass…

Apart from the bandits after dark, at 6 pm vehicles cannot function without lights and rougher roads are often cut into curved mountain sides creating a cliff drop on one side. There are rusty motorbikes and scooters about. It is odd that just outside my little flat the learner bus drivers do their manoeuvres on the very slight hill there. It is fun watching them scrunch about and learn to control their buses, although that engine noise isn't great on a morning when I want a lie-in. Seeing a new breed of drivers: women too, is a novelty since all machine operatives here are men.

I am struggling with this giardia parasite a bit and luckily now I know where to buy the stuff I need over the counter. On one occasion lately, I had to go home early as I felt so rubbish, and was shocked when I slept on well into the late evening: sheer exhaustion. The antibiotics tend to rip a few good bacteria away along with the nasty stuff so my guts are struggling and I am losing weight as I get over a bout of this. It doesn't add to my mood and I need to eat a bit more to gain an inch or two…ooo. More home-made pan-cooked cakes will be needed. One evening, I tried steaming dumplings in the pan but sadly they were stodgy. I ate them though…I need to bulk up a bit. However careful I am with my own cooking, I have to be polite and eat what I am given when out and about so it is easy for me to end up with some bug or other. Ho-hum.

The Olympics are getting closer. It is the talk here as they have rivals in the Kenyans. Plus, it is in the magical utopia for these people: *London;* that great city paved with gold.

I am not sure if the Ethiopians will figure there, but am hopeful. A neutral topic of conversation is helpful now! I am still being involved in conversations here about the London riots last year: what was our Prime Minister doing going on holiday and leaving his country? They just don't get it. Mind you they don't do 'holidays' as such as they are all too busy keeping alive so they don't understand that one either.

When I return, I definitely will expect you all to handshake as they do in Ethiopia! I heard that there were worries about shaking hands at the Olympics and catching germs or something: how silly! There may be nasty diseases around the world but I have not known such rules as Ethiopians for hand-washing and care over contact with hands. As volunteers, we have had to learn the protocol for meeting and greeting. When meeting for the first time, a firm – seriously squeezing-firm – right-handshake is good, but hold your right elbow with the left hand if showing respect while doing so. If you have just washed your hands and they are wet, or you know your hands are not clean, you offer the back of your right wrist to touch instead. If you are meeting a good friend, then you touch right shoulders while shaking hands…I just love that one, it is so friendly and happy, and really good mates bump shoulders twice. Ethiopians wouldn't dream of having a drink or eating anything without washing their hands properly first – so just remember that next time you reach for the biscuit tin at your coffee break before thinking of criticising others! Having said this, we all carry and use chemical cleansers for hands and I use mine at any time of the day. There is a medic over here who is teaching children mainly to keep their fingernails short and to scrub them, as statistics show 8 out of 10 nails have parasites underneath. Aggghhh. I have decided again somehow to 'up' the care I take.

Three volunteers in the area are VSO and the rest are from the US Peace Corps, while some others pass through visiting each other, so that adds to the people I see here in general. There are some German volunteers who are in their late teens and come over as gap year workers I think, so they are quite different and inexperienced. Apart from Barbara and John, they are all single, linked with a hospital or the Education sector, are good company and it is relaxing being able to talk freely without being careful how I say things, or having to speak, so, so, slowly. The two doctors are due to leave shortly so we will have a get together in a restaurant before they depart. Sarah is moving further south in Ethiopia to carry on her work in the gynaecology department. Some of her stories of childbirth complications are incredibly scary and upsetting – not for the squeamish. The FGM of course has a lot to answer for in this department too. There are political issues, bribery as well – even for positions of power in colleges and so on, but we say nothing publicly and watch and think.

Somehow, we gather once a week for an early evening meal and I still meet Barbara mid-week just to talk about schools and office grumbles and frustrations. John works as a self-employed translator and since his work is computer-based he can work anywhere in the world – viruses and electricity permitting. But it does get lonely for me and weekends can be worse, there isn't the shopping therapy option here but I am hoping at times like these I have that stickability factor to see me through. So, a mooch about town is often my break from chores – I am not in much of a hurry at the weekends and can cope better with the beggars and shouts, and later, if I can meet up in the good old open-air trusty pizza place with some VSO friends, that's always good. There are new ones from Canada I have been keen to meet but one family's three-year-old is unwell so they are stuck. Tricky enough for an adult settling in as it is but a child would be so hard. Hmm.

The post office is a bit of an obsession and I am trying so hard not to call daily. Stamps are sold in small denominations and are the lick-stick variety which means when I send a parcel, I have to leave a large space for these. The prices for sending and receiving are random along with the form-filling to retrieve 'large' letters sent to me. My friends and family know I enjoy sending and receiving handwritten letters. Somehow, I feel connected through letters, always have, and now in this place, I really need that sort of intimate friendly connection. It's the handling of the envelope, the choosing, the touch and thought that has gone into the writing, sealing, posting. My sisters and brother, my really good friends where I live, but most of all my very precious children have sent me things. How I treasure every single bit of them! From the holding the package to the careful opening when I am alone to savour the moment, surprise contents, letters and cards, the variety of carefully chosen things sent out to me; I get quite emotional. The packaging is also very important as there isn't any here, not a card shop or piece of wrapping paper to be had – why waste time doing those things when you are struggling to fetch water and gather food to eat? But there hasn't been much arriving for me for ages.

Then, some posters came in a large tube as a result of my request for free stuff from galleries and museums in England. I had some Dickens portrait posters which will be hard to distribute but brainwave, I thought the school libraries rather than classrooms would be the answer.

One Friday, I was due to go to a school quite a long walk away. Going via the office first to pick up some papers was just as well as a massive meeting I didn't know about was in full swing there for all principals and supervisors. However long I am here I still can't get used to their unplanned un-diarised way of getting along. Telepathy must be good! But that meant my school trip would be wasted. Barbara just called to see me as her office was also full of people in an unexpected meeting there too and they needed her space. I called at a school library but it was shut, so in town, a new pop-up bookstall selling and lending English books was SO grateful for the Dickens poster. I decided that if they had the drive to try to set up a bookstall, they deserve a lift.

The weather is changing more now. Thunderstorms are regular and a full drenching is to be expected. Streets are well drained and cleaned by all of this and now I appreciate why the very high kerbs are in place – keeps the river on the road as well as pedestrians safe from wandering traffic. Some Ethiopians simply put a plastic bag over their hair to keep dry. Horses and carts have well-worn plastic bags fixed together as canopies when they haven't enough sacking to hand. Some evenings as the sparks sizzle along the open wires between buildings and we have power cuts, I use my candle supply and keep my laptop charged and ready. The light show in the dark across the sky, as well as the wiring, is dramatic. Easy meals of omelettes and spinach can be cooked quickly when electricity allows, so I am coping. I have made a friend of the very young mum who runs a small shop opposite the office entrance. She has her tiny baby behind a sack curtain there but speaks amazingly good English. Her older daughter – must be about six – tries to talk to me when she is there helping in the shop; her eggs are pretty tasty too!

I'm running out of books to read: the record in my diary of every book is getting longer plus I am re-reading some as I have no option. I need to do a deal with other volunteers and frisk the head office when I go there next. My sister has sent me the entire DVD set of 'Monarch of The Glen', plus I have 'Jeeves and Wooster' and all of the Black Adder series on my hard drive, so I am really trying to pace my viewing of these programmes as they are so comforting when I feel rubbish.

One evening, I had different entertainment. Two huge container lorries arrived opposite to deliver some massive gym equipment to the new unfinished extension being built just down the road linked to the Axum Hotel. They had no fork-lift or drop tail-gate, so the chaps swarmed about in groups lugging the stuff somehow into the shell of a building, they dropped one piece – so dangerous – struggling, shouting and groaning as they negotiated builder's rubble and sand heaps. Three large pieces are left outside covered in plastic; they can't be sited yet I suppose.

Here the school run is just that: no cars, they run. Some children live an hour's walk away from their nearest school so often they run both ways. I never saw a car carrying children to school in Mekelle so from that point of view the roads were empty of cars. But since there would be thousands of students walking to any school, the roads would be filled with children at certain times of the day and then the runners would have to slow to a walking pace as the crowds grew. They all carried their meagre quantity of books if they had any, some done up with string, the lucky ones have a drawstring Manchester United, Arsenal or Chelsea FC bags. Most would have a large, heavy water bottle to carry – the sort of plastic container which formally would have held oil, not necessarily an actual water bottle since no Ethiopian *buys* water. Once on a bus trip, we were advised to hide our small plastic water bottles as that would be the only thing the children would think of stealing.

Since I tend to visit schools in the mornings, I try to avoid leaving at their lunchtime as they all walk home and it is then that I get the Pied Piper moment, followed and hassled by students practising English phrases which can be awkward. One fierce Principal didn't get the full obedient response by his students to go straight home without following me, so he saw them off with a few rocks, then went to the bucket to wash his hands! I have learned this particular man was held in solitary confinement in darkness *for six months* at the time of the uprising. There is history here which must make a big difference and it wasn't so long ago either.

A typical school has its large fenced or walled space comprising the gated compound with its flagpole area, some with some trees for shade and a football pitch marked out with stones and rough goal posts surrounded by the Nissan huts for classrooms. I have already focussed on the uplifting flag ceremony in every school at the start of the day but have been to more than one school where the guards at the gate beat latecomers to the school flag ceremony held at 7.30 – 7.45 and belittle them badly so those turning up near flag time make a really mad dash for safety into the compound. Overall, the flag ceremony itself does give me an idea of the care, discipline and staff interaction within the school. In most schools, about a third will be orphans from HIV/Aids families and it is where the proportion is higher that there is more bad behaviour.

The huts do have really wide metal roofs for shade and protection in the rainy season and these too would help to preserve the outside walls where there may be the huge accurate diagrams for geography, the periodic table, *all* imaginable biology and each of these being painted in bright colours. Where there are younger students, the words may be in English but otherwise, it is all in Tigrinya. However, poorer schools are quite bare, may have no doors and are generally very depressing. Don't worry, where there are newly planted areas, they are secured with lots of barbed wire. Outside the school walls are the ladies selling nuts, carrots or berries by the handful.

School Principals are up against poor funding and supporting the very poor students when they do not have much themselves. Freshly painted classrooms, exercise books, uniforms for orphans, new equipment and pens – they all use biros all the time – are usually funded by other parents in their community. The Ethiopian government pays schools a tiny annual amount per student: equal to the price of a small packet of crisps in England. Therefore, when I go into schools, I watch lessons and am looking to see how I can help the teachers be more creative, more active in their lessons including using what they have readily around them to lift their learning such as bottle tops or even beans. After working with a combination of Principals, Cluster Supervisors and the teachers, to improve their lessons, I hope this in turn will help their results and behaviour improve as well; bored children the world over, or those who cannot simply achieve the expected level being pushed at them usually become naughty! Only I had a serious different problem in one lesson concentrating – a really noisy pigeon entering via the window regularly to feed its young chicks in a nest directly on top of the blackboard!

But it isn't all good news for teachers. In one school, a groovy young teacher nearly cried when I gave him his feedback noting the lack of discipline and chatting students. Oh, dear. And yet in the next school, I saw the best lesson ever. There it helped to have a keen collectively interested group of teachers wanting to improve the lot of their children in spite of their problems. After that, I decided I would clear out the office stash of resources and give a fair amount to the schools. I am being told we are moving offices 'very soon' all the time so this is a good opportunity. Teacher trainers in England colleges have a tendency to store resources to demonstrate their active teaching through workshops and so on, and here it is the same, but seeing these schools so devoid of any stuff makes me think it would be better out of the office and in the classrooms right now.

In my local little school, Lemlem Daro up the hill, the one with a strong headteacher who arranges her students to do performance sessions to impress has connected with me again. I had the bright idea that I could get a class to exchange letters with my daughter's school near Brighton. Brilliant. It fits the English curriculum – a treat in both countries. However, letters here are rare and they need teaching about what they *are* in the first place. Letterboxes? Postman? Whatever can they be? My lesson there was very difficult and luckily, I had an idea written down to direct the teacher who was also at a loss, but some included in their writing: 'Copy the following' as well as the multiple-choice phrases listed: 'I like to play football, help my mother, do my homework after school'. Anyway, we eventually got there and I had the option of postage back at my favourite place: 400-birr airmail or 36 birr 'special' post (that's just overland as the usual post). No contest. I also managed to get them to pose for a class photo and the teacher plus supervisor were very happy to push to the front and to be centre stage for such an unusual occasion for them. They are so lovely. Some children are wearing rings made from palm leaves to remind them of fasting and Holy Week. I made a mental note to stock up on foods ready for shop closures as they are bound to be shut for this massive event. One thing I treated myself to was a tin of Heinz baked beans I found in a shop! That cost me the equivalent of a day's wage but it should last me two days if I can keep it cockroach free and cool enough.

Technology for me lately has been dreadful. I was back at mine one early evening and couldn't register two top-ups cards I had bought for the internet. Wasted money, no contact possible. 'Skype' again is on high alert by the government here as possibly being banned so I have to be cautious, but I am having problems connecting both ways. Then I had four phone calls from an unknown number and with weird content. I am now learning on this old phone how to block callers.

At the office, a young teacher (young enough to be my son) called at my room. He was a bit too pushy, asked for my Facebook address, emails and so on. I told him sorry work isn't emails and Facebook and my private is just that: private! At least he apologised but kept chatting, ever hopeful!

Then one Saturday evening I had the deputy of the Meiweini school rang me too.

"Where are you? Are you OK?"

Oh dear, he's coming on to me and I have to be so careful.

"I am out with my friends." (Not) "Can we talk when I call at your school next week?" Hmmm.

Meanwhile, a teacher in another school I was helping also wants me to go around to his house. I told him to ask his wife when was the best time, perhaps he will.

After another surprise office closed-we're-having-a-meeting day came around, luckily for me, it wasn't in English. I was invited to take tea with them all afterwards and stupidly said I recognised the place as Ato Mulu had taken me there before…oops. He was embarrassed and I learned a bit more about how I had better be careful. Goodness, then he asked for extra English lessons! I suggested conversation practice in the office which didn't go down too well with him. Hard luck matey.

My return visit to that first school Meiweini was tricky. I didn't see the young teacher, thank goodness, but the deputy shook hands then backed off so that was good. The cluster supervisor was there and she's great, I really get on with her. We had a very productive chat in their tiny staff tin shed, cushions softened the rough benches around a clothed baskety table in the middle. I had tea in a tiny glass loaded with statutory masses of sugar. Washing up is done traditionally in a series of three small bowls of cold water while the teapot is on the charcoal boiling all the time. (I do think this is where I am picking up some of my stomach bugs which isn't great.) Through the hole in the tin wall, a couple of children sell orange juice in recycled small bottles. I had a laugh with two old guys in there with their walking sticks and made sympathetic noises to the cook who showed me her badly cracked heels in her nasty plastic shoes. This school really has its problems with an intake from shift primary schools as well as coping with shifts itself in some of their early secondary classes. How can they ever achieve good grades when they effectively get only half their education? I have talked to this principal before about assessing using value-added results rather than a blanket grading and he can see the difference.

A couple of weeks later that deputy was different: moody and sulky. I had just observed a lesson where some Grade 2 children were fighting and totally out of control so I wasn't in the best of moods.

"You haven't been to see me for ages." Big kid. But I had better be careful. He probably didn't believe me when I told him I was going there tomorrow actually, but I mustn't give the wrong idea either. Bugger.

After that, I went to the school library around the corner and gave the librarian a Dickens poster. I explained who Dickens was, showed him the two copies of 'Great Expectations' in his library which wouldn't be great reading for Africans but in the end, he understood the idea that Charles Dickens was special. He was delighted and immediately got his pot of paste out and slapped it up on the stone wall – a bit crooked but there clearly to stay.

My visit to Meiweini the next day was met with mixed lessons. The teacher in grade 4 was disorganised, no plan, no resources, smiled a lot. In fact, some teaching was wrong too – 3 o'clock taught as 9 o'clock and vice-a-versa – for people not having clocks in their daily lives at all, the numbering round it must be even more confusing. A boy who had been yelled at for getting it 'wrong' was winking at me, I circulated doing my best to help while she marked books oblivious. One boy was shouted at for knowing very little, but I gathered he had recently arrived from the Sudan border war zone so was targeted a bit for not being a local Tygrinian. Another threadbare child was yelled at earlier for not knowing how to spell the word 'five' – it was the 'v' sound that was so hard, but with no resources or direction how can they grasp basics? At break, the staff had an emergency meeting to raise cash for a local family whose house had accidentally burned down. I gave another teacher there written feedback which I try to do for them, and she was very happy with that; I hope it is useful for her portfolio. Then a maths lesson impressed me with really tiny children understanding the relationship between $4 \times 5 = 20$, 20 divided by $5 = 4$! In another lesson, a mid-primary group did a comprehension exercise in both Amharic and English together so the two supported each other. So, it wasn't all bad! It was a good 30-minute walk each way and I popped home to shower and have lunch. The afternoon was a waste of time; the principal had locked up and gone, the Grade 6 class I was supposed to see wasn't there, I trudged back via the market and nearly got back before the heavens opened again but at least being soaked close to my place wasn't too awful!

There is potential to sit about in between these school visits doing nothing. Now that I have accessed the VSO store of English books, I have been able to read through different textbooks generally used in classes (when available) and now I have decided that I would write short easy to administer activities linked with the chapters but I realise I need to produce them as hand-outs. The interaction between students and teachers as I see it is where the problem lies so this should work. If I am able to get a few activities used around Mekelle schools, delivered either at workshops or to the clusters in person for feeding down through to the teachers themselves then I will be happy. Now I have another angle to my work here, it feels better and finding schools shut or unable to see me doesn't feel such a blow or waste of my time.

Towards the end of this month, three events happened.

First, a good friend of Ruth's planned to come by with her boyfriend and I would put them up in my little lounge. The anticipation was ridiculously exciting for me, they needed advice on what to look out for in Addis Ababa as well as tips on travelling about. They stayed at mine for two nights catching a few sites I still need to see myself in the Tigray region before moving on north to stay in Axum. We ate out one evening after their exhausting touring but I did my own thing during the long days. I struggled to make a pointless trip to the post office. Then was invited to join a group at a hillside restaurant a good hour walk away for me but probably by luck the thunderstorms prevented me from going; I also tried to go to the Museum Palace but that was shut for refurbishment. Meanwhile, I was becoming more tired myself. At the end of their visit, as they were about to leave, a message came through from their bajaj driver up the hill to say he couldn't get close enough to mine due to the regular bike race outside, so they had to say rushed 'goodbyes' and hurriedly left, struggling up the hill to catch him while I waved them off feeling absolutely really down and rubbish. Very empty and flat. There is a lesson for me here, I think.

St George's Day is the second event. Every church will have this patron saint shown on a beautiful as a brightly painted mural depicting his dragon-slaying riding on his white charger, but I confess I am enjoying the 'St George's' beer! Although they celebrate him *every* month the whole church procession and band marching, flag flying, call to prayer over the speakers, feasting and festivities on the key annual date is massive. St George is the patron for a few countries including England, but I am sure they celebrate him the best in Ethiopia.

Easter was the third big event for me this month. All through the Saturday, live animals could be seen being dragged, carried, given a lift in a bajaj or perched over handlebars…to their prospective final resting places. The church calling to prayer again going mad and people out and about getting prepared for feasting fun is all part of the preparation. I had a phone call on my phone I didn't recognise so I ignored it. Some of us walked to the monument on a distant hilltop before going for a lunchtime pizza – well we ordered ours at 12.15 and the food arrived at 2.10. There are more beautiful brightly embroidered ceremonial umbrellas around this weekend; carried by priests to shelter the higher-order religious dignitaries, they are quite spectacular. Barbara rang me to tell me my landlord, Hailom, had been trying to reach me. Oops. I then agreed to go to his house for lunch and as he has no transport, he met me by a hotel I knew on his side of town. I was very nervous about the return trip as he lives on the edge way past the town in the wilder countryside. Luckily, I had a few gifts ready of a tea towel and sweets to take wrapped in used paper but all bright and ready to go, so I was organised and had no option but to get on with it.

His house is tiny but new and full of furniture embellished with shiny fabrics and lace. His oldest daughter is 30, she works away from home and he is worried she will never get married. There are two younger daughters and a son, all of whom speak excellent English so they translated a lot for his wife who was so lovely and happy I was there with them at this important festive time. The dining area was very cramped and I assumed we would eat together but we couldn't actually fit around the table so we ate in shifts. I ate with Hailom first – or rather he talked and they all plied me with food and drinks. Hailom runs a factory for disabled workers. He is an amazing man who somehow manages to make a living as well as give disabled Ethiopians a life – and there are plenty of those here, many young otherwise fit war veterans apart from those suffering from work-related accidents.

Apparently, they used to live in the flat I actually rent so that is a little extra income from VSO but he is another great supporter of our VSO in Ethiopia. Imagining a family with three children in that tiny flat where I am now swanning about in it on my own. Very humbling. Food-wise, as expected, the main meat dish was tough (as they can't hang their meat and it is butchered in a hurry), the sort of mince dish was very spicy, plus there was another stew of meat on chopped bones, and after weeks of fasting and being vegans there is no vegetable element today! Injera bread piled up ready for finger-eating, plus a sort of cake bread to use to sop it up. I did my best, but clearly, they think I don't eat enough and are worried about me. The drink on offer with the meal was a cloudy yellow liquid with bits in, called 'sewa' and it tasted like it. It was imperative I drank red wine too as I was told they had bought it especially. When I related this story to the office, they were very impressed I drank and ate all this, and they loved the picture I described of straining the herbs out the beer (sewa) through my teeth!

Their coffee ceremony was set up in the lounge on the floor along with the sweet biscuits and popcorn to help down the three cups. Hailom's younger brother and his family came next. His two children were much younger, one was a baby who was breastfed or given bread constantly. All very happy, calm and loving, it was brilliant and relaxed. It reminded me of our Christmas, the telephone calls to relations was continuous while all family and friends gathered giving presents – Hailom's wife absolutely loved the tea towel, so that was great. The niece attends a cluster school I regularly visit so I will look out for her next time.

My return trip was fine. They saw me onto the line taxi and made sure I was safe. I yelled 'woraj!' properly when I wanted to 'stop' to get out in the town centre, and I walked speedily the rest of the way through main streets back to mine.

Monday was back to work as usual with the cleaner making a good job of the animal blood all up the stairs, and the sales of freshly removed animal skins on street corners pretty much all over. In my next letter, I managed to bag up some local shiro lentil curry powder to send to Tom too. I know he will really like it. Double bags got the smell down a bit but it took a lot of lick-and-stick stamps to send to Canada! Plus, a result…there were two parcels at the post office; one full of simply nice things from home and the other with posters in from the Natural History and St Paul's Museums in reply to my begging letters for anything! Perfect.

Fifth Month

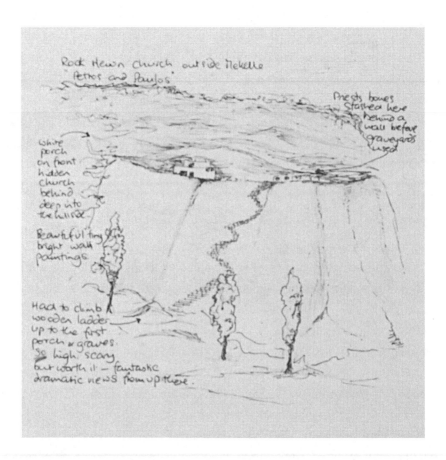

Rock Hewn church outside Mekelle
Petros and Paulos

Priests bones stashed here behind a wall before graveyard used

White perch on front hidden church behind deep into the hillside

Beautiful tiny bright wall paintings

Had to climb wooden ladder up to the first porch + graves. So high scary but worth it - fantastic dramatic views from up there.

May Day, a national holiday and I was up too early, very excited to be going on a trip out of town! The day looked perfect too: sunny and breezy. I had prepared my lunch, water and 'tourist' clothes the night before so I filled the time doing washing before going to sit outside on the front steps watching May Day processions: decorated buses, flag wavers and people in their best white suits and purest white decorated dresses. (Still don't understand how, in their washing facilities, using a bar of regular soap, drying over a dusty line they manage to produce perfect gleaming white clothes!)

Nine of us volunteers were in the transit van booked to take a trip back in time to pre-Ethiopian days of Abyssinia, see some of the famous rock-hewn churches with our local guide, Gere, who knows his stuff. Our route took us high into the lonely mountains of Tigray, past a swing bridge used by farmers and cattle, hanging precariously over a gorge very far below, and on through mixed landscapes of rocks and small cultivated patches surrounded by cacti hedges. I was clicking my camera like mad through the windows. It is so stunning out here.

These churches are literally hewn out of the cliff rock face and can't be seen easily from the path below so a guide is essential. Medhene, our first church, is whitewashed and tucked into the rock face behind a graveyard but is very much like a 'Hobbit' house. What is typical of these churches, apart from being a really amazing place, is that they are hard to recognise from the outside but open up inside like a magical tardis. All have their wooden doors over the entrance, window holes, embroidered drapes, wall paintings, a nave, Holy of Hollies and replica Ark plus a chapel for services. The second, Mikael Melehayzenghi, was really hard to spot from below as it was set so high well above a small extra chapel at the base of the cliff face. The track rose steeply upwards but it was well worth the struggle. I loved the little carved windows looking outwards from the dark to the vivid blue sky and landscapes outside.

The third, Petros and Paulos, was the highest climb. It is clearly popular with tourists and the chancers trying to get us to buy their guide services were all over the place but our local chap, Gere was good at sorting things out for us. One lad continued to hassle us even as we drove some way with his arm thrust into the minibus window! The church was a good climb up a long series of wooden ladders and had a small walled area nearby where priests were buried originally (admittedly that part was a bit freaky). Not all churches allow women into them and a porch serves as the space where female worshippers could congregate. This one had an extra white porch added to the outside but the rest was carved very deep into the cliff face. Treading carefully, we could go in to see the really fantastic detailed bright wall paintings, as well as the amazing views of the countryside way beyond into the distance, which made the scary climb both ways well worth it.

Exactly how old they are: who knows. We Europeans only realised these churches existed relatively recently so they still feel very much untouched by our touristy trail, but some do date back to the 4th Century. Religion before that time has many stories attached to its upheaval so hiding these places of worship well was a very good idea. The first bishop was instated and Christianity was made the official religion from AD337 when Abyssinia was ruled apparently by the twins: Saizana and Ezana. However, from AD 750 Christianity really grew while Abyssinia continued to have links with the Holy Land and Persia, but not all was friendly between them. A Falasha (Jewish) Queen Yodit led an army to destroy Axum and thousands died as a result. The Zagwe dynasty that followed was based near Lalibella, and since Zagwe was believed to be a direct descendant from Moses, the country became a more stable Christian empire.

Incredibly, most churches are still used as regular places of worship and have not been destroyed. I say 'incredibly' because it is quite a mission climbing up the cliff face in the heat and wind to the cave-like chapels, sometimes with the aid of a set of rickety wooden steps or a handy pile of rocks, and as ever, accompanied by the old priest we had to pre-book for each church (thanks Gere, again.) In addition, a group of fascinated locals each wanting to gawp and put their hand out for a tip afterwards sprang out from nowhere near every church. I don't blame them for gawping; there we are tooled up with fell-walking sticks, wearing our sensible climbing boots, and there they are in their slip-ons or bare feet beating us up to the top every time!

On our way back to Mekelle, we went through Negash. Apparently, Negash is said to be the next best place to visit after Mecca since one of Mohammed's wives is supposed to have been welcomed to live there. According to historical stories, Mohammed himself decreed that Muslims and Abyssinians would always be friends. Inside we saw where fifteen special Muslim priests are buried – or rather laid to rest within a massive cage under beautifully embroidered dark velvet cloths. I confess it was a bit bizarre really being next to so many bodies (skeletons they must be now) under what amounted to a cloth, but had to give total respect.

All in all, it was a brilliant day full of awe and exciting new things. Gin and 7up treat time and try to relax as it is work again in the morning.

The next day was back with a jolt as I went again to Meiweini school in the south-west part of Mekelle to be met by a very grumpy Principal.

Why didn't I observe Grade 6 as planned last time? I tried to explain it was cancelled, I had tried, but nobody was there. He was pretty cross, made worse by the presence of the cluster supervisor. That head has lost my written feedback of all the observations too, so OK, I will rewrite that and include a carefully worded addition about the Grade 6 lesson. Just an extra thing, while I was in discussion with the sympathetic cluster supervisor it was very hard to concentrate as she was poking her ear wax out with the spikey part of the blue biro pen top, checking her progress on the lid tip from time to time. Most disconcerting, and it went on for quite a while during what was a serious conversation!

Later that week, I was relieved to go to poverty-stricken Alene school in the north-east area where they try so hard, listen to ideas, enjoy their children and show respect. How I want to help this school. It is the large secondary next door that has those books for very young readers that I would like to carefully shift over to this Alene school. I can also get my Education office chap with the drill to come in to put up blackboards that are propped up on chairs, and a few stranded wall boards which lie unused too. There is so little electricity here and they have no tea-making facilities. The Principal spends her money buying me a cola and biscuits. Amazingly generous.

My pay. We are paid a minimum wage which would be given to an ordinary teacher but our rent is subsidised and that way we are slightly above the run-of-the-mill teachers here. Everybody is aware we have some savings ourselves otherwise we couldn't cope really but obviously that can vary. I know I have brought clothes to last me the year and I don't intend to spend on luxuries like haircuts – wouldn't let anyone near my head with a razor blade or scissors anyway, and I save a bit by not having to pay for a maid. The electricity and water are on a meter so that bill comes through periodically and the guard gets his big grubby ledger out, catches me before I climb the stairs and we discuss what I have to pay. Before we left Addis, the head office gave us a start-up fund and so I haven't had to think about my pay until the end of the month. My office doesn't seem to be bothered about it and I have had to ask quite a bit and try to fit in with them. The one shared office car is often the manager's taxi, but I seem to be able to swing it so that the office finance guy can sort out a lift for me to collect my money from another office miles away on the other side of the city. I calculated I was given 1,650 birr initially for a couple of months which was way lower than the 2,500 due which caused yet another debate. Each month-end has been a cat-and-mouse thing and I have had some pay.

This month I was told: yes, finance office trip is ready.

So, result, I manage a lift and I do get there, wait my turn in the long slow winding queue, only to be told there was none for *me*. The right bit of paper has to be authorised and passed at the right time then it can go ahead. I had to make a joke of it to the cashier who knows me by now.

"Look, you have that briefcase full (she does, she brings a stuffed briefcase into the room like a bank robber!), but here is my purse!" And I show her an empty purse.

"Ha ha…but you come back on Monday afternoon please then we can give you your money."

Monday happens and I am unexpectedly stuck in my little office surrounded by nine naïve keen London students who want to interview me. A massive storm followed and the rivers of mud happened through the streets: no car until I paddled home at ten to six.

I am doubly cheesed off right now. It had been an up-and-down sort of few days not helped by the storms. I have missed talking to Tom this birthday week but have to keep my laptop fully charged in case I can skype between connections but also the evening films which I can watch are a comfort really. Obviously, the electric shower doesn't work either so it is buckets and cold washing as well as thinking ahead for meals, candles and early to bed.

It was finally Tuesday when luckily this time the lady with the loaded briefcase wasn't off sick, the paperwork was in place, it wasn't a national holiday or office meeting, she peeled off my correct pay in 'monopoly' money and I came back with a full purse stuffed inside my secret pocket.

Basically, anyway, I know I pay in shops or bajaj taxis over the odds. I am a white person clearly not a local and unable to barter as they do so I know I am ripped off, that's how it goes. My home savings are my income really as I don't anticipate living off market lentils and veg the whole year. But by this month, at last, I feel I have got my pay on track from the £20 a week to £30 which I am due. Time to celebrate!

The streets of Mekelle, the capital of the Tigray region, are clean and tidy because the women keep them that way. This is probably true in many towns across Ethiopia, where the street cleaners in their yellow cotton overalls who push their loaded iron barrows and brooms are women, the café workers who brush water about to keep the dust down and the ones who perform the coffee ceremonies are all women. When I walk about – at my usual speed – I keep an eye out for any potential problems or people who are actually unwell (I think you can guess what I mean: being naked or partially clad is a big clue), so I can avoid confrontation with someone not keen on foreigners like me. Oddly, I have had more trouble with girls and women: name-calling and stone-throwing isn't out of the ordinary here. Like the known 'mad' female teacher who threw rocks at me the other week. On one early morning visit, I was hit a couple of times by a couple of small girls and although my loud "Oi!" stopped them in their tracks, (women are quiet here as a rule), but for a 20-yard throw I was quite impressed with their accuracy! St Mary's birthday was this month apparently, women of the town ready to party, so there was another meat-fest plus bones being fought over in the street by local dogs, and I think the knock I had on my door really late was to join the corridor party.

Women of Tigray wear dozens of beautiful, neat plaits (sheruba) tightly braided off the forehead and billowing out loose at the shoulders. Some more elaborate creations are for special occasions where the middle three braids are padded and sometimes henna or colour is applied. A very fine plait is also somehow threaded across the forehead…I am still puzzled as to how that works and try not to stare too much! My landlord explained to me once about the strange smell that country women have…it is the butter they put on their hair as a sort of tonic, I think. I didn't say that in the heat it didn't do any favours for me but hey ho that's their tradition; the odour is pretty grim but now I know.

Jewellery is worn mainly by women usually on any special occasion and is silver or gold with amber and glass: round, very heavy and chunky, some woven into their sheruba. The diverse people of Ethiopia wear many different styles of clothing as well which usually reflects their climate and economy. Thick cloth and drapes are useful for the people of the highlands, not many skins of wild animals are used as they are farmers here in the north; the animals we associate with Africa are used more in the southern parts. I see some ladies coming in from the country wearing greyish heavy cotton in layers to the ground, whereas in the towns the cloth is white – but all have their traditional heavy colourful detailed woven decorative borders. Although in modern towns the western style of clothing is seen on a daily basis teamed with a locally made scarf, they do all wear their regional clothes for festivals and so on.

Carrying weighty things high on their backs, shoulders or occasionally their heads is quite common for women too. I have no idea what they would think of our prams and buggies: nothing like it is seen here at all. The baby is carried in a tightly wrapped scarf on the upper back until the child can walk, and some exquisite leather baby-carriers are seen on country women decorated with seeds, or with shells from the country Djibouti on the coast. The babies are quiet and content, their young mothers happy and full of smiles as they chatter together. They are never brash and raucous as some western women can be. I can't speak for other East Africans but I have to say the Ethiopian women are quite beautiful. Perhaps because they are mixed with Middle Eastern blood somewhere way back in history. They are tall, slender from top to toe and with chiselled features including massive eyes – which Ethiopian art replicates almost in a cartoon style.

Mulu from the office asked me once, "Does your mother wear the same clothes as you?"

Great. I must be looking dowdy! It may be in part to the large brown sequined shawl I wear as white is supreme here.

VSO Head Office have asked me to email a few notes on what the challenges are. Goodness. I am thinking I do have the 'stickability' to see things through, being a role model to other women I hope, but probably key so far I like to think I can empathise with people and have certainly learned to be more patient or slow down when I see there is no point being stressed especially about quick results. The local office quite enjoys my humour and light-hearted attitude…long may that continue.

But this month, my female teacher mode included: washing by hand in a grubby bathroom in buckets, moving hot water when available from the only hot tap in the kitchen to wash/mop/clean. The food issues about what to eat, no fridge, what is available. Watching my money always as well as my guts – which still aren't great. Mental note: ask for Imodium from home and maybe dried quorn could be good!

Before I arrived to work for VSO in Ethiopia, I realised that women would have different lives and I would have much to learn, both to fit in as well as work around sensitively in schools. I am still on that learning curve! Women here, when away from their family and homes, are generally shy and lack confidence.

One Saturday, I was invited by a young office chap to a celebration for the birth of a baby girl along with a few from my office. He was chuffed with a picture I had painted more than the wrapped gift, of a local hidmo house but with a cartoon style Arsenal gun on the roof – he is an Arsenal fan and they really liked the clothes line picture of her baby things I had painted on the inside.

For the event, their street was closed off with piles of rocks for the inevitable big tent, and the long stream of guests receiving a welcomed plate of food. I rather hoped I would see the baby but didn't. Instead, the happy parents arrived dressed actually in their wedding clothes, to sit on two thrones at the head of the tent surrounded by gifts mainly of bottles of various drinks and I added my gift of a pouch of sweets! The meal was served by the women and continued for *over two hours* so they must have been preparing it all for simply ages beforehand. Needless to say, I was the only white person for miles and was a spectacle anyway, but I did the right thing: ate the flat-bread injera and chilli mixtures all with my right hand, I was perfect and didn't lick my fingers ever, plus I drank their dubious cloudy sewa beer, along with the rest of the crowd. I am told a first-born is more special here if it is a girl since the girl can look after all members of her family as she grows older. Common sense.

There are plenty of issues a girl has to face here in the education system alone. In schools, there is a steady increase in absenteeism up through the years or grades and more girls are kept down year on year as they become older to complete their basic education. Some dawn Saturday morning schools also exist in towns for girls only, since they are the ones who need the extra support. My local school runs a two-hour session before they do their household chores at home most Saturdays for girls who have missed school due to ill health of a relative, or who are too shy to participate in a large mixed class and have fallen behind. I couldn't imagine our teenagers getting up early while their friends are asleep. It is a hard call for the teachers too. The teacher I observed this time was fed up as I was causing them to be even shyer with my presence, so I livened things up a bit by staging a mock interview between us. The next teacher was an older guy who was also struggling with lippy teenage girls acting up because the content was too hard. It happens, so between us, we simplified the lesson with some word games. The 22nd August is 'Girls Day' in Tigray apparently, go girls!

Women teachers are accepted with lower grades as it is more difficult to achieve necessary certificates…I could go on. I had picked up on the recent meetings in the office around the manager's long table that something special was being planned. My counterpart did fill me in a little that things changed in schools from May onwards and they were organising a showcase of secondary school and college work.

Typically, the event rushed up on me and I heard about it just in time but surely the planning must have been going on by my office for quite a while? The day came and I was officially told to be at the office early to go together to their 'Festival of Education'. The school around the corner was hosting it so I knew a lot of people there as well as my office team. It was a treat to see so many inventions displayed by students from age 10 and was really thrilled to be shown amazing complicated machines by budding female scientists. Hearing some aspire to be an engineer or an architect was really pleasing. The day consisted of an opening ceremony with bands and marches, schools and colleges had a small area in the compound for their 'stalls' to display their inventions and working models while the Sunday was dedicated for the prize-giving beginning in the local hotel with a great gymnastic display, stunning dancing and great singers as entertainment. My landlord's factory has an apprenticeship element so were qualified to show their machine work at the festival too which was very good to see. In fact, the prize-giving was at 8.30 and I arrived promptly to find myself next to the president of the university, a German. So there we were, the forenjis, best friends, in the front row. For the next three hours. During the event, I saw some schools I knew well receiving prizes but I had no idea what for, and my landlord, Hailom's business also received unexpected prizes naturally making him incredibly happy indeed.

The entertainment that followed was well presented: gymnastic displays, musical groups and dances, and I was truly impressed. I didn't realise there would be food but while we waited outside, the hall was neatly transformed. It was another massive stew, bread and beer event, and I wished I had left an hour before eating but *Whatever,* I thought, *best get stuck in.* Added to that I was shepherded to the front of the queue with Hailom and the German as the white forenji guests! Afterwards, Hailom's driver friend was called for and he whisked me back to his house for a coffee ceremony which I had to down fast along with the traditional nibbles accompanying the three cups of stewed coffee as his brother wanted us at his place next for his coffee too. Their rooms were very different. At the brother's, we sat in a row on the four chairs while his wife and children sat on the mattress on the floor opposite us. I was very good and smiled a lot until at five we had yet another chilli stew and bread with his sewa beer, I could have done with a water but, oh well, yet again I just have to get on with it. Then a bajaj into town followed by a much-needed walk to settle my guts back to mine completed a crazy long day.

I had to feedback my immediate thoughts to the office and made them laugh about all the dubious sewa varieties I had strained through my teeth and the triple coffee sessions I had no option but to take to wash down all that injera!

Rather than give a verbal response to my office, I decided to write something they could mull over and look at and share between them. I had a few photographs printed that I had taken that day and gave them to a couple of schools I had special relationships with as well as my landlord and the office staff. They have not had that before and were so happy.

They were also thrilled with my written report:

Education Festival 19th
20th May 2012

Event notes: Valerie McKee

The Mekelle City Education Office staff should be congratulated on a brilliant event. It takes a huge amount of forward planning, preparation and organisation to put on such a big festival – and then to clear up afterwards.

Not having seen such a festival before, I have a few thoughts about it which may be of use.

The venue for the Festival was ideal. It is central and must be easy to access and prepare, the people of Mekelle can all get to it and spend as much time there as they wish. It was spread out and big enough – any larger, then in the heat, not all exhibits would be looked at carefully enough. Also, if the stands were any bigger, the schools may be tempted to fill them with not such good quality items and the better ones could be overlooked. I was glad for the shade inside each stall!

As I have visited schools, I have been proudly shown inventions and machines in science departments and can now see that it is driven not only by the student and teacher interest but by the forthcoming Festival. Knowing they would be competing and that it would benefit the school as well as the students, gives them a focus which is excellent. Then, as I studied the finished products, discussed with enthusiastic teachers plus the 'inventors' themselves, I became very involved in the process and thinking behind each individual project. It was thoroughly interesting and well worth every minute.

The prize-giving on Sunday was also exciting – even if I didn't understand the language behind it, I still felt involved. There have been many occasions when I have been at large celebratory events and it is usual to have a few performances by students by way of introduction. The number and variety of acts chosen were perfect and the quality of each was extremely high. It was great to see some of the schools I am now very familiar with receiving their awards so I can imagine how they must be feeling, and it gives others something to aim for and realise that they too could achieve next time around if they make the effort.

I especially hope the science teachers of the schools are congratulated as well since their enthusiasm inspires the next generation.

I was not expecting lunch and although there was a gap between the prize-giving and the lunch, it had to happen: how to transform a hall into a dining room for so many in a shorter space of time would be a miracle. The food was fine – even for me, a forenji!

There are a few thoughts or ideas which may be of interest for the next Festival, (the third one here may not be so easy to adjust):

1. *You should be proud that the Office does this massive undertaking every year and so advertising that it is, for example, the '6ᵗʰ' or '7ᵗʰ' Festival would be a good thing and raises the profile. If such an important event as this is regular, then showing that on the notices is a good thing. It also makes sure that not only Mekelle has it on their calendar but that the excitement will continue through the year as it is talked about and preparations are made.*

2. *I am able to recognise the uniforms of many schools now, but since English is a goal for schools and in Preparatory science is used more often, I would have liked to see the English written names on all the school stands or stalls. A few more labels in English would be good too, but at least the basic names in English?*

3. *Having had the difficult task of preparing and judging inventions myself, I know how hard it can be. However, in the inventing, it is good practice for sketches of the development of ideas and of the workings of a machine to be available alongside the product. It shows how the mind progresses, how changes have been made to improve something at the experimental stage – which is a normal process – and how the public sees the final product, particularly, as some of the moving parts may be hidden inside a sealed box. It is extra work but a good habit to get into: to record the process and the engineering ideas behind a machine. The Art College displayed some really good drawings with their new brushes but schools need not have such quality diagrams, just an outline would be a good idea. Then, in the judging, there is evidence of how it was created as well as by whom. In England, it is no different: I know too many parents etc. who would get involved and influence their child's work.*

Again, well done to the Mekelle City Education Office and thank you for a really exciting weekend!

Opposite my office is a large restaurant which apparently specialises in large cultural evenings with dancing. Barbara and John organised a table of us all and I wasn't really keen as I can't seem to be able to enjoy the meat here – lately I have had to be polite and eat quite a bit of chewy stewed meat and I feel I need a break! The day after that office meat-fest I was really poorly… But I was wrong, this was such fun. There were traditional dancing groups and we all joined in – even the children, which was brilliant – a bit like Ethiopian line dancing with lots of shoulder action. We all wore any traditional costumes we had and got involved in everything there. The food was ordered on entry and the meat which was hanging in the butcher section at the entrance was hacked off the carcasses, weighed and taken outside for barbecuing. Although not cheap, it was totally yummy, not spicy or hot so guests could add their own chillies as they wanted. I had sheep kebab and tsahali which was a mini sizzling clay pot over its own charcoal fire. There was a lovely salad and nice bread plus the usual injera if wanted. Barbara and John have met another volunteer but he's actually from Winnipeg. He was shocked someone actually knew all about the place so I enjoyed chatting about my son's life there too. We shared a tiny taxi back so it all ended safely and not too early which was a change for me.

The weather is seriously wet now and electric storms so dramatic I am used to turning off the lights – if not blown anyway – and just watching the light show outside, and that's not just the forked lightning but the electric sparks jumping along the street wires. Sometimes I can't move outside as the roads are awash with mud which is good for cleaning away toilet messes in the massive storm drains and fine if it's the weekend, but not great if I am out on a school visit. A couple of lessons I have seen lately were perfect for my active weather reporting. If they can't count properly, they know the words for thunder, wind and flooding! In spite of the weather, the women are up and down ladders lugging sacks of cement and mixed buckets for the builders to use as they work their way ever higher, wearing their usual long skirts and headscarves. Modern style concrete buildings are filling some spaces between the traditional hidmo houses and the hotels opposite are a fascination for me. A foreman may appear periodically with a clipboard and a hard hat but everyone else manages in rough ordinary footwear and floppy clothes balancing on narrow poles as necessary, so it is actually scary.

I made them laugh in the office this week. Back at my flat, I had become fed up with the bang banging on the ceiling above. It seems to be early morning, very early. I thought it was too much like rats scraping about and tapping over my head. I have tried knocking on the ceiling with the broom handle to frighten any rodents up there, but sadly no change. Then it dawned on me: again, things are hard for people to adapt or take on Western methods here. They are used to chopping food on a flat rock outside, but put them in a building upstairs they still need to chop food somewhere and the marble floor is ideal. So that's it: the women above are preparing food as they know how – on the floor above my head! The office loved that when I confessed. Barbara too tells me that she had real trouble stopping their maid from preparing food on the floor but to use the table they had bought especially. The lovely plastic table cloth made it easier to clean and covered the splintered old table-top. Then, a stroke of genius, recently I thought I would take the whole set-up apart and clean it. Oh yeah… Brilliant. I had found where the cockroaches were nesting big-time! This is no time for the squeamish as they have to go once and for all. With the rainy season deteriorating and the cockroach problem getting worse as they sought cover, I was convinced they were coming in under the door, but this find hopefully will sort it out. I apologise to the flats below as I whipped out the old table drawer and ran with it to the tiny balcony and tipped it over the edge. No doubt some fell into balconies below and for that I am sorry. Scrubbed and sprayed and dried out; the drawer has been replaced but I will check sometimes to be sure I have no repeat performance. Truly grim.

Meanwhile, I have slowly brought back sand in my pockets from various builder's piles to fill a couple of plastic water bottles which I can use as weights! I am worried that I am not as fit as I could be and as I have a lot of time indoors, I need to fill my time productively so a little circuit training is now in order.

Tsitsi and I have decided next month we will accompany each other to travel further north to see the sights together for safety as much as anything else, so that's something to begin planning. The Ethiopian Airline office is a lovely place to hang about, we are, as is usual in Ethiopia, organised by a guy with a stick to move in turns nearer the desks, but I tend to shuffle along the rows of chairs chatting with anyone. Part of the trip will be by air and part by bus. I am finding I am getting to know the airline staff, and amazingly the same people may be the stewards on the flights or at security desks in the airports which is probably why they know their job so well.

After my jolly session at the airline office, I was delighted to find a parcel for me at the post office. My old glasses, DVDs, sweets, contact lenses and two articles on FGM: thanks, Jeanne! More laughs on the way home buying tomatoes and eggs we had to leave quickly as the woman's barbeque set up for her coffee ceremony suddenly started smoking *so* much, we were all choking! So funny. Then it was a delicious tea of pasta, avocado and scrambled egg…yum.

Sixth Month

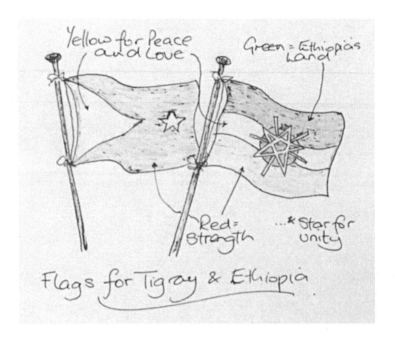

Yellow for Peace and Love

Green = Ethiopia's Land

Red = Strength

...*Star for unity

Flags for Tigray & Ethiopia

Northern Ethiopia is also known for the dramatic highlands, it's farming and village lifestyle and although there is not the range of animals about which we tend to associate with 'Africa' – giraffe have moved across this continent further west for the time being – but there is still plenty to see and marvel at. On our return from the last trip, we saw a few caravans of camels – about 50 camels tied neck-to-tail, all sedately walking from Mekelle market to their work or temporary homes in the country; knowing that just one camel would cost the price of a truck, we did debate which form of transport would be a better option in these parts. Meanwhile, either using a pick-axe by hand or with the aid of an oxen and what amounts to a medieval plough, the ploughing and planting of these Tigray tiny stony fields is complete.

The rains have paused pretty much and we have sunshine again for a few weeks. It is still over 20 degrees through the thunderstorm sessions, so with any luck, we will celebrate a good harvest when the rains stop again at the start of the Ethiopian new year: September. My washing is drying really fast on the little balcony. But maybe I should be honest and say it is just getting thinner with all my physical scrubbing! I have to tackle it when the water is on as weirdly it is the turn of water rather than the electricity to be on or off these rainy season days.

This month has begun with a more serious ill me than I have ever been before. Barbara's landlord, Ephraim, again came to my rescue, and he promptly walked me to his trusted pharmacy for appropriate parasite antibiotics. It's taken another course to clear it, I've been well behaved, not eating dairy – there is little to be found here anyway – but I've been left pretty weak so my school visits currently are shorter and not so distant, for a couple of days at least.

Tsitsi and I need to discuss our final travel plans as she is to meet me in Axum and we travel there separately to fit with our ability to take time off work. The journey will take a long day on a bus to get there so that has to be factored in. The regional chap, Ayele, is visiting us now with his driver in tow so we opted for a pizza meal out which I thought should agree with my guts but the service was embarrassingly slow and we actually nearly fell asleep waiting for food to happen! The following day, Ayele wanted to discuss my staying in Ethiopia for longer as I seem to be working well and they really like what I am achieving, so I took a chance on my food intake and have his choice this time of the Ethiopian lunch before he left for Addis. At least it arrived promptly.

It is a big deal for me going to Axum in the north not far from Eritrea on the bus. I am hoping to have enough cash ready for the trip which I will secret about my person and I practice this ready. Tickets for a long trip like this cannot be bought in advance, even two days before, as I discovered after my dash there one day. They laugh at my organisation and tell me to relax, it's too early to get a ticket. The office is changing tack as I am told this week it is exam season now in what appears to be every school in the city and they are assigning invigilators so I feel superfluous; going away now is a good idea after all. I did try to fit in a reshuffle of the local secondary school Atse Yohannas's library English shelves, but what with the disinterested librarian and the removal of rat nests and rodent poo, it was a trial, to say the least. I need that holiday!

One day to go and I trek back to the bus station office and am allowed to buy the ticket: yippee! Still no water in the flat so I recycle what I can and add bleach to the clean-through before I leave the place in the hope that at least some of the cockroaches will think twice.

Axum

My five o'clock start is scheduled so it's still pitch black. I scuttle to the bus station fast ignoring the 'hello sister' from a persistent voice in the dark and reach the locked depot gates. Phew. I crouch down with other women trying to blend in. We wait, nobody moves. And we wait.

Suddenly, it's all systems go. I speedily suss out the right bus for Axum and rush on, grab a seat by the window for perfect views and smile a lot at the woman next to me with her goat squashed under her knees. They travelled next to me for part of this journey to be replaced by a man in threadbare clothes carrying a lot of boxes which he shoves between us and under his seat and feet. We're in rows of five across – small people these Ethiopians which helps busses pack in more travellers. The whole hot squashed trip is six and a half hours, it is bumpy, full of hairpin bends, occasionally very close to the steep drop down the valley.

I really am loving the scenery changes through Abi Gras. We have a toilet stop here which I reject: it's a case of bobbing in turn in front of our bus. No, I don't think so, thanks! I had visions of the white forenji's toileting being the talk of the town. On to Debre Damo and finally towards the northern city of Axum. The skyline changes from peaks to more level highlands – patterned with stepped fields hugging the sides, all being planted at speed ready for the imminent rains – to amazing flat-topped mountains at Axum. Sick bags are passed along the craggy switch-back route. It is pretty hairy in parts and the sheer drop by my window isn't something I want to dwell on. Next, I am prodded from behind for the shared large bag of wraps of the drug 'chat' which I decline, but I see the driver is pretty keen to take part and seems to be the main user. Goodness, let me out! My journey ended suddenly as I didn't recognise the stopping place and called 'woraj' rather late, *totally* the wrong end of Axum. This meant I faced a fast, terrifying evening walk or rather trot with my bag back along the road again. Thank goodness for the texting phones we have as I was able to make contact and adjust where I was to meet in Axum town. The relief was huge when I saw the volunteers waiting there for me, it is guesswork as to who they could be but a white smiling face is a clue! Beers, food, lots of talking then bed. Okay, I am sleeping in the VSO's house on blankets on the cold, solid marble floor…I am beyond caring.

Kings and Emperors of 'Abyssinia' as it was back then, ruled their country from different capitals in northern Ethiopia. Axum was the first notable seat of power at a time when regular trade took place between similarly wealthy countries: India, Persia, Arabia, Rome and Greece – it was the Greeks who named the people 'Ethiopic', meaning 'burnt face'. The name Axum comes from the original ruler: Aksumai who apparently was the great-grandson of Noah and the following generations of the line lasted, some say, up to about 97 generations. In the eleventh to tenth century BC, the Queen of Sheba ruled Abyssinia and Yemen. Not only was she very powerful and rich, but she also had a relationship with King Solomon of Jerusalem and they had a son, Menelik. Much to Solomon's anger, it is said that it was this Menelik who moved the Ark of The Covenant from Jerusalem to St Mary Zion church in Axum where it is said to still rest well-hidden there.

By the end of day one, I still cannot believe I have walked through the Queen of Sheba's palace, trying to think of how it could have looked all those years ago. Unbelievably, the actual base, courtyard, pool and walls still remain to wander around and we were the only people there. It is true! Today I have walked on the very same stone floors as the Queen of Sheba. It would be great to see a computer-generated idea of it all when it was in action.

One of those three wise men at Bethlehem, Balthazar, was said to be from here at one time too. It was a bit later on after the birth of Christ that this kingdom of Axumite rose as the most powerful state between Persia to the west and the Roman Empire to the east and was then converted to Christianity in the fourth century. The history of this place is mindboggling and I feel like a kid in a sweet factory.

The first stelae field or graveyard we saw was the oldest with its massive (tree-sized) worn gravestones leaning in all directions. Knowing there are even more dramatic stelae to see tomorrow is so exciting. We are surrounded by incredible stories and looming in the distance is the mountain missing a serious chunk from which these stones were quarried before they were moved into position by elephants and rollers.

Guide books will tell you of what a technologically advanced civilisation Abyssinians were at that time, but it truly is fantastic. Next morning, we began by visiting the free-standing, carved, solid granite stelae over tombs of ancient kings and princes. There are quite a few ranging in size, the tallest being thirty-three metres high and all put there somehow between the first and seventh centuries. At that time when Christianity was relatively new, the carvings show both sun and moon reverence as well as Christian crosses – hedging their bets on the afterlife would have been a good call. One stone obelisk has support systems around it as it was only retrieved in 2005 from the Romans who way back when had cut it into three bits to transport it away.

But to walk easily down fabulous steps into the tombs beneath these stelae, complete still with original air vents, rooms ready for burials, doorways and places carved for hinged doorways, all made from such massive stones perfectly carved to fit – no cement; well I am still in awe. It is just stunning. King Bazen's tomb (Balthazar) is among these too. Add to that, the biggest one fell down in the construction over its tomb. It lies where it fell and the tell-tale cracks in the structures underneath from that tumble are still there but it is safe to explore. Can you imagine the angry shouting that would have accompanied that engineering blunder! There were few visitors to the site that day so it was a surprise we bumped into a yet more like-minded volunteer. Fun times.

Axum is a lovely town with plenty of 'normal' life going on. Cobbled streets are being laid, palm trees and flowers line the main avenue complete with sellers of carved crosses, camels trundling through and the usual beggars. I am pleased as I have bought a colourful woven basket from a shy woman in the market nearby; I will treasure it forever I am sure.

Yet more tombs again that afternoon. Added to that we saw such beautiful artefacts: glassware, gold, ivory, bronze pots, coins. Then it was a trip on foot out up into the hilltops as far as we were able in the heat and dust to see a few massive tombs and tunnels which haven't yet been excavated thoroughly and are preserved, waiting... Down into one cave, we were lucky to see the equivalent of the 'Rosetta Stone' only this one had translations of Greek, Ge'ez and ancient Amharic on each side, and as such has helped scholars understand these languages.

From the top, as far as we could walk, the view was amazing. Far away into the distance, the mountains of unsettled dangerous Eritrea and the odd plume of smoke: what could be burning there? Doesn't bare thinking about. Since 1960, Asmara and the access to the Red Sea has become very important to the powerful nations and although Ethiopia wanted to keep control, the Italians were driven back into that part of Africa and the never-ending conflict has continued resulting in the deaths of at least one hundred thousand Eritreans. Below us, the winding pathway into the nearer countryside was scattered with families walking from the Axum markets: women loaded with baskets and pots, men carrying their sticks, donkeys, children. In the calm, we heard them chatting merrily as they walked however many miles home. Alongside the path on our descent sat a strange rectangular reservoir, apparently, it's the Queen of Sheba's baths which is still an important site for pilgrims and baptisms, and we marvelled as we too wound our way back into the town.

Again, after talking carefully in Amharic or stilted English, meeting up with other volunteers and chatting freely in English is great. We share stories and experiences which certainly helps lift spirits. I am cross with myself because I haven't brought foods from Mekelle which are not available here: peppers, beans and aubergines especially. The VSO education volunteers here have looked after us and with their local knowledge have been perfect hosts.

I love Ethiopian airlines. The airport treatment focusses on high security and I don't blame them for that, we don't argue being moved along by a rifle through the many X-ray machines barefoot holding onto un-belted trousers. But the inflight experience is fine, I left my scarf in the airport and it was brought to me on the plane which was more impressive as we took off south for Lalibela early: again the plane is ready and everyone is seated, no point hanging about on the tarmac. All passengers are keen listeners to the safety instructions as many have never flown before and I have often had to help with basic seat belts or calm terrified travellers. Although I have to weigh up the difference in cost of a bus versus plane, I am beginning to clock up a few loyalty airline 'Sheba miles'!

Lalibela

We had pre-booked a guesthouse from recommendations and haven't a VSO to meet up here so it is up to us to get sorted. The waiting taxi guy was to be our driver, guide and landlord for the next two days. Tsitsi is black, although not East African, she is clearly African it is still a surprise to me that she experiences what amounts to tribal racism taunts directed at her. Ethiopians don't think twice about commenting on a difference in shape or colour – their skin colour isn't nearly as dark as other parts of the continent. Be prepared for 'You're fat' or 'You're thin', and since the Chinese are here in strength as engineers mainly, I clearly don't look African so, "Oy, China," shouted in my direction is regular. Some volunteers confront the caller but I don't bother; smiling helps. I did ask my office counterpart once why this happens, asking if I looked like a Chinese woman. He leant forward, studied my face for a moment and said my nose wasn't quite the same which I suppose was true. "What about my eyes?"

"Oh no, it's the nose."

Oh well, I will keep smiling and hurry along.

My friend wished she had taken a picture of my emotional expression when I encountered the twelfth-century first rock-hewn church at Lalibela; I do recall I was totally overcome. From the road, if there were no modern shelters to protect these astonishing eleven ancient sunken churches, you would simply have no idea where to look as they are accessed from lower levels or by connecting tunnels. They were literally excavated directly downwards into the mountain below, creating hidden two or three storey free-standing buildings. Good old St George who figures a lot here has his special, stunning, 15m high, cross-shaped church which is the one seen on most advertised travel pictures of the area. Luckily, his has no need for the extra 'World Heritage Site' roof protection. And these churches are not small buildings either: they are a good size, have chapels in them, plenty of pillars holding a vaulted roof, different levels of windows, the odd baptism pool – just amazing. Some churches are as sponsored conservation projects by other countries and some are protected by 'World Heritage'. It took the best part of our two days touring and immersing ourselves in each church, learning about their special differences, trying to give each time to appreciate them and their museums. Some have documents that are incredibly ancient and at times, have had to be buried or wrapped and sunk in wells to hide them from looters or anti-religious raiders. How these survived until today is a miracle in itself.

The downside was the dreadful hassle from clever children beggars: 'Buy me a dictionary', 'We need a football as we have nothing', or even 'My mother is dead, give me money!' There are large notices written in English here telling tourists not to give money to beggars otherwise they will never go to school living off their street donations, but talking to some visitors – and there were certainly more here – they were taken in by these cheeky children.

I have been able to sleep brilliantly in this guest house thank goodness as this travelling has been so tiring and here, I have a proper bed! With more tourists here, there are more eating options but there is one incredible place, the relatively new Ben Abeba restaurant – I saw it on a BBC programme after I got back (Ben means hill and Abeba means flower). It looks 'Gaudi-like' and is set on a crazy hilltop, not everyone liked the looks of it but I loved it! The food especially the delicious goat burger was an amazing treat. It had wacky stylish toilets that had doors and flushed(!), fountains and 360 views. I only hope it doesn't become too groovy for its own good.

Gondar

From King Lalibela's seat, we flew west to Ethiopia's next capital: Gondar. Since the Egyptians were keen to try to annex the whole of the Nile for themselves, and the Blue Nile flows from here, it was a good choice for defence. Between 1635 and 1855, the troubles were between European Catholics (mainly Portuguese at this time) and Ethiopian Orthodox Christians. Apparently, during King Fasil's reign, he banned all Europeans from living in Ethiopia except one single Frenchman in 1770! The large graceful medieval walled castles perched on the mountain must have been a perfect palace until late 1800s when Emperor Menelik II moved the capital south to Addis Ababa. Walking about Gondar was a mixed experience of beauty and calm and poverty. I have to admit, I haven't felt so nervous about walking around anywhere in Ethiopia as badly as I have in Gondar. We were hassled on arrival, were ripped off every time we tried to buy basic essentials and it felt generally uncomfortable out in the town streets. I'm still pretty pissed off I was sold expensive phone credit cards that I didn't know had been already used. Grrr. Photographs of life around you in this country are tricky at the best of times. I am not an ordinary tourist here and have seen most things so the argument with the treadle sewing machine man in the street about how much I should pay for that privilege of capturing him on camera wasn't great. And yet, other people were lovely. The woman with her loom was keen to show us her skills and turned out to be our taxi driver's sister!

The Royal Enclosure was something else. No, it isn't a racecourse feature! Norway has taken on the conservation of this religious place which was really an elaborate chapel set in a huge bathing area like a wide moat, surrounded by incredible tropical forest jungle trees rooted into the cliffs at angles – which rather reminded me of Anchor Watt in Cambodia. For anyone, it is a spacious beautiful oasis slightly off the tourist trail which was well worth the visit. A good calm interlude.

I'm pleased the whole trip through Tigray started with the ancient history in the north moving through the centuries to the more recent, found in Gondar – a good call.

Staying with another medic volunteer turned out helpful for Tsitsi as she prepares to leave her Ethiopian placement. I am beginning to pick up that actually leaving Ethiopia isn't as straight forward as it could be elsewhere, ha! I am not quite at that stage yet.

Preparing food for a large in-house medic volunteer party planned for the day I leave was part of the house share chores but chopping a big sack of onions really finished me off that day. Well, that was until my taxi to the airport cost me a rip off 150 birr – hadn't a choice as I was clearly a sitting duck. But result: my taxi from my airport to my own flat cost a mere 3 ½ birr. You win some, you lose some.

Mekelle

Phew: my flat was untouched – I always have that panic that I may have been burgled every time I go out – so I could relax again. In fact, the seeds I had planted in that broken plastic bowl and old lemonade bottle on my tiny balcony have actually sprouted. I am very excited to have some rocket and tomatoes of my own so moved them into the bathroom for less heat and wind which is pretty strong again these days.

Returning from any holiday is really hard. I found it incredibly difficult this time. I found I was unexpectedly sad and teary.

My family life back home is in turmoil, my divorce is still plodding on at a snail's pace, I miss my children SO much, I'm struggling with crying and I want to skype more but can't, the timings too don't make it easy. At least they seem to be doing well and I should take comfort from that, but I feel rock bottom, rubbish.

I walk about glad to be back in Mekelle rather than all the other places I have seen and still feel lucky on that score. After the rains, the vegetables here are really good so I have spinach and potatoes from my little shops as basics for all sorts of exciting meals but yet again am having to take antibiotics for yet more parasites so can't drink alcohol for a while. Running out of cash isn't great either and an 'incident' at the bank for some security reason there meant it has been shut for a couple of days. But success: I tried the ATM machine for the first time for a few birr but had the brain to change my pin number straight away after that! On to the post office to find that Jude had sent a newspaper from England which was great to receive, but I confess, in my mood reading about the London Olympics build-up made me even more homesick.

Also was a bundle from my Ruth enclosing letters from her school addressed to Lemlem School, the one I am trying to link here, and since exams have taken over schools leaving me a bit 'jobless', I'm keen to go straight there to share them. In Ethiopian English books, they try to teach the meaning of the post and what a letter is all about, but for them to actually receive one is so unusual that they were more thrilled than I can say. I am sure those Lemlem Daero School children will always have their own letter proudly displayed somewhere in their homes. An actual piece of paper addressed to them personally…well it may never happen again in their lives as far as anyone can see. Unfortunately, they insisted on replying there and then, and I had to practically dictate reply sentences, yet another repeat of multiple choice for them to copy down on bits of paper which weren't quite as personal, but as the teacher was also on his letter-writing learning curve, I just couldn't do more. These replies I took back to the office, trimmed each up as they were written on any scraps they had available, matched names with two classes from Ruth's school and went to post the lot straight away. Since being here, I have learned to package letters better. The space I have left for the number of stamps again is tricky, but I am sure they will appreciate these African antelopes jumping over the package.

The old palace or Castle built on its hilltop about 1890 continues to be a great place for us volunteers to meet up whatever the weather. By Ethiopian standards, it isn't bad for my afternoon cup of green tea – albeit shuffling around the courtyard hugging the shade of the building but keeping sight of the fantastic views is a treat. I can go there alone safely and for me, it isn't a long walk really, so if I time it right, I can walk back again to mine easily before the dangers of dusk rear their scary vibes. This weekend Barbara had some ex-volunteers to meet there so that turned out well, plus we were able to make proper plans for our trip down to Addis Ababa for the jubilee celebrations at the British Embassy next week. That helped cheer me up. I wouldn't miss the event for anything even though it was another flight and expense! We left in the evening so I shared the bajaj home afterwards. The small bar opposite mine has started the dry season with banging discos at weekends. Please let me sleep?

One local small school invited me to give lesson feedback in their tiny staff meeting which was tricky. The poor new teacher was *so* pathetic I can't see him surviving in a bigger more aggressive school situation, but they agreed with me to try one thing each week and not attempt the whole list in one go. We'll see. Then on to another really needy school for younger children in the process of being rebuilt so they currently share the space by managing a shift system, using the sweaty tin huts and thus enabling the local children to at least get some schooling. The teachers again are a lovely bunch up against it with so few resources: four books to share in a class of about 50 children isn't great.

The Education office is now pretty empty of personnel, it seems they all have their scheduled invigilation duties going on and I am now beginning to pick up that after this they close schools and all get on with farming. Not sure where that leaves me but I have my ideas to continue creating active lesson pointers for the dull English textbook led lessons.

Two days in Addis Ababa

Embassy day arrives. An early start by the god-fearing bajaj driver up to the airport. It is a struggle in that thing and each time I cross fingers! It makes me smile; the chatter we have about the church and Jesus to 'distract' us as he leans forward willing the pathetic engine to get up the hills. All fine, easy trip down to Addis to check-in bags for the overnight stay. We have a couple of hotels here we can rely on for safety as volunteers, which is lucky. Did a bit of shopping around with Barbara before getting as glammed up as possible for the event was fun. Scarf shopping is good here and we know the best places now and which grubby drains to avoid too. Even in the capital, they don't do tourist nick-knacks: postcards? What for? Holidays and post mean they are a waste of time. Trinkets and gadgets? How could they help feed a family or be of any use? There is nothing that doesn't support everyday life really but I am thrilled I managed to buy three tiny clay guinea fowl in a random market, hope they weren't made in Kenya!

Then, what a fun party. The red, white and blue theme was brilliant: marquee drapes, red and white wine, flowers, serviettes, cake icing made it a great party…and bizarrely there were the local giant tortoises wandering unphased through the gardens searching for fresh grass. I am keen to talk to as many people as possible and I met quite a variety of government or university folk – some it seems to me don't go anywhere without their driver and don't go where there are 'poor people' so they are quite interested in our chit chat about street and ordinary volunteer life. How the other half live.

It has been a while since I really ate myself silly but I was up for it regardless of what anyone thought and confess was one of the last to leave. I ate properly sliced bread sandwiches – cucumber yes! Three pieces of Victoria sponge cake, lots of exciting nibbly bits, drank two Pimms, one red and two sparkling white wines. I probably talked a lot but hey ho. Knowing the Brits had celebrated the

Queen's Jubilee which was shown out here to us all and the giant tortoises on a large TV was a great way to connect, and along with my stuffed state really helped lift my mood. The return trip just as good and back to the flat to unpack my cute black and white clay birds.

Mekelle

School visits are not worth it at all now so I'm pushing paper. Barbara and many others are planning to return to Britain for the Olympics period and I am not. I say to them in the office when they ask because they know most volunteers don't usually stay in Ethiopia during British or Ethio school summer holidays, the way I am feeling if I go home, I wouldn't come back again. It is a very difficult time. I have discovered a charity school in the northern part of the city which teaches very poor children, of older freedom fighters in particular, and runs a summer programme. I need to investigate this Nicholas School and how they are fixed over the summer.

Classic sixth-month working week goes like this…

Day 1

I met up briefly with a young volunteer, Brittany who has been working with the Charity Blind School in the north of Mekelle. I haven't been there as it's another one not in the Education office brief. Our office thinks she's odd – she does chatter a lot (more than me) that I have to pick out the relevant bits it is true. Brittany is making books for the school. Apparently, the children in her school go directly to begging once they leave so keeping them in the education system for as long as possible is important, but the governance sounds extremely dodgy. Actually, there is a lot of blindness in Ethiopia for many reasons, but the office does say many would be able to see if they have basic spectacles. However, in addition, there are no smallpox vaccines in many parts here and so it does result in much of the actual total blindness. It's really a sad struggle.

The Addis office have emailed me a lot of working questionnaires to download and print then have completed by my office. Oh, that's great! Paper is in short supply so again I have to I buy the paper pretty much exactly to the piece I need, then get the office staff to complete each one. They make a lot of excuses, but through random conversations, I now know there is actually a VSO meeting planned there in the not-too-distant-future. Hmm, that's news to me.

Over lunch with Barbara she says she will get me a super-whiz medical kit from Addis as I will be the only volunteer here over the summer. Eeek. She will try to get a few teaching books from the head office too for me to work on as I need this summer project to work.

Evening electricity is intermittent and European football games are on TV but I'm not sure if we beat Sweden 3:2! My laptop is playing up and I'm getting messages which are a complete mystery to me from Microsoft about renewing programmes. I really do not need this extra worry.

Day 2

I walk via the office to a school to deliver their report as requested. The school is completely locked. Only Grade 4 have been let in to take exams. Back to the office where I am trying not to appear rude to Solomon who is too touchy-feely in his Ethiopian style greetings – awkward. Then home for a long lunch break!

Walking that afternoon, I go in the other direction to Mailiham school, to their library. It's locked – but surely it needs to be open for study during exams? Then a massive thunderstorm happened. A grade 8 student saw me and called to me through their door invited me into little their coffee ceremony on their classroom floor there. How kind! She insisted I shared a large portion of their personal bananas, apples and fruit nibbles too. I discover in the conversation that there is an IT room here too but that's habitually locked to keep out the dust. I need to have a look at that, although by all accounts they are the heavy older computers which are not all working apparently and were a 'gift' from abroad, however having an IT room whatever it may be gives the school an advantage and status.

There is a special martyrs service for those killed in the fighting just 30 years ago at the Hawelti monument over the other side of town near Nicholas School. I probably should have gone – but in the dark? Alone? Solomon and others there? Decided not to go but to get up early and make the morning gathering just to tick that box.

Tea was plain rice I cooked mid-day and a tin of tuna luckily still in my cupboard.

Day 3

Crazy early muddy walk at 6.30 over to the monument. There are particular occasions when the Hawelti monument is a landmark for the people. Apart from the incredible views and the thought-provoking museum, it is usually a very quiet empty place – the highest point at the heart is the focal point but it is also surrounded by gardens (in as far as Ethiopians 'do' gardens). I absolutely love every bit of it. It is an extraordinary massive structure visible for miles around, a golden ball on top of a huge cogwheel supported by four pillars each carved with mottos and palm leaves gleaming in the sunlight. Close up, it is amazing. I am really impressed by the statues on either side: so moving and simple. On the left, are groups ordinary struggling distressed Ethiopian men women and children and a donkey then to the right, there is a tank with a few wounded or marching soldiers.

I am so glad I went to this historic Tigray moment… I climbed the back steps, found a large group of women on one side so joined them and crouched alongside. Many had their tiny babies in papooses high on their backs as is tradition, and nearly all carried a farming tool or similar – I even saw a few pickaxes.

In front of the structure is 'Martyrs Avenue' and it was up these steps a series of about seven wreaths were taken and laid while the Mekelle brass band played a very long version of the 'Last Post'. The wreaths were so huge – being made from large palm leaves and local flowers – they had to be carried by groups of people. Then there were long speeches and suddenly, without warning, everyone disappeared over the back to plant trees! I wondered about taking photographs but maybe not this time. All in all, it was a meaningful commemorative event. Ethiopia has really had it tough and this Tigray region, in particular, suffered quite recently. Although I was invited to coffee by a woman I had only just met I declined as I wanted to remain up there for a while before going back to the office. I was so deep in thought as I had been left alone, that I wandered into camera shot of the TV film crew I had no idea was there. Now today, I find I am famous. Nothing is edited so I'm there on the regular TV channels ducking about behind the man with the mike on every single looped newsreel. The office guys saw the recording and are asking me why I didn't say something on camera: they wouldn't miss that opportunity to make a speech through a microphone that's for sure!

The bustling town with its beggars, animals, traders and smells brought me back to earth and the Post Office lifted my mood as in my tiny box was a funny card from Ella that took six weeks to get to me but was well worth the wait. I bought a few vegetables, trekked back to the office again and managed to get a few VSO questionnaires completed which is difficult as they are hardly around to do them. They are getting cross with me asking but I am supposed to email the responses to Addis asap. Tricky.

I wrapped a few pencils and a notebook for the student I met yesterday and walked over there to give her a 'thank you' gift. The girl wasn't around so I left it with the odd-job woman tied up in a dull paper bag…wonder if she received it?

There is a new volunteer, Katherine, working with the 'Mums-For-Mums' charity and lives quite near me which could be good. I showed her where to buy essentials and which places to avoid. She's twenty-six, never been out of Europe before, travelling on her own. We're all going together to an American's summer leaving do on the other side of the city so we all planned on sharing bajaj drives and foods. Should be fun.

Day 4

The talk in the office is all about the Olympics and as ever, the Ethiopians are only interested in beating Kenya at absolutely everything by the sounds of it. They are bowled over by the sights of London – makes them feel a bit behind the times. My counterpart is not often in the office but when he is, he talks about GREAT Britain and how much they love Tony Blair. I think he gave a fair amount of money to Ethiopia which is so important to them and the bit they will not forget. The young driver, Daniew, who is also the office odd job guy but annoyingly for him he is the first one they shout for when they need computer help. They think I'm a whizz too now since I fixed Mulu's computer by turning it off and on again. Now Daniew has my permission to work quietly in my office – it's the only time he can have peace! Planning work doesn't really happen here so for Daniew it's the same every time an emergency blows up or something goes wrong, they literally yell for him. At least he is quiet and we both can get on uninterrupted.

With my parasite antibiotics, I have to be dairy-free for a week afterwards which isn't very hard for me at the moment. It's just a case of not eating those cheese triangles in my omelettes or having milk in drinks I may buy since I have no fresh dairy available to me and no fridge anyway! Ella's Bombay potato mix sparked up my dull tea this evening.

I can't believe it. Head office have asked me to get my lot to complete yet another fresh questionnaire. I still have three of the others to collect so put a mental hold on the new request. I can't ask my lot to do more at the moment.

Day 5

Woken by an annoying noise above my head again; this must be a huge amount of food she is preparing and the chop-chop-chopping on the floor is particularly loud. But I suppose again when there is no flat rock available but a lovely large marble-style floor space, why not just get on with it.

Saw the funniest thing this morning. There are a few old-style bikes around and one guy today was carrying a sheep on his back for a celebration meal, no doubt, but another had a plank over his shoulders *sideways*, like the Angel of The North statue pedalling down the road! Luckily, the road wasn't busy.

Wrote loads of letters home (it makes me look busy in the office!), and walked to the post office which was worth it again as a tasty parcel from home and a postcard which *took six weeks* to get here.

I am bored with being told my office is moving…still hardly likely! Barbara's office has actually moved now and she has to choose which way round to have her desk in the new open planned space. That was quite fun making suggestions. Then they scratched the new floor heaving their battered old desks about. There is no air conditioning so paper is being stuck over the lovely new blue glass windows and there are plenty of them in this groovy new sparkly office space. The lift is only for managers and important people, so it is up and down the stairs we go!

Day 6

We didn't need to take much food to the American's lunch do after all. They had loads of cheese and wine which was seriously unusual for here and so yummy. We played volleyball in their yard and I didn't disgrace myself at all. Haha! We had to catch a bus back to ours and got in just before dark which was perfect. Football: England vs Italy on TV but we lost on penalties. As the grudge against Italy is still here, the office was sympathetic on Monday even though Italy were, I thought, better that day.

Day 7

It's the weekend. I had a dreadful night with café disco blaring out. Wonder why their electricity problems aren't the same as mine. I'm not happy with an early knock from my landlord who wants me to pay a bill – electricity or water I'm not sure until I read his big ledger later. So, it's a bank trip for the last cash I have there as my pay isn't made up properly this month either. After that, I had no choice but to watch Barbara shop for scarves knowing I can't go out this weekend without funds, but on the bright side, it would do my stomach good I suppose.

Chores again but very slowly today. Skype is a punishable offence we have been told and we're all waiting to see if it is true, one or two years imprisonment we have been told because the Ethio telecom wants the monopoly on calls across the world from here, and they still don't trust Skype anyway.

Cooked a great batch of pan Welsh cakes for my treat trying to fatten up a bit. Cleaned the flat again and watched Monarch of The Glen DVD set for comfort!

Things are changing around with this weather. The high winds have bent the metal structure and finally blown a massive billboard down into the main road to the bus station and everyone is just manoeuvring round it! The advert is actually for using sweet potatoes as a healthy alternative, as Ethiopians need to try more variety of crops and not just rely on their 'teff' grain – it is this teff that fails in the dreadful droughts they experience here, but traditions and palettes are hard to change in spite of these famines.

Eating in the streets? You just don't! In a country where food is not always available, it isn't right to treat any food in an off-handed way which is how they consider eating whilst walking along, outside in the street or simply away from the formal eating places. Wherever they eat it is organised and may be sitting in a group on stools or rocks, or together at a table. Street 'food' would be a surplus of fruit or vegetables sold from a barrow or box prepared for eating, but the customer sits on a nearby rock or stands by the vendor and has a conversation while eating it there. It was good to see, for example, students selling cactus fruits they themselves had collected and were selling them to passers-by during their school holidays or a farmer selling her fresh carrots to school children by the school gate. We could learn much from these people about healthy street food!

Seventh Month

Street food and
deliveries (with flies!)

Household tasks definitely suit my Saturdays. Where I am isn't a particular malarial area but we are all issued with mosquito nets and have supplies of pills for travel elsewhere. This week, spurred on by the attractive red blob on my chin, I decided it was time to organise that mosquito net above the bed just in case. Found it buried in the cupboard, cut carefully out from the packet. Hey presto, mine isn't a nice 'princess' sort of round one, but a large square thing that needs lots of hooks and string and an octopus to sort it out. Only one hook is up there in my concrete flat ceiling. Bugger. Eventually, as the bed is stripped – it is Saturday remember – I shift the mattress so I can balance on a chair on the solid wooden bed base and shove two more hooks somehow into a couple of cracks I've spotted in the ceiling, then attach strings. Genius! They had better stay there or I'm doomed. I know why I should have bought that dodgy chewing gum off that urchin this morning. Now for the octopus part: tie four strings at once onto my three available hooks and balance the lot so it is the right height and everything is in place. Two hours later, it is looking about fine so I descend carefully and rearrange the mattress. Making the bed again underneath is tricky so I bundle the net up out of the way. Done it: a nice blue net all trussed up by its string thing ready to thwart the insects over the orange sheet, blue and white weird-shaped VSO issue pillow and nasty green felt blanket. What the hey. Then I top it off with ridiculous big bows at the ties just to compensate in an abortive attempt to make it look vaguely pretty. All ready for insect deterrent. Resourceful or what?

But have you ever slept under one of these nets? It is quite an irritation having to position every little thing you may need in the night next to you within reach and *inside* the net: book, water, head torch, glasses… I am beginning to think perhaps the square sort may be better than the one-hook-round ones after all as I have corners to use to stash the night-time requirements, but this does hang a bit low over my head and I have to sit up very carefully so I don't drag the whole thing out of place. It is also important not to be touching the sides during the night or the whole net effect becomes pointless. Mosquitoes can poke their bums and jaws through if they are in direct contact. However, I don't use it all the time, and often bundle it up above my head.

I had a lesson once at a stop-over in the country. No problem I thought, non-malarial place, and ignored the mosquito net hanging there all ready to go. In the night the insect life was just fine, but I put my hand out on the pillow to find a friendly slug for company. Lesson learned: nets are good for *all* creature attacks!

Some mornings I wake tired from all the night disturbances mainly here dogs barking or shagging, I'm not sure, but either way, not the best sleeping tonic. I don't cope with earplugs so have to tolerate noisy moments after dark. A bitch on heat in this place is just a target for a growing pack of random dogs and I always hope it doesn't gather below my window. This morning, early, I am awoken by a distinct weird buzzing in my ears. Buggers: insect life again? Wrong. It is the church calling to prayer nice and early and I never thought of the similarity until now! I check the mass of net above hanging there just like the Blue Whale in the Natural History Museum…maybe they have 'do not touch' signs because their hooks aren't fixed so well into the ceiling either! I made a mental note to buy chewing gum later on my way to the bank.

My evenings are better now too since my sister sent so many DVDs including the original Sherlock Holmes. I make sure my laptop battery is loaded ready for power failure and am glad I bought the extra safety booster in Addis. Barbara has a posh TV connection and they are able to watch the tennis so if I get there in daylight hours, I can watch some Wimbledon action, but I confess when Andy Murray cried at losing, so did we! I prep food and make more Welsh Cakes too when the power is on. These badly fitting metal windows don't cope well with the horizontal rain either. I have flimsy curtains strung up and I have seen them actually blow sideways too at times – we even had hail – so seeing my mop flying over the balcony into the distance shouldn't have been a surprise! To keep my bed dry now I have a sort of old plastic sheet and a towel draped across it on the window side, and keep the broom handy to swish the puddles about hoping they dry up in the heat. Quite bonkers really. Fitness-wise I am using the sand-filled bottles I devised for weights and move furniture so I can skip in the lounge using a spare washing line for a rope. God knows what the people below think… I could be 'chopping veg' I suppose.

Work has taken a turn as they prepare to close for the farming season. I continue to visit the Education office and chat with my counterpart there who is still surprised I haven't gone home like other Britons. I confess I have lied and said I am meeting my family in Kenya…they assume it is my husband too. I do still carry the photograph of my happy family so they think I am 'husbanded' and not available for marriage. My name here is Miss Valerie and it took a while for me to realise in Ethiopia the family name comes first rather than our way round, tagged on the end, and since the Biblical name is important to Ethiopians, it is obvious to them the religious word comes first: Solomon, Moses, Haile, Valerie!

Home connections are up and down. The old family home is still rented and the tenants are kicking off about electrics so my ex can sort that surely? I've done everything else. My three children are really struggling in their own ways with our separation. Tom's very adrift out in Canada but has a lovely partner with her local family so at least I can hope he can be supported by them when feeling shitty. I really feel rubbish when I try to get my head around it all. Emails and paperwork have been winging their way to the ex-husband who isn't enjoying it, to say the least, but for me, there are no short cuts and I want closure. Not long now.

As education volunteers, Barbara and I are held in some esteem and we were invited to a prize-giving at Nicholas School which I found a really odd event indeed. There were a lot of disabled veteran relatives in attendance, the 'fortunate ones' on crutches and in wheelchairs. Bearing in mind these people have no money, this expense on these occasions seems quite out of place. Is it American influence? Maybe. There are similar bizarre events creeping into our English systems, goodness knows why.

These were six-year-olds. Dressed in Sunday best with a proper black gown over and juggling a mortarboard on their heads, all collected progress certificates, the better able were given huge ruck-sacks but the six top 'students' received gold prizes and bouquets not just for being 'A' star grades, but also for supporting the less able during the year. The backdrop of their neat school block on four floors behind with the standard educational wall paintings was fitting, and yes, there was a lot of coffee and cake. However, watching a war veteran balancing on his only leg while juggling a set of crutches so that he could present a prize to a very small child and shake her hand is very humbling. I had much to think about in my fifty-minute walk back to my little flat.

The office is aware of the charity run Nicholas School and although not in the state school remit, they are full of admiration for the work they do. In spite of the location, I have said I will work there over the summer when I get back from my two weeks in Kenya but apparently, I have to ask permission since I am paid in part by the Education Office who are happy I will work hard regardless, but also VSO who may not agree. Luckily, after some debate, they are all happy – better than me going home for the whole time.

But in my discussions, I also discover totally by chance that there is a whole new set of English teaching books coming out for their new year. A completely whole new set for teachers and students. After a lengthy talk, waiting around on separate occasions, lots of signing of papers and so much smiling my face hurt, I am able to get one of the education chaps – avoiding any personal 'debt' for the loan, hmmm – to lend me a few of these with a couple of the parallel teacher books. They are so different from the last educational material, it is incredible. The active ideas I have been working on no longer fit the weekly input from these books so that's a wasted effort. What I think is needed now however is a translation of the contents so it is teachable. At the moment, I really cannot see how the teachers will be given help delivering this subject matter as it is such a change and so *English,* which not all teachers speak fluently; they will need a lot of help. Thank goodness I have it all to hand before the months lock up when they disappear to their farms!

In less than a couple of hours, it is possible to walk right into the hills around Mekelle. As I say, you need a guide just to be safe and sure you don't get lost, but it is really good to be out. The countryside is beautiful up there especially now that it is very green and full of colours. The cacti have flowered and their fruit is on sale along the streets in Ethiopian towns, as is corn on the cob, barbecued over open tiny street charcoal burners. Don't get too excited, I tried it and it's a bit chewy but seems to sell well! Sheep, goats and cattle are herded up into the hills to graze. The little farms have a one-roomed stone and straw farm building for the family (cooking is done as usual over charcoal next to the house, and they don't have a lot of belongings or 'stuff', so one room for night times is plenty), plus another round hut is there for the animals. A few vegetables are grown near the house and a protective wall or tall cacti hedge surrounds it all. Unfortunately, corrugated iron with a few rocks to hold it down is the new roofing material, so that in the sun it heats up and then in the rain it is incredibly noisy. I have yet to see a hyena but did see a wolf on one trip and they are both a real danger for farmers. I am keen to see hyenas but not sure about the ones paraded about down south in Harer with hyena men who apparently put their heads inside their mouths for a fee. The birds are lovely exotic varieties and I have given up trying to photograph them (I decided I would cut up a bird book for pictures when I need a record as they look so much better than my efforts!). Town birds survive somehow like those little hoopies in gardens with comical Mohican feathers on top. I have kept my eye on a pair of cranes nesting near the bank on a rickety roof and they now have two noisy chicks to feed. Good luck with keeping those alive! Starlings, the iridescent colour of kingfishers and sparrows here have either deep red or bright blue chests and tails. There are plenty of other birds from very small bee-eaters to larger birds of paradise and even larger vultures and buzzards wheeling overhead or strutting in the fields. I'm used to the birds of prey everywhere in towns now; I think they feed off pigeons and whatever is lying around. Needless to say, the plants are amazing as well and it is weird seeing the small exotic house plants we tend to in our English window sills as very large shrubs and trees with the most brilliant flowers. The flowering trees lining the streets have changed on from purple to fist-sized orange ones that later produce massive bean-seeds dangling from them. We had one bean pod I remember back in the music percussion class in Cambridge, so now I know exactly where it came from.

Due to thunderstorms, the flights to and from Addis have been pretty haphazard. Just to be prepared for anything I spend an hour queuing, or rather shuffling between chairs in the airline office to buy my flight tickets in the local travel office bringing forward my forthcoming Addis flight by a day, and booking an overnight stay in a safe Addis hotel to be sure I catch the correct flight to Nairobi.

The bank has reopened so I decided to join the line there next for currency, suitably embarrassed however by the guard calling me and waving his stick indicating I should push forward past the enormous zig-zagging seated queue to the front bench. Plenty of others glared as I moved on up! Oh dear, an older white woman volunteer gets it again. I gather no visitor is expected to wait for the locals here; can you imagine that ever happening in England?

"Hey, you look like a foreigner, come up to the front!" I think not.

Between all this queuing, I call into my office and try to see my team. It appears there are rounds of meetings that I know nothing about and are obviously not recorded anywhere. Barbara has a workshop involving our Addis coordinator so I attended that one and found, by chance, my office lot there too. We had a yummy lunch at the cultural restaurant nearby and I could sense my people were watching me intently yet again to check out my eating habits using fingers and injera properly. Then the boss guy suddenly caused a fuss apparently with a bit of chilli in his eye! Goodness, everyone was dancing about in attendance and the waiter was called to have a close look and wash it with water. How anyone could see anything anyway in the murky lit place is a mystery. In the afternoon we had a small group activity, I made sure I took the lead and presented the flip chart to demonstrate I am able to do this! Afterwards, there was another argument about where to eat before the Addis group flew back. My line manager, Gamunzadik is so calm and placid he goes with the flow but I could tell he was extremely fed up with a woman visitor from Addis causing another fuss about menus. It's a treat, its food!

Fabulous response the next day back at the office with my half-yearly reports, all typed and at great expense to myself printed one each on my paper, delivered by hand to the cluster supervisors too which took a lot of walking around the city. Then I whizzed to Barbara's office before their summer break for their first coffee ceremony in their new office. The full ceremony was underway with herb grasses and incense burners spread on the floor that is already messed up with dragging desks about and badly patched staining to cover the scratches. The coffee and nibbles were much needed though *and* I got home before a crazy overhead thunderstorm which was a result.

Since Barbara and John are leaving for their Olympic tasks in London, I am being given a key to their place. Apart from the fact that their address has a locked safe deposit box where volunteers can retrieve specially reserved vital money and tokens in case of regional emergency, they have kindly said I can make use of their facilities over the summer. After their departure, I tried the gate key and couldn't get in so over tea in the Axum Hotel I met Getnedt, the chap managing the place for the landlord, to explain and organise better keys. I paid for our tea and now he fancies me. Bugger. Their maid, Mehrat shuffled all the way to my office in a dreadful thunderstorm to meet me to arrange for a key copy. The office translated the problem and together we went to a key cutter in town. No electricity = no keys cut. I gave her enough money for two keys and the cutter bloke told me there were two different keys I would need anyway to gain access so I didn't feel quite so thick! Poor Mehrat, a lovely lady, so gentle and kind but was coughing badly. I felt for her. As I talked to her quite a bit today face-to-face, I appreciated how truly beautiful she is and I never noticed until now as she hides away or keeps her head down. She agreed to deliver to the office for me at her convenience but Getnedt keeps ringing me, his latest topic is trying to get me to dismiss Mehrat from her job so he can employ his own mother. I don't think so. I know the landlord, Ephraim very well now so I contacted him and he's sorted it out in no uncertain terms – I wouldn't want to be in Getnedt's flip flops. A few days later, the keys arrived so I went round and although nearly broke my fingers trying them out, it was worth it as I could help myself to their shower and fresh avocadoes and herbs before the slugs get stuck into the crop.

My flat stinks more at the moment and with poor electricity, the water pumps don't work so I can't flush the pipes or drains…keeping the bathroom door as shut as it can be is the only remedy right now. There is only so much bleaching and bailing water I can do! I am sure there are even more cockroaches scuttling about but perhaps it is the rain flushing them out of the crevices. In the office, the mice seem to be increasing in numbers, flooded out of their usual hiding places I am sure. Better spray the flat with dreadful toxins again before departure to be sure they don't take over completely. On that note, I called to see my landlord to give him my dates for Kenya and deliver a photograph I had taken of his family at a previous coffee session there. He was so happy. Since Ethiopians don't do photographs, it is already on the shelf for all to admire straight away. Unfortunately, I had to be polite and was force-fed more spicy dishes with injera when I would rather have given my stomach a rest.

Preparations for Kenya is pretty much done. A few creepy guys numbers are already 'blocked' on my phone but I do need a break from all these hassles. Volunteers Bob and Pam are staying in Barbara's to keep an eye on things for part of the time and the keys work! My laptop is stashed under the mattress; the water barrel is empty now so fresh Kenyan water will be a dream.

Mekelle airport departure lounge is an easy routine for me. I am used to the many x-ray machines every step of the way, the gun-waving soldiers, only flights of stairs for access, shoes, belts, scarves, jewellery off procedures plus the two simple cultural shops and the one pre-flight café. Finally, the long walk across their tarmac from Mekelle airport to the plane steps, past burned-out ex-army planes used for training, is always incredibly windy.

The larger Addis airport has even more security and apart from being bigger, all around is an odd mix of cultural and international. Obvious VIP lounges, a chapel, small mosque, guards with serious guns everywhere, x-rays on entry, before and again at intervals after check-in, then again before boarding are minimum requirements. There are cafes, but also the random pop-up Ethiopian coffee brewers complete with their scattered herbal grasses, incense burners, charcoal fires and traditional baskets all laid out on the departure lounge floor are quite popular too. Small shop units line the walkways as they do in any airport however many here are vacant since shopping for pleasure or for luxury goods just isn't the Ethiopian norm. The museum-like display in one shop unit of coffee beans, baskets, local cloth, stools and sacks of sweetcorn husks will always stick in my mind as the rats were having a fun time in there feasting on all of it! Corridors are wide and lined with plenty of proper fully reclining beds, there are stairs and temperamental escalators, male and female toilets – no disabled or baby facilities as yet – and all of it spotless since the women with mops and buckets are constantly working. Checked-in baggage itself varies too from taped laundry bags to paper-wrapped things and even very large colourful woven coffee baskets arc taggcd for transport. It all gets a bit messed up as the conveyor belt is tiny so man-handling happens a lot and bits do come adrift in the process. The other funny thing for me is the departure gate process where TVs are for cultural adverts or displays of a new road somewhere with a car on it rather than for relevant flight details, so as usual, I have to be alert for unannounced changes and keep my ears open to others' conversations. It's quite normal to have to sprint to a completely different gate to catch a flight.

Kenya

(A brief overview of my stay while out of the country)

Kenya was far more English than I thought it would be including driving on the left, their ability to read and speak English (including swear words) and even using shillings too! Although we have most African animals in Ethiopia, there are no giraffes left so I really enjoyed seeing some in the reserve just west of Nairobi. We cycled up there on one mini-break and with the quiet early dawn, everything looked fantastic, relaxed and natural, so close as well. The giraffes really look like trees, wandering majestically about but also seeming prehistoric. Zebras are great and warthog families dashing around are funny. I have respect for water buffalos and wouldn't go too close to a baboon troupe either…but all really brilliant to see. Impalas are beautiful and the bigger gazelle, like deer also very shy and elegant but with twiddly horns, are stunning as well. Ruth and Marty came to Kenya to be with me for part of the trip and they went on a full safari too where they saw the rest – elephants, a leopard and lions.

Apart from meeting up with my Ruth, which was absolutely great, a few days by the Indian Ocean was excellent for me as I am not near any seaside or delicious fresh fish in landlocked Ethiopia. Negotiating violent beach blokes' little gang lands was also another experience so we were lucky Emma (the same friend of Ruth's from Cambridge University who had stayed with me earlier this year), took over all of that side of our dangerous hassles. But the real threat of a machete attack can take the edge off a beach walk back to base. When the tide was out, the beach was covered with rock pools that attracted local shell collectors. We were told that they also gathered beautiful live shellfish which was not so good; all of these are for the western jewellery market, but at least they collect by hand and not machine…at the moment. I will think twice before I buy clothes or beads decorated with shells any more in England.

We heard on the BBC world service about 58 ordinary farmers had been killed in the south-east – near the beaches where we had just been – in a dispute over grazing rights. What a tinderbox it all is.

I also went with Emma a few times to the charity for street boys in Thika where she has been placed for the past couple of years. The charity helps get 9 – 14-year-olds off the streets where they mainly sniff glue and truck fuel, it helps them settle into school and gives psychological support too for six months. Being in Nairobi, Thika and around towns meant that I mixed with local people and learned their ways a little more – like the music and incredible noise along with regular religious teachings from Bible readings from the front of the bus. Once too, I was forced off a bus before reaching the bus station by a typical policeman in a mood, demanding passengers pay a 'fine' in addition to the usual fare – that was very weird for me but not unheard of here. It was really interesting noting the differences between countries. Sadly, I should have anticipated the purse pick-pocket coming as I was squashed onto a small line-bus sharing the plank-extra-seating-thingy across the central gangway, but I was so very sure I had my hand firmly on my front pocket the whole time. Buggers. Grrr.

Kenya is so westernised and way ahead in its development – in some ways, this is a good thing. But I felt I couldn't relax when out and about, and the traffic, noise, pollution, fatty sugary foods…was something else. I already have my money hidden in different places (shoes it is for me, I'm too skinny so a bra is a non-starter), know how to squash onto an overloaded bus, luckily I am good at dodging cars when crossing roads – having big speed bumps on the Kenyan *dual carriageways* helps, and I'm not too bad at haggling over the prices, but it does all get very exhausting.

The Olympic opening ceremony was fantastic: Emma had recorded it to watch with me on my arrival. I also shared a celebratory bottle of proper wine with her as my divorce email had finally come through too! In the end, packing to return to Ethiopia where my friends had temporarily left me all alone was not as difficult as I imagined. I had had my break, seen another country with all its quirks and faults but most importantly, I had lots of my family hugs: totally necessary right now.

Onwards and upwards: literally!

Mekelle

Back to the airport, blown into the building with its dust and heat once again, waited at the only carousel to see most of my bag coming through – the strong strap round the case had disappeared and the buckle was in bits. I hung on in case the strap came around but sadly it did not. Taxi hassle as usual: "150 birr?"

"No, I generally pay 60."

We worked it down to 100 but it became boring and luckily another in the queue moved in and we agreed to share at 80 birr between us! That's more like it.

Why was the guard so very keen to carry my bag on his shoulder up to the third floor I was wondering? Then he explained my landlord, Hailom had been in. They are old friends since Hailom had lived in that flat. The smell of varnish was overpowering. All woodwork even the bed had been repainted. As I rang him, keen to find my now missing laptop he told me he thought how clever I had been to hide it under the mattress and that he had it for safekeeping. That was kind, really as goodness knows who could have had access over the past weeks, however, he couldn't get it back to me for a couple of days. I managed to disguise my distress, told him the place looked lovely and made an arrangement to meet him in town. The gap in between, without having any contact with the wider world and receiving friendly messages was dreadful and now a bit of a blur. Holidays always bring me down afterwards with a bump and this I could seriously do without. I had to do chores but there is no electricity or water until I could persuade the guard to switch it on and then work out what to do first between power-cuts. Drinking water, as usual, is priority, so I tried to collect water on the tiny balcony during thunderstorms. But Kenyan Chorizo and cold baked beans gave me a lift that's for sure!

The next morning I was awoken by loud banging on the doors along the corridor slowly coming towards mine. Sounded like the doors were being repaired; it was so fierce. I flung on some clothes ready. Then my door shook. Three policemen were checking occupancy, permits and ID. Since the state controls all telephones, they wanted to look at mine too. All a bit 'Big Brother'. As I was up early, I could only do my exercise routines and then have a bucket shower before shopping for a few fresh veggie things.

Hailom was really keen to know my opinions on Kenya, enjoying the stories about corruption, theft, sea-side scams, expenses and so on. He quizzed me about my photographs on display in my flat, plus he was pleased I liked the varnish and repaired curtains, but wondered about the wardrobe key, he had no spare. I explained that I had to keep it locked in order to keep it shut at all. Pity about that though I discovered as the roaches had had a fun time in their new hidey-hole while all this was going on in the main room around them. Added to that, before I even went away the Microsoft messages were becoming more threatening and imminent so I felt that had to be fixed as quickly as I could; but how annoying knowing it was to be a very slow job reloading with Ethio slow connections and the cost of every single second being connected by a mounting pay-as-you-go expense.

On balance, I was glad to be back here in Ethiopia, even if meat is again limited, the water has been off and on and the electricity cut out just as the Ugandan marathon runner was finishing! Think positive: I'm not needing to wear flip-flops again to avoid crunching on the cockroaches – maybe they are dwindling in numbers at last; drowning possibly? However, with my emails and messages up to date, my evening TV programmes up and running, I am making myself feel rejuvenated and ready to set to work to make my impact on teachers and classrooms as best I can in the coming months. The six-month report finalised and sent off to Addis Ababa and my planning ahead is thankfully sorted. I will have to bite the bullet and do the 'workshops' they want for the new teaching materials published in this incredibly difficult English; I just hope VSO can come up with some money as the teachers cannot do any training unless they are actually paid to attend, plus are given a notebook, biro and of course, a bottle of water!

Six Month Report to Mekelle City Education Office for School Visits

Mekelle city education office

Working with the CPD Department at the Mekelle City Education Office

I arrived in February 2012 and became quite quickly part of the team at the local Education office. Having no directive, I created my own programme pretty much based on a routine of classroom observations and feedback linked with the current three CPD targets found here in Mekelle namely: to achieve better results, to enhance active teaching and learning and to improve behaviour. I found myself telling all in education these three are linked and if one – active teaching and learning – is improved the others will follow. I have given whole-school feedback to schools where I have seen a range of lessons plus their library, science provision, outside environment and (very importantly, for my assessment of behaviour) their flag ceremony. I have had plenty of positive comments from both the schools and the cluster supervisors. Apparently, they have been sharing the points I raise amongst themselves as well which is great. I have found all schools here keen to know how to improve and happy to hear suggestions. Having said that I have not adopted what I can see as the 'Ethiopian' method of swathes of criticism; instead, I offer more targets, positives and suggestions, which I would usually expect to put forward in an English school feedback.

I was already thinking of creating material to run parallel with the USAID teaching books for the second cycle schools in Mekelle to give some guidance for active teaching and learning, but a new set of books was delivered in June which covered this aspect amply, so instead I spent much of the summer familiarising myself with the content of these books. Instantly, I could see difficulties in the language involved and have since had meetings with cluster supervisors and department staff to make them aware of these problems in order to direct their support for their teachers. The teachers themselves with local NGO volunteers should shortly be attending my workshops to give support and guidance, after which – along with the NGO volunteers and myself – between us, we can follow up in schools giving class support.

English observations have been carried out, verbal feedback has been given immediately to the teachers and Principals unless otherwise noted. Pedagogy centres, libraries and science laboratories have all been seen where they are offered as a facility to the school. I have been accompanied by a member of the Mekelle City Ed Office to the following schools: Elalla, Meiweini, Gereb Tsedo, Alene, Atse Yohannes Elementary and Atse Yohannes Preparatory. All the cluster supervisors I have dealt with appear hardworking and are loyal to their schools, wanting the best for their group.

General points I have noted when giving feedback which I think are relevant to all schools:

- More English generally to be signed around the school: notices, on buildings/doors in the school and labels for painted diagrams.
- The blackboard area is a focal point for teaching and learning and should be used for key teaching aids. Hanging spaces for current lesson information, keywords and so on, on either side at the front is a good plan to adopt, some have no hooks available.
- Pay attention to the height of all displays and writing: can it be seen clearly by those it is intended to attract, is it readable, is it too high and out of sight or too low and covering sight-lines of the board?

- Group resources into subject areas for easy access and use them. Update regularly and remove old worn material.
- Regular use of small chalkboards for paired or individual work as well as other physical teaching aids should be used more often.

School: Meiweini

Notes: Teacher seen 3 times: Almuch Tesfay, feedback given in writing. Cluster supervisor met with me after observing her also to compare notes.

Library seen on 30.3.12. It is very well organised and easy to access materials there. Not many students were present when I visited. Science laboratory with the assistant has been visited twice and active lessons happen there, a good variety of work displayed proudly. Well organised pedagogy centre seen twice. The supervisor is a geography teacher so not always easy to access materials, but a few poor old English resources were seen.

Since observing the 'C' grade 5 group, I have given the G5 teacher (Zafu) sets of alphabets for small group activities.

My visits to Meiweini have been met with a mixed response. The school needs to have support with its teaching and learning but only pockets of the teaching staff are receptive to or understand my suggestions. The day before Easter break, I visited the school and many of the staff were missing, and the lesson I went to observe simply didn't happen. Having part of the school on a shift system must make it difficult to keep a cohesive teaching staff and it takes a strong Principal to do this. I have met with the Principal on a few occasions and he has been friendly if a little preoccupied. My first report given to him was lost. The quality of teaching is very varied throughout the school so some teachers in higher grades have a difficult task raising the standards there. The library and other central resource areas are well-stocked, however resources within the classrooms need a lift and relevant teaching materials should be made available for all classes 1-4 since what is there is old, worn or missing. The pedagogy centre could support this also with lifting the profile of English around the school, there were no English resources in the centre at the times I have visited. Although the students come from a variety of backgrounds, it is still important to insist on punctuality and respect for the whole school which is not a feature at Meiweini.

School: Atse Yohannes 1-8

Notes: Library 28.3.12 assessed, revisited 24.5.12 locked, revisited again early next morning and cleared more English books with the help of the Librarian and Principal this time who is positive and listens to my ideas. Some books allocated to G1-4 classes as too young for 5-8 library use. We moved the English books to central lower shelves for easy access and displayed a poster.

Full meetings with 1-4 supervisor, Kalayou Kindaya: 15.3.12, 16.4.12; with Principal: 10.4.12, 24.5.12

The driving force in this large central school is the Principal who is energetic and wants the best for his students. He is actively involved in most events and is always keen to work to improve the school further. The teachers are mixed in experience and commitment but the Principal seems to be focussing on the best practise to lift teachers to a good standard. Grades 1-4 have nearly all worked on my suggestions regarding displaying teaching materials and a more interactive style. Grades 5-8 vary in quality of classrooms and teachers need to arrange the furniture to create a good learning environment and come equipped with teaching materials for lessons. There is too much reliance on the textbooks or teacher-talk and the Principal is frustrated by this, although the Grade 8 teacher (Ato Sisay?) was active and delivered good lessons. The Saturday sessions are difficult to monitor and the teaching is equally varied in quality.

School: Lemlem Daero

Notes: Links made with St Peters School, North Chailey, England. Two sets of letters written and replies delivered to G4 class. New names sent to England, but with Principal and staff changes, continuation may be difficult.

The Principal has been the driving force in this school and has a clear vision for the whole – teaching and learning through the school environment right from KG to Grade 4. Her energy is obvious from the record-keeping to her staff involvement and lifting their teaching. It is difficult to make suggestions for further improvements although some of the general feedback comments do apply. There are too many resources in most rooms, which apart from being at an incorrect height so they interfere with the sight of the board, they are confusing. I have not seen a full lesson at Lemlem Daero and although I was shown around a few times, only a small part of an English lesson was demonstrated to me each time. The grade 'A' students are clearly defined and others are not necessarily involved actively with the lessons, but their learning is supported by the materials and whole school teaching and learning spaces. I have enjoyed my visits to Lemlem Daero and making links with a school in England has also been appropriate with such a forward-thinking school. Whether this will be able to continue when the Principal is moved and Grade 4 teacher moves to Grade 1 will be another matter.

Eighth Month

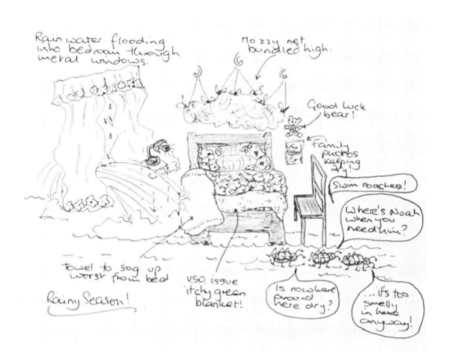

As I typed my regular bulletins home, I was glad I had a surge protector – for non-IT-whiz people that is an extra box plugged into the supply that stops the electrical things going bonkers when the electricity is cutting in and out mainly from thunderstorms…for the life-support laptop, it is a must. There were times I had the torch in my mouth focussed on the keyboard so I could continue to type! The pool of tears would be huge if I had no laptop.

I missed the closing ceremony of the Olympics and hoped to see it on YouTube if not too long to download, but I heard from the guys at the office that *Great* Britain did an amazing job. They really are in awe which is nice. Beating the Aussies in the table is quite something for me, but for Ethiopians, they were ahead of Kenya and 2nd in the Africa stakes so they are reasonably happy. John and Barbara came back briefly which was lovely to see someone and eat a bit of meat together in a cultural restaurant, but they're off again for the Paralympics in London. Hello; Goodbye.

The thunderstorms are even more serious these afternoons as their year comes to an end. The sparks outside, flashing along the low-slung wires sticky-taped together across doors and windows are lively and bright! A pigeon, struggling to get some respite on my narrow windowsill although he is messy and probably full of germs or mites, did gain my sympathy in the downpour. One time walking through the town, I bargained for an umbrella. Great price I thought, but the guy was probably keen to get rid of this one. It was bright pink nylon and had ridiculous big ruffles all around the edge so for rain it was useless as the water stayed on the top in puddles, then was hard to empty and dry out back at mine. Oh well, even though it could have fizzled up in a flash of lightning I suppose, it certainly wasn't a boring umbrella. I continue to regularly slosh water about the bedroom floor encouraging it to dry up as it pours in through the metal windows. Returning from Kenya, it has been quite a contrast as it is not their true rainy season at the moment, but here it has washed away the accumulated filth. New Year in Ethiopia starts in September and celebrations coincide with the end of this rainy season bringing with it their spring and the return of the African burning sun, so for these people New Year next month makes perfect sense.

Mekelle doesn't have many tourist sites to speak of. It is a working town. There is the Palace of Emperor Yohannes IV dating back from the 1880s in the centre and the modern monument in the Hawelti district but that is about all. The Ayder School here also has a museum of dreadful mementoes following the bombing they suffered in 1998 during the most recent war with Eritrea and I have yet to go to see that school. It is a bit of a walk and I have been warned by the office guys that it is not a very safe place to trek to alone. The Orthodox Christian faith is strongest here in northern Ethiopia and since Mekelle is a good stop-off point to visit the hidden rock-hewn churches of Tigray, some touring visitors do stay over briefly. It used to take a week for the camel trains to lug salt blocks into Mekelle market from the Danakil desert, but now it is trucked elsewhere from the edge of the Danakil so that traffic has largely ceased. However, Mekelle is the centre of the Tigray region with its flourishing university and airport. I find the aim of many younger local people is to get away to their capital city where they hear there are good opportunities. This means, although Mekelle does not have much of an influx of new citizens, outsiders still come here to see the sights.

Being the obvious white foreigner here is very interesting at times. Within the African continent, Ethiopians can tell who is not an Ethiopian, and if you study the actual colour and physique of different Africans – the Olympics has been good for this – you can see they vary in skin tone, facial and body shape. When I first arrived, I had to get used to being called all sorts of things, admittedly I don't mind 'sister', not keen on 'mother', okay with 'forenji' whereas 'China' is still a mystery to me.

Then, if *I* have to describe someone – forgotten the name or something – I am asked if they are black! Come on, asking *me* if they are *black*? Mostly, I make it a bit of a joke but they seriously do consider the tone of skin and true Ethiopians are noticeably paler, have different more Middle Eastern features and of course, for various reasons, are very skinny. Here it is absolutely fine to suggest someone is fat, thin or put on weight: they will not hold back from telling you, weight is an obsession. There are as many sets of scales between here and the bank as there are beggars: true. Where these gadgets all came from, I shall never know. And then there is the bank itself. Having negotiated the numerous street trip hazards, had the bag searched, a pat-down coupled with remarks on how thin I am for a white person, bomb detector scanning also completed by a female guard, I can then think of joining the massive queue inside the bank. While waiting one day outside, I was fascinated by a chicken's attempt to re-join its owner. What a struggle. It was obviously 'lunch', had its legs tied together after being sold on, but it wasn't allowed into the building and was dumped on the steps assuming it wouldn't move off. Incredibly somehow, that determined chicken actually made it up the bank's front steps!

Dairy notes for one week this month:

Monday:

Woke far too early worried about Microsoft warnings. I am on a countdown of usage apparently. Feel more in touch after skyping Tom who is struggling with shoulder problems (rugby again) but sorting out their Winnipeg house purchase. Ruth is stripping wallpaper and clearing their new house in Brighton now that they own that, all great news.

Walked the 50 minutes to Nicholas School, observed two lessons, made notes for improvement. Strode back just before the heavens opened again then dodged the rain to the office after lunch. Wrote up observations which I could have done back at mine but I need to be seen in my office, I think.

Back and cooked tea just as electricity went off so painted a card to post with Kenyan key ring to Tom. Trying to collect water in pots on my tiny balcony is a farce with the wind blowing about everywhere but I'm running out of water and that's another problem. Took pictures of what has become another amazing brown river rushing down the road outside. At least all open-air the toilets down back alleys along with the storm drains are having a thorough cleaning. Can't read in candlelight so watched short 'Black Adder' (again) – a great tonic!

Tuesday:

Nicholas Charity School observing again. Office, bread shop, but then took shampoo to Barbara's and Pam let me in to use their shower. Feels so much better. Lugged a canister of water back to mine as supplies running seriously low. Afternoon: persuaded office finance guy to take me over to their head office to get some pay, but surprise: none there for me. I showed the cashier woman there my bread rolls and told her I wouldn't starve tonight…don't know if she got the joke.

Home, tried to wash clothes in a thimble of recycled water. Word processing my messages before emailing copies is saving time and trying to avoid crazy messages warning me of possible shut-down.

Jeanne and Polly back home have found a little, empty terraced house for me to buy! Checked it online and it seems perfect. I'm now trying to persuade the estate agent in Willingham that I mean it, I want it, I won't let him down, sight unseen, I will buy it. That has to be sorted now as it's too great an opportunity to miss. Keep going faithful laptop please, please, eh?

Wednesday:

Nicholas School with an interesting Special Needs group, I think all should have one-to-one reading but the poor frustrated teacher is struggling without strategies hoping drilling and kindness will do it. At least this teacher is thinking of gentle approaches to the uphill struggle.

When will I get a proper hug from people I love and miss so badly? Oh dear, not feeling great right now.

Post office letter I wanted to send cost more than I had in my purse. Plus, they opened the tube I had carefully packed up to send Tom with an injera mat and some small placemats (which here are woven fans for barbecue fires) so I have to repack that in their sight, apparently, to be sure I don't include prohibited items like knives or dynamite. They are a bit surprised I want to actually send abroad such domestic household items. Bugger. Finance office: shut till two, double bugger as I had to hang around the church wall opposite where all sorts goes on. Huddling down was impossible this time as I was avoiding a mad chap chucking rocks anywhere and everywhere. Finance woman turned up at 2.15 and surprise, surprise, actually paid me something! Not the full amount due but better than nothing I told her; she still didn't get it. Picked up a card from Ella when I returned via the post office which was entitled, 'SMILE' making me feel slightly better, and bought bread and cheese for tea in the cutest tiny shop where the lady knows me where we have a cheery attempt at a conversation. Walked on to be tapped on the shoulder by a girl. Did I remember her from the Mailiham School? Yes! She was the lovely girl who invited me into their coffee ceremony during a storm and she wanted to thank me back for the gift I left for her. That was pretty amazing it actually got passed on as well. But I was very touched, resulting in a mood swing for me again: so incredibly emotional again by the time I got in. Frying pan pizza style tea experiment – dry-fried bread drizzled with whatever I could lay my hands on in that cupboard – wasn't too bad and at least the electricity stayed on for that. Goodness, I am missing home so much and knowing there are GB Jubilee celebrations back home in your streets are not helping either.

Thursday:

No wonder I felt down. I was warned flu here would be much worse than the GB variety. Skyped Tom on the other side of the world as I was up that night! My attempt to collect rainwater in pots on the tiny balcony is a total failure – I think the wind is completely in the wrong direction. Better think of a different plan. Went to the office, told Gebre I was sick but I would need money for laminates for my workshop preparations. Returned via the shop for food supplies. Straight to bed.

Friday:

Morning lazy start probably shouldn't go anywhere but struggled into the office after lunch. A weird young dog was following me, I couldn't flick it off, and some passers-by realised it was yucky and snapping annoyingly at me so I chucked rocks at it till it ran away…the wrong way up the by-pass. Oh well.

Friday afternoon, massive meetings in the office outside my little office door. This week there have been many meetings in the Mekelle City Education Office as they are organising which teachers are going where in the city for their new school year and what the school budgets will be. They leave it till *now* – don't ask me why, or how any teacher can plan for their next term in advance, but there you go. It is like a chess game. Principals have been in and the noise level has been quite high. Zemenface, the deputy here is incredibly loud anyway in everything he says.

By Friday pm, I am stuck in my little office next to the meeting room making my 'new-book-plans'. The pressure to hold workshops is huge now from the office so I can do that with a lot of preparation. I decided to check next on the 'Teaching Aids' (resources to help teaching to you and me) since these new books are very prescriptive. Yes, amazingly, they do give each unit of work Teaching Aid lists. However, they seem to all be leaflets, blackboard chalk, newspapers or magazines. (Not that magazines are a known or even an easily accessible item here.) I also saw 'resource persons' – by that I think they mean to get into school some person who can talk to the students about their work etc. Then suddenly I came across in the 'Health' unit that the teaching aid suggested would be actual 'patients'! That cracked me up and I started laughing loudly. I couldn't stop. Gebre came in to see what the joke was and got it so reported back to the meeting next door… Then I discovered the 'Adwa War' unit's list of necessary teaching aids: 'spears' and 'arrows'!!! I was crying. The meeting had to stop for a bit, I needed to explain what I was doing and why I was laughing, luckily, they got it and some agreed it was mad. I had to take a walk to calm down (it's the little things), but bloody hell what can I say to teachers?

Back in the flat I tried my hand at popping my own popcorn. Not sure if my teeth are up to it, though with seeds that never popped and that pan was a bad choice as now it's a burnt crusty mess. Oh pooh!

It's all change.

Right now, the Ethiopian Prime Minister, Meles Zenawi having been flown to Belgium for treatment for some unspecified illness has died at the age of 57.

He was from Tigray as is his wife, both were ex-guerrilla fighters for the Tigray Peoples Liberation Front in the seventies and eighties. Later, he was elected as Prime Minister under a new Federal Constitution early in the nineties. There was another election in 2005 and he was put in power again but with a much-reduced majority and I haven't quite been sure if that election was untroubled. Meanwhile, the problems with Eritrea have rumbled on and the Ayder bombing in 1998 shows how dangerous the whole situation really is. The state funeral will be held in Addis once the body has been lain in state and the arrangements made. The BBC world service reporter said that he had been in power for 20 years and although very unsmiling with an unclear human rights record, he believed in Ethiopia and pulled it around after so much civil war. Around the world, the worries are for an upsurge of trouble mainly from Sudan and Somalia bordering Ethiopia, but Eritrea in the north and Kenya to the south aren't great neighbours either. The deputy Heilemariam Desalegn is to step up but he seems a bit weak plus nobody seems to know much about him either.

This is incredible.

The head of the Ethiopian Church, Abune Paulos *has also died*. He worked with Meles Zenawi as a team and the Pope has been on TV talking about his importance to the Ethiopian Orthodox Church, links with Rome and so on. The funeral preparations, lone flute playing on blank TV screens, general quiet in a place without much noise to speak of is eerie.

Therefore, the country will be laying to rest two of its most important, influential and strong leaders within a short space of time. Yet again, it has been an incredibly sad period for Ethiopians and I feel for them. Lurching from one dreadful disaster to the next, it has been only in the more recent ten years that the record has been marginally more stable. However, all their neighbouring countries continue to have border issues and I am sure the wider world watches and waits to see how things will work out in this part of Africa.

Never has there been a peaceful handover.

I'm nervous.

The TV is all black curtains, black-clothed reporters talking about how amazing the PM was or re-runs of old interviews. Background music is continuously a recording of the lone shepherd piper – random flute notes but lovely. The office people were very sad and teary, Gebre sent me home which is what I wanted really. Went via town to try to stock up on food but many shops now are boarded up, and where I managed to buy a few tins the shopkeepers are all red-eyed and emotional.

Apart from electricity and water on, I have filled every vessel and my barrel to the brim, charged the laptop, cleaned the flat using boiled water…it all helps to shift the flu to the back of my mind which will wear me out if I let it, is my way of thinking.

Stuck back at mine I've done my tax form as far as I can – it uses too much downloading all the stuff so I'm hoping I have done enough; emails sorted to date; a nervous but ever attentive VSO head office are emailing me with links to sign in with British Embassy and reviewing emergency preparations…looking around there isn't much to pack in a hurry. Kenyan coastal farmers are a tinderbox waiting to happen. I have to remember those unhappy 58 farmers killed over grazing rights a couple of weeks ago. The Ethiopian controlled telecom is flashing up messages: 'Ethio Telecom expresses its deepest condolences on the death of the visionary leader Prime Minister Meles Zenawi and wishes strength to his family and to all Ethiopians'.

The next few days were pretty similar. The only unusual thing was that my chap, Ayele from Addis came to see me on his way around the region checking on volunteers, but he really likes the cultural restaurant in Mekelle so arrived in time for supper at six – after dark here but he invited me too which was great as tasting meat is a treat. The place was pretty empty and quiet with all that's going on, Ayele ate his 'meat-fest' at speed and some-how I kept up. Shockingly, I was back at mine by 7.30 which after a restaurant moment using Ethio timings is quite an unheard-of speed!

Outside after dawn in the street, a procession of about 150 people walked past holding candles and pictures of the PM, chanting I know not what. There are a few armed police patrolling daily but this is changing to soldiers jogging past and the odd truck-load of cadets. There is a barracks on the hill; I'm hoping young untrained recruits know how to keep the peace? They are very young and a bit keen on their weapons.

I have charged up all my electric things and again filled every water container. No disco in the night, the streets are deserted the next day, no call to prayer, no building construction shouts. It's eerily quiet but I slept well. This goes on for a few days and I just sit tight.

Then tragically, comes the announcement of the funeral of the Head of the Church, Paulos. Although experiencing double shock of losing both of the highest, most important people here in a matter of days, they are taking it carefully. The Pope, the African Council of Churches, the deputy PM are all sending messages of calm over the only TV channel available so I hope the people are listening. There is no movement at all outside mine or in the town. All is very quiet. Then a whole day of the funeral for the high priest Paulos in Addis Ababa arrives and is televised. Everything is white. The embroidered headgear worn by women in mourning on their stunning white clothes is beautiful. The high priests and all involved in the Orthodox Church look amazing in gold cloth and bright colourful cloaks shaded by their vivid embroidered ceremonial umbrellas. The armed forces are very much in evidence too.

I have made a decision!

I will begin to prepare for the 10K run in Addis in November. I must turn this around to positivity. I have my trainers here unused so far and although I couldn't possibly run outside, particularly at the current time, it would be awful being hassled by children, dogs, the general public apart from the fact that I would have to wear such a lot of clothing to cover myself up, I have what I need. So, the plan is to measure this tiny flat – I have a ruler!!! Then to figure out how many 'circuits' could amount to a kilometre. I could do stretches and try to vary it a bit so I don't do the same turn round the table or twist at the sink and mess up my rhythm. Plus, I have a playlist ready for a jog: I warm up to Cold Play 'Paradise' then I'm off, what more do I need?

Outside it appears there is some activity. Okay there are a few trucks loaded with shouting soldier recruits waving flags or random groups of local people marching and chanting, but a few shops appear to be open after that funeral so I venture out to the office via a street shop for supplies. A few fresh vegetables and more tinned food would be a good plan. Yesterday I had a chuckle as I ate up the last of my eggs and beetroot in an omelette…I did eat the lot but it did look like a fresh road-kill, it was so vivid! They are all there meeting teachers again discussing in huddles, occasionally weeping but overall there seems to be some work happening. After all, the schools go back in a few weeks and life goes on – Meles Zenawi would have wanted that. Solomon is weird and touchy-feely again. Yuck. I dread him wanting to ask me something. Just because he got me the new curriculum books from the store I am not beholden to him! Zemenface is nervous about signing the VSO request for funding workshops now that he has read that the office would be liable for medical emergencies during the day. Really? How likely is that! A 'mad' teacher came into my office once to sit and calm down. I had overheard a slanging match about her inconvenient New Year placement which was nowhere near her own home, and I recognised her from my classroom observations. I checked my notes: "I may just beat the students to the door after this one" was my recording then!

Laptop worries are doing my head in so I'm ringing Microsoft often. I'm spending so much on Ethiopian run pay-as-you-go telephone tokens at the local kiosk that the woman can't believe her luck. It is likely that the Addis office IT chap loaded a trial program onto my laptop which had six months life: now expired and having to restart remotely, between thunderstorms, intermittent charging availability. Marvellous.

The City Office here has had various bursts of different crowd gatherings. Once the teachers knew where they were to be teaching – some didn't even know until the day before they had to start, and others didn't necessarily agree, then we had a government pay scale change and they all flooded in for the extra cash. Now, it is the teachers who have *upgraded* themselves over the summer holidays on their usual cramming courses wanting their personal pay-rises. It hasn't all gone smoothly. I know some of them and have made the office staff laugh as I re-read them my classroom observation notes from last year: 'she scares *me*, I don't know how the children are feeling' was still the best one!

Meles Zenawi's state funeral day was pretty much the same format but there were even more dignitaries present along with more sparkly canopies and awnings, even displayed in the cathedral decorations and draped over the coffin, the processions and the final burial.

The rest of the days at the moment follows much the same routine:

Sit in my office when I can get in or have a chair there for writing my translation of the phrases in the new teaching materials.

Sort out a training programme based on the New English for Ethiopia books and workshops.

Write a brief to explain my ideas for helping teachers.

Jog around the flat.

Read. (The same books over again if necessary)

Keep an eye on water supply, bringing back a bottle refilled if possible from Barbara's.

Watch jolly DVDs when I can.

Type ahead of myself emails and home messages in case…

Plan meals carefully, top-up food supplies from stalls if open and we agree on the price!

... That's it really for about ten days till the day of the burial and everything appeared to calm down.

Eighth Month – Appendix

Now I am ready to present my workshops

My introduction to my full paper written on the new teaching materials

Approaches to Teaching and Learning
Valerie Mckee

The problem:

A lack of understanding and grasp of the wider implications as the new 'English for Ethiopia' textbooks for both the teachers and students are introduced to second cycle schools.

Objectives

To have an overview of the progression in the new curriculum from Grades 5 to 8 *(ages about 10–14)*.

Having achieved a better understanding of the new books, to be able to support teaching and learning.

Methodology

To prepare a short introductory programme involving relevant experts who are in contact with, and assist schools directly: certain key zonal office staff, school managers and cluster supervisors. This can take the form of a presentation within a meeting followed by direct detailed support as laid out in a paper.

A new approach to teaching and learning: embracing the new 'Teaching for Ethiopia' textbooks.

These new books have immediate colourful appeal. The variety of material, the interest and pace contained in each given unit are added improvements. Within the group of the second cycle, the 5 and 6 grades are paired together as are the 7 and 8. The timings of the lessons fit well within the two semesters and coverage is possible using five periods a week providing the teachers begin immediately.

But there are 'comforting' similarities with the old USAID materials: lessons are taken in 'steps'; there are answers detailed through the exercises; the content delivers well-structured grammar, drama, picture clues and the subject matter is modern. Not only is the material relevant to today's student, the teacher's introductory sections are also excellent for their professional development as well. Syllabus charts and learning objectives are presented in a variety of places within the Teacher Guide – helping them initially to locate these will be useful. The four basic elements of language teaching and learning have a more equal emphasis in the new books, and since this balance is directed it will be even more vital that the educator speaks less themselves and engages their students more, which is a tall to ask of some current teachers.

Unfortunately, there is little indication for homework activities and no directed extension for better-abled students. Other challenges which I foresee will be mainly related to the more problematic English language presented here plus the phraseology is tricky too. (The vocabulary lists are not particularly helpful.) Often, the sessions include the use of reference materials: much preparation will be required using both the Teacher Guide and Student Textbook in parallel. I suggest that all involved prepare well ahead, organising resources, arranging vocabulary aids, creating a stimulating learning environment – a whole unit of work would be ideal, and schools may have issues here.

Changes in routines such as these always cause initial worries and criticism, but once teachers become familiar with the layout within each Grade book, where to locate different material and so on, they will gain confidence. It is really important that the schools use these books right from the start and the supporting network in the City Education Offices, School Managers and Cluster Supervisors are fully aware of the difficulties they face as they do so. There will be teething problems, but together we can work through these, and ultimately prepare the students for the next steps.

Proposal outline

**New Textbook Teacher Training Based in Mekelle September 2012/2005
Aim: To support the transition to the new English for Ethiopia textbooks in
use for the second cycle grades 5-8: a whole-school approach.**

A. Managers and Cluster Supervisors

Knowing the cluster supervisors and some managers will need to be fully
aware of the changes in English teaching, I have designed an overview session
which would last approximately two hours – without a break. That could be
extended if additional time was required for a break and questions or further
discussion.

Each of these sessions would include the following:

- Introduction, aims, objectives
- An overview of the new materials: both the Teacher Guide and the
  Student Textbook
- A comparison with the old books
- Making a start
- Syllabus, layout and differences
- The English language challenges
- Preparation: planning, resources, mixed ability
- Conclusion and impact on teaching and learning from Grade 1

B. Teaching staff

Since the teachers may experience time constraints or problems attending a
whole day course, I have prepared a variety of time tables that can be tailored to
their needs.

The whole day course designed to give an overview for Grades 5 to 8 or a
combination of Grades and includes some participatory activities, a 30-minute
break and one and a half hour lunch break.

An alternative shorter training programme is possible and I could deliver this
in half a day, for example, a morning, 8.30 – 12.30 with a 30-minute break
included. For this, I would suggest the sessions are pitched for teachers within

the groups 5 and 6, or 7 and 8 since their teaching focus is slightly different – but it would still be possible to combine any grades if required.

Each of the teacher sessions would include the following sections:

- Introduction, aims, objectives
- An overview of the new materials
- A comparison with the old books
- Understanding pace and how to begin
- A study of the Teacher Guide
- A study of the Student Textbook
- Activities and exercises within the grades
- The English language challenges
- Preparation: planning, resources, mixed ability
- Conclusion and impact on teaching and learning

Where activities are included in the teacher training, they would focus on both groups: 5 and 6 and 7 and 8, and include a discussion session to share feedback in the group. These activity sessions would take approximately 45 minutes to carry out and would benefit the participants.

The location of these training sessions is flexible and I think depends on numbers and accessibility. The office has a good-sized room for about 40 teachers, but it may be preferred for them to be held within the clusters and have localised, smaller groups. That may make it easier for teachers to reach, attend and a better option. Either way, I think 40 participants in one session is probably the largest manageable group: bigger groups slow down the proceedings.

Costing the training notes:

- The exact number of five to eight teachers in each school and cluster needs to be calculated.
- ND Teachers could be excluded since they (hopefully) will be aware of the new English materials.
- If the whole day workshop option is chosen, then per diems need to be calculated. Localised training may avoid this issue, and the half-day option may also make a difference to this cost.
- Notebooks, pens, water would be budgeted for also.

- The cost of photocopies of material and resources lists could be limited to one set per school and cluster.
- Preparations completed:
- 1. Presentation to Managers and Cluster Supervisors, PP and flip-chart
- 2. Presentation to whole group 5-8 teachers, PP and flip-chart
- 3. Presentation to 5 and 6 and 7 and 8 separately, PP and flip-chart
- Presentation plan and approximate timing for each of the above three scenarios
- The notes for each section included in each presentation
- Resource list for new teaching: hand-out
- Feedback hand-out

Ninth Month

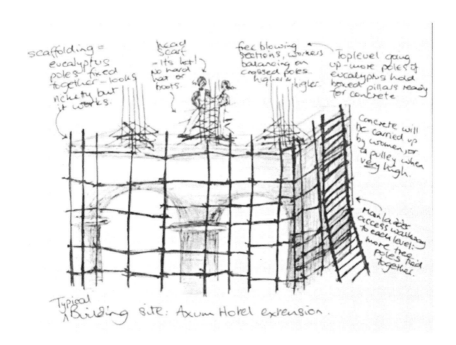

Street scenes are changing.

The orange 'tulip tree' flowers in full bloom yet again look stunning, especially from my balcony. I have created painted picture cards to explain back home how incredible they are to watch while attracting bees and fabulous butterflies. Sneaking my camera out one morning, I managed to capture pictures of the pretty cobbled back streets complete with stone seats and beautiful one-roomed stone cottages – I'm still very cautious so I don't release the unlucky 'devil' in my camera.

Bin collectors are rarely about with their yellow trucks and I wonder what is actually thrown away here since absolutely everything is reused, but they do wear full-length yellow overalls and substantial Jedi-like hoods and masks to do their jobs, so what hits the dustbin eventually must be pretty ghastly. Children kicking a bald football, an emaciated horse with its cart, a bloke handling somehow a heavy truck-thing loaded with beers and colas, bikes with their handlebars laden with everything from tree branches to chickens or a goat for the next celebration. The poor sheep I saw strapped to the roof of a small bajaj was desperate to escape, nutting itself madly on the taxi roof. What a life! (Or death?)

Since no Ethiopian walks about eating, they are squatting down near the seasonal vegetable sellers on street corners munching on the fresh oranges and prepared cactus fruit. These must be really sweet, as the massive fly population feasting on the pile of empty skins nearby is huge and to be avoided by passers-by like me actually. I did try a cactus but not keen on the pips: like coping with a mouthful of lead shot I decided. When shopping, the Tigrinya language is different here and although I tell them my brain is full, now I am old, I am trying to get the guttural sounds which they find very amusing. I can sort of count to ten but I'm proud I have mastered the throaty challenging 'oon-khoo-la-leikh', before carefully carrying a couple of eggs home.

There was once a railway through to Djibouti on the coast which was a valuable link for this country with the wider world but in the troubles here it was put out of action. There are no other communication links other than the roads such as they are, and planes. Within Mekelle, there are relatively newly cobbled streets but uphill towards the edge of town traditional dirt tracks are the norm: dust or mud depending on the season. Italian influenced tall palms and other smaller flowering trees line all the relatively wide roads which is a beautiful way to provide much-needed shade. Italy tried to take over Ethiopia during the late nineteenth century, and in spite of the famous battle of Adwa which they lost and coupled with a massive petition for peace drawn up in Rome in 1896, the Italians pulled back into Eritrea land but they did leave their mark in the Tigray region. The newer cobbled roads do look lovely, keep the grime down and seem to be durable for vehicles, but I feel sorry for the horses pulling such heavy loads as they skid up and down on shiny cobbles. Some kind cart owners tie a spare wheel to the back axle as the 'drag' stops the load whizzing away too fast for the horse, and a few kind owners will be seen helping push a loaded cart up a slope. More often, sadly, it is the whip is all that is needed to get things moving. Black Beauty's life was a stroll in the park compared with these horses. Donkeys seem to have different rules and can get themselves from A to B without much guidance regardless of the debilitating load of charcoal or straw.

Cars began to arrive here in Mekelle about ten years ago; not many can drive let alone afford a car. In the office, they are shocked to know that I can drive.

Pedestrian accidents are usually caused by people themselves wandering about, stepping into the path of the few passing cars, who in turn haven't the skills to avoid them anyway! There are also bicycles: either the Sunday lycra-clad groups of men racing on their superbikes like swarms of bees, or the old push-bike that you hear squeaking along. The television makes me chuckle as I am used to such brilliant filming skills back home. Since being unwittingly filmed and never edited out while up at the Hawelti monument, I am regularly on TV, so I have told the jolly travel operator around the corner I can sign autographs, for a fee: I'm learning!

Barbara and John are back from all the GB Olympic events and full of their fantastic time over the summer, we celebrated with a tasty steak sandwich and delicious chips together at the Axum hotel. Another day with their friends, we shared a chilli laden meat pot in a tiny local place, which I struggled through and luckily got back to mine in time for the stomach explosion. Not great. Oh well. Plain rice and hard-boiled eggs to compensate were my next meals! Ups and downs continued with losing the handle on my homely Mrs Beeton mug which later broke completely. RIP.

Although thunderstorms are still happening, they are beginning to spread out a little: Ethio New Year is nearly here! Receiving lovely emails from everyone back home work both ways for me and this contact is vital but some of my emails haven't 'sent' properly. Unbelievably, Microsoft is working on it *still* for me…fingers crossed.

This month I called at the Ethiopian Airlines office to check out prices to Bahir Dar as I want to go there and see the Blue Nile Falls. I haven't enough air miles to cover this, so need to plan. If I am to take a trip to Addis to do the Ethiopian Run in November, I can't afford or fit yet in another outing but I am definitely doing the run.

Ethiopians work very hard. Plus, machines just don't happen here: we are still mopping, washing and sweeping by hand, manually bashing with sticks and rocks where needed. With the road building, some clever planner decided to put a pretty grassy central strip along one of the longer bypasses near me. It fascinates me how the small teams – mainly women – now tend the grass by hand with battered shears and rakes. Their equipment is so old they may as well be using scissors. It is too narrow to tether a donkey or to have the grass eaten shorter would be a good option. Men do use treadle sewing machines, a man sharpens knives while his lad pedals the weirdly shaped bicycle grinder, and strangely I have yet to see a *woman* in a wheel chair…where are they, I wonder? Yesterday one of the wheelchair-men caught my eye with his customised base: an old plastic patio chair attached to wheels instead of the regulation seat. Surely, they aren't *that* uncomfortable that fixing a plastic chair in its place is a better option? Maybe they are. Or maybe a plastic chair is a better status symbol although having a rare wheelchair anyway is pretty up there.

The absence of machinery also makes for a quiet life. Whereas on holiday in Europe I wouldn't want to have a hotel room facing a building site, here there is no problem with noise since workers all use hand tools and carry things about between them. The only change is during lunch break when they muck about by the roadside and relax – that is a time I avoid passing by as I am an obvious target for whatever English phrases they feel like practising! There is the rare cement mixer I have spotted, plus a hoist for lifting buckets of concrete on another very tall new hotel, which like any machines are operated by the men. In fact, the whole building site thing is quite fascinating. The structures are concrete shells which are eventually filled with breeze-blocks, metal windows and glass. Trucks deliver the basic materials in piles next to the site if the gravel for the concrete is not the right grade: well, just get a man to sit on the heap and sort it out piece by piece with a hammer and a strong rock. Obvious.

Eucalyptus tree branches which grow pretty straight are used for the scaffolding and ladders, and these poles are moved up to the next level of work as needed. (The worn-out branches are eventually taken off by a cart for charcoal production.) So, from their arrival off the open-top truck at seven o'clock in the morning with their shovels and hammers, until five at night, the place is quiet – just a hive of activity with everyone swarming over it carrying concrete up heights on funny little stretchers and hand mixing a heap of cement, seven days a week. I did see a hard hat once – just the once – but generally *any* footwear coupled with a shawl and long loose clothing to keep off the direct sun is all that is needed.

The new extension to the Axum hotel down the road is pretty much opposite me so I get a good look at how it is progressing. It now has its 'scaffolding' about five floors high and I watched the latest builder up there tottering along it like a tight-rope-walker in his blue wellies chipping breeze blocks into shape as each is passed through the gap to him through the top floor window. He is cementing each in with his hand trowel: just leaning over, using the bucket of cement that had been winched up there roped to the scaffolding. Bonkers. The next week when they reached the sixth floor, suddenly, they are wearing high-viz jackets. Goodness, no helmets or other changes…easy to spot when they drop off the edge perhaps, plus there is no screen for pedestrian safety below either: beware the falling brick if you choose to walk anywhere near a construction site. As the buildings opposite gain height, they can see straight into minc so I'm having to keep my curtains closed all the time making it pretty dark. All for a trendy looking high-rise building!

Another notable trait is that Ethiopians are quite tactile. The initial bear hug and ultra-firm handshake plus right-shoulder-bashing I am used to now. However, holding hands, linking fingers, wrist grabbing while walking along or greeting others is also normal. Men of all ages do this more and then hang on and don't release, whereas women tend to have their initial hug and let go to talk face-to-face. It has taken me a while to get used to this, my very stiff upper lip British reserve and all that, and now I have problems deciding how far a 'friendly hold' is just friendly and not too 'touchy-feely'. You can imagine how I jumped when a bloke in the office without warning, leant over the desk with the speed of a lizard tongue to touch the birthmark I have high on my chest and ask how I acquired it. *Whoa, steady on,* I thought! I suppose blemishes on white skin look so different and maybe although very pale, it could be mistaken for a burn scar. I have kept the patch well covered ever since, plus have moved my desk so I have a decent barrier between me and visitors…but there is another guy who somehow manages to squirm round to my side… I'm still working on covering this angle.

Post funerals, the office hasn't been exactly whizzy although I think the teachers are allocated now, thank goodness, ready for the new term. There is still a tension in the air and I did congratulate the office that they seem to have made their transition from one much loved Prime Minister to his deputy without bloodshed or worse. There has never been a calm non-violent change over historically so my fingers are well and truly crossed.

The temperature is rising from 20 degrees back up to 28 sunny days ahead. The wind is rising too so the dust clouds return with a vengeance. *Still,* there is some talk about moving to 'the new office' but again we wait. Needing something to do and to make a change from writing about the New English books, I have begun to pack a few boxes in my office; I must shed some of this stuff – better being used in schools than hiding in a cupboard.

The new office – I have seen it – is in a complex towards the desert so I would miss this lovely rambling garden area around these huts. There is a goat tethered here now ready for killing soon I am told; a pomegranate tree the size of an apple tree is laden with fruit. I discuss this with the office people and they are shocked I would think of eating the pomegranates as I am told firmly: 'they are for rats'! I pick one and one chap is brave enough to taste the seeds I offer around and is actually positive about it, but there are no more takers. What a waste. Different cultures do have different views on what is food or what should be left alone and I suppose we are the same. But in a country where famine is a reality, it is a shame good food is wasted. The other interesting thing in the office garden here are some massive caterpillars. I have observed them as time has passed. The ones that fascinate me the most are about the size of my forefinger and very hairy. A strange webbed construction as big as a rugby ball has been hanging from a branch and it has just begun to spew out small versions of these caterpillars. Incredible. I have asked around but they don't seem to have noticed it.

VSO also need an update on my work here so that bit of creative writing is to be done also, but they will understand it will have been tricky working alongside the funerals and rainy season school closures.

Finally, it is Meskel! Meskel is Amharic for 'Cross' and has been celebrated in this area of Africa forever! Happy New Year 2005 over here. It will be celebrated as I discovered over time…for the next *two weeks*!

I have now been informed by my office manager that children will not return to school until the Monday after Meskel for their massive flag ceremonies and teaching resumes the following day. This means in effect that children will have had no school for four months.

The lady sweeping the stairs gave me a traditional circle of yellow daisy flowers woven with what I recognise as 'sticky-weed' which works really well to wear on my head! It is the Gift of Jewels festival too, something to do with the Queen of Sheba going back and forth to King Solomon in Jerusalem. Either way, there is a lot of feasting to organise with freshly killed creatures and loud celebrations that will last a couple of weeks along with the headaches, plus usual collections of recycled skins and bones heaped on streets corners. The water and electricity is still intermittent but I got out to visit Barbara and John for a Hilltop restaurant visit, and another time I managed to check out my landlord's family. There is more going on in my week right now.

The training in the flat is amusing. I have figured out if I do one and a quarter-hour jogging, it means 220 circuits or 3-4 miles. I should be on track if I up it to two hours' worth. Counting it all is funny as I have a collection of pegs and bits which I move on the kitchen table each time I pass so I know where I am with it all! Disciplining myself to do this is a good focus and the push I need when I am feeling down – which, to be honest, could be is the majority of the time at the moment.

A typical week this month of sunshine and showers, muddling through:

Saturday

Barbara and John have a local friend who knows the hills around so well and we decided to get out there for a walk, early this time, before the sun heats up too much; John is a bird watcher so he's really made up. What does it for me is to find a few baby toads climbing about in the tall damp grass. So cute! The countryside is still very green but I can't take photos well enough and the variety of beautiful birds continues to amaze.

Halfway, along one of the few tarmacked bypasses, the one running by the dodgy bus station is blocked by a marquee for a wedding. A few rocks in the way indicate there is no through route and traffic will just have to do its own thing. Nobody complains, it's a regular feature to use these areas for gatherings and just because it is no longer a dusty track through the centre of a community doesn't mean it stops the people holding functions there.

Got back to watch the BBC three o'clock kick-off which was the Stoke v Man City game on television, and although the picture is still fuzzy with the red versus a blue kit, I cope. I still really enjoy that bit of England for a couple of hours anyway in spite of the pop-up ads by Ethio TV which appear on the right of the screen squashing the elongated players and action into the other half!

Sunday

Ran 5.5 km today, thinking more about my stride and footwear I ought to go to a bigger field to try if I could… Washing done in limited water. Breakfasted on different recipe scones I trialled in a crummy new pan I had to buy to replace the burnt one. Wow: they were a great success! Completed tax form: finally. It had better not be sent back as I'm feeling clever. Watched 'Eat, Pray, Love' as I feel I can cope now, proud I didn't blub too much. My walking sandals have ripped the toe so nearly broke my fingers and needles as I struggled to mend them. Back home I wouldn't normally enjoy canned sausages but today it is a different story. However, there were only five in there when the label said six, I feel cheated; mash and tomato soup packet though was delicious. Ironing managed as electricity on and no candle needed for reading before sleep. A good end to the day. Things are improving.

Monday

Up with a crazy 4.00 call to prayer from the orthodox tower so found my brain thinking about our alphabet design, and how difficult it is for learners or those struggling to read to get their head around. Now I have seen it stuck onto classroom walls I can see some shapes or pairs of letters that in our alphabet sit together are so hard to remember or tell apart: ab, ij, pq, vw, mn. Then learning the sounds which for people with different throat or guttural speech is very tricky, for example phonetically: s and z; f and v; but i and e in all their forms beat the lot.

As I was up so early, I reviewed my latest paper about my New English books and my idea for VSO funded workshops before setting off to the office with my plans. Saw an older guy on my way who tried hard to tap me for sponsorship to finish his distance learning second degree. Goodness, the poor chap said he had to leave with depression so never finished it, but it is a 'sorry, no' from me.

I arrived all ready to be dynamic but found a coffee ceremony being prepared which I wasn't aware would take place, so I dashed back to mine for a bag of sweets to share and my lunch sandwiches ready for the long haul. Apparently, this one is to celebrate the festival of the 'Finding of The True Cross' later this week. One manager asked me why I was 'keeping' the wrappers from all the sweets we had eaten? I explained I intend to bin them carefully. It is because actually, I am only picking up the litter. You lot habitually throw everything on the ground and these are not biodegradable, as you will find when you become (sadly) more westernised and the plastic hits this country, not to mention the carbon monoxide and factory emissions. In the natter over three very stiff coffees, I am told to prepare a proposal for immediate training. Plus, oh, there is a competition for the likes of our office workers to present a talk for the Annual African Conference. The conference is being held at the Barhir Dar University in October. And the closing date is in a few days. Actually, there is a prize too: it includes a free trip to the town and Blue Nile Falls! Why didn't I know this?

Like everything, it's a steady accidental osmosis process and luckily, I am about with my ears wide open. There are times when the coffee certainly helps.

I shook all the way home, said 'no' countless times to kids asking for money – when are they going to school? – to eat the popcorn I am getting better at cooking and drink water in an effort to clear my thoughts.

Tuesday

I can print a few things in the office I am told as I now have the secret code to the printer. I am taking in the paper I need as they have none, so I can buy it piece by piece at the shop around the corner. The manager actually came in to ask me for more sweets! He enjoyed the others so thought I would have more for him. Worth a shot I suppose.

Gawped a bit at the felling of a massive eucalyptus tree in the office entrance. It involved two guys in flip flops and no headgear with axes, chisels and some ropes. Demolishing the whole thing took two days. They enjoyed me taking pictures of them which was weirdly amusing really, we have manoeuvred our walk around the branches and mess but the smell of the fresh sap has been fantastic.

Barbara tells me their office has decided to work Saturday mornings too in order to follow deceased Meles' hard working example. Hope my lot don't follow that idea. I simply can't sit about Saturdays as well! On my route today, a happy group from a football team were dancing about holding their cup which was fine until they tried to pressure me to sponsor their team as they were clearly winners! Saw the worst horse suffering in the road too. Thin, lame, sore and blind. I have been told that if a vehicle hits it and kills it, the driver is liable so when these poor animals are close to death, they are usually shoved into roads with some hope for a money payout. Life isn't great for anything really. Then reached mine to prepare myself yet again for no water. This has been for two days now and I wasn't ready for that, I stupidly thought the water shortage times were over. Bother.

I have had such a bad stomach again – giardia parasite style – I may need to visit the pharmacy for more gut-ripping antibiotics. I wasted the shower water yesterday but today collected what I could to clean the floors…once again trying to keep the 'roaches away. Electricity off yet again so this time and I couldn't use my laptop this evening. Back to reading by candlelight.

Wednesday

Early panic by me about the Barhir Dar competition rules so emailed VSO hoping the Meskel festivities don't shut down all office life in Addis as it seems to have done here. Then more Meskel flowers given me by a girl on the street, so cute. Fiddled about aimlessly in the office again, few people in there but they are impressed I even turn up.

No letters at the post office but the pharmacy was open, thank goodness, for the medication I need.

Late afternoon loo dash to Barbara's then out with them, Peace Corps volunteers, a few from the hospital too so it was a good crew, to watch the religious 'finding of the true cross by St Helena' which apparently happened in the fourth century AD called the Demera procession and goes with this Meskel time of year. (It appears to be like our bonfire night but a totally different and for me justifiable reason!) It was, as I had been told, absolutely amazing. Hundreds of people had made their way up to the hilltop and lit a massive bonfire up there. We stuck together as we were among a huge crowd lining the streets watched the activity up in the hills from below. The hordes of people up on the hilltop proceeded to carry flaming brushwood flares as they carefully wound their way down a rough path, somewhere there were beating drums to add to the occasion. It looked like lava flowing downwards and lasted probably about an hour. After that, it was back to Barbara and John's where we feasted on pasta. I can't drink alcohol with the pills I am on so probably the only one with a clear head by the end of a great evening to negotiate the shared taxi home.

Thursday

The aftermath of the festival yesterday means little done outside and more Meskel festivities and feasting today. I called in to a school which had a few classes running and gave them an alphabet letter set from my office stash. The visit was certainly uplifting, bring it on! Agreed to meet a new volunteer from the north of Ethiopia for a meal at what is usually a good place on the hill but today it was awful. For chips, we had crisps, rubbish bread and what was supposed to be meat? I *had* my glasses on and still couldn't see any meat! Complaining isn't possible here, well not by a forenji anyway.

Glad I had my laptop charged as VSO have sent the competition rules: full research paper or similar is required. I rewrote my 'New Approach: Embracing the *New Teaching for Ethiopia* Textbooks' overview as asked, tweaking it all to focus on how to address updating cluster supervisors in the new language and methods, before resubmitting it – a bit late but hey ho, they should be used to that around here by now.

Friday

Goodness, why isn't that horse in the road not dead yet? It's struggling on its side in the gutter now deep in its own waste and blood. I can hear hyenas in the bushes over the road as I hurry by.

Arrived in time at the office to answer a call from my VSO manager. They have sent my paper on to Barhir Dar but cannot currently fund my workshops or the laminates I wanted for classrooms.

There are meetings in the office about the coming year's curriculum for all grades! I can't believe this planning.

Yeah, a productive visit to the post office to find *four* parcels for me from England, they must have been hoarding them here. After all the form-filling, I am so crazily happy to get them home. How clever: a new purse and rubber gloves, chocolates, instant sauce packets, a new water bottle, tummy pills and paracetamols…thank you, friends and family! XX

Saturday

The crickets are buzzing again. Hotter weather definitely on its way. Water was on again which was great, and in spite of my lack of energy, I made myself run for half an hour; so pleased about that.

Walked to the Castle Hotel on the hill to see a few wedding parties up there. They don't seem to be having their 'do' there, but are taking turns to use the lovely old backdrop for their photographs which is quite a good plan. Each group has it's borrowed car with ribbons and flowers, the bride is always in a Cinderella-style white dress and bridesmaids in red similar puff-ball dresses. All very lovely, as they then set off in the cars around town honking horns and shouting as they happily circuit the streets before they hand the vehicles back. One bride's dress was so big she couldn't fit into the groom's car and had to stuff into the taxi with her bridesmaids, so the groom went ahead on his own! Another bride lost her hoop from the petticoat and I was on hand to step forward and helped her with my handy safety pins to hold it together.

The sunset views up there are stunning too so it was a relaxing cup of tea at the end of my day before I dashed back to mine to see a fuzzy Stoke v Chelsea football match. To top that, I was so happy to read today's set of emails from friends and family plus I managed to skype Tom in Canada. Planning such calls can be a bit obsessive so it's a good thing I made it, otherwise...

Sunday

A new volunteer, Olive, is in Mekelle from Ireland. We went together to the Atse Yohannas museum but a 'helpful' bloke sprang out from nowhere to guide us – for a fee of course. The whole palace, built in the 1870s, is under refurbishment and he didn't get it that I was worried about ancient parchments and artefacts being stored in a boiling hot tin hut nearby in the meantime. There were really interesting exhibits: clothes, costumes for their mules and donkeys, swords, armour and plenty from Queen Victoria, who they seem to like a lot here. [By all accounts, the British were aggressive and not particularly helpful before this and sadly the Emperor Tewodros II failed in his attempts to unite Ethiopia which was quite likely a factor contributing to his suicide. However, the next Emperor Yohannas IV was a better diplomat and gained British support partly because of the conflict we were having with Egypt over the River Nile.] My favourite thing was the Ethiopian king's royal bed. Made from juniper wood, collapsible for war transportation, but it is set up on high legs like stilts because the king had to be raised higher than everyone else! A random bloke there tried to tap us for a dump of cash so he could go to London and we had a bit of a laugh together actually about it; but sorry, no. All good learning for Olive too.

John and Barbara have persuaded me that I need a break and to go with them to the Gheralta Lodge for a weekend late October. It is true I need something to look forward to but the cash flow is a problem. John will lend me the money for the deposit...ooo too tempting, so: 'yes please'.

There is such a thing in Ethiopian office jobs as 'annual leave' but that is a break only from a regular office job and then it is usually spent at home or visiting relatives in Addis Ababa. Generally, families have a close local support network: children move around the corner; the taxi driver in town will be the brother of the guard for the block of flats; the shopkeeper will be the daughter of the cleaner; the shoe-shine boy's sister will be selling cactus fruit on the next street. There are a number of hotels being built and I do hope they are eventually occupied: it will certainly not be by Mekelle folk as the men will be quietly guarding them equipped with their little bomb detectors, and their family lady members will be cleaning them – by hand, naturally!

Tenth Month

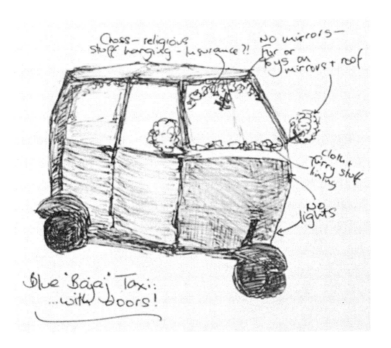

So, it's back to a sort of routine now: early morning 'training' indoors; heat; scurrying between the office, schools and a proper loo somewhere; Wednesdays still connecting with volunteers for our 'meetings'. There is still a tense sense of 'waiting' and political nervousness in the air, the army are maintaining their presence on the streets, but I am glad others are around having returned from their holidays and Olympic jobs back home. Knowing the drop-safe in Barbara's courtyard was always there as a back-up plan for speedy-escape-emergencies wasn't quite enough to relax me!

Barbara and John dipped out of a trip they booked early this month suffering from too many infected flea bites. One good friend, a Peace Corps volunteer, has left for good with depression. It happens. I really appreciate how low a volunteer can get and am glad I have mustered the drive to get on with my life here – but don't get me wrong, I don't feel any better than others and they are to be congratulated on giving it the energy they have. I recall the initial grilling we were put through in London while applying for these jobs and now it really makes sense.

School terms are in full swing and I am feeling positive about my work at most schools, the poorer Mailiham Secondary School in particular. It is quite a walk across town. One day, as I passed their local church, there weren't the usual number of beggars and locals kissing the walls in prayer, instead, some local women had spread their rough old sacks or large fresh leaves on the dry earth, and laid out their meagre produce to sell: just a handful of red chillies, one or two lettuces; a small bag of bark chippings for fire…so desperately sad and sparse. Really makes me reflect.

Mailiham school has helpful staff, and the primary Alene next door who I enjoy visiting on the same trips over in that direction. That Alene team is amazing and really happy to work with so few resources as they try hard to teach their very needy children. I realise a variety of texts with some simple English is still important at whatever age here but they were just overloaded. Now that together the Mailiham librarian and I have separated and stacked up a lot of books that muddled the shelves for their older students they are ready to pass all on to Alene. Suddenly, at one visit, the librarian looked a bit sheepish, and the deputy head comes to tell me that the committee needs to approve the giving over of these books.

"Oh! Which committee?"

"It hasn't been put together yet."

Great. How frustrating. Just when it was going so well. This mention of 'a committee' tells me that they are clearly stalling and expect me to back off. I know that here schools are given credit for their *quantity* of resources regardless of their usefulness or relevance so that's a brick wall now and anyone may as well give up, but not me! I will keep plugging away and have a word with my office guys too.

How good is this? Once, I was assisting a special needs teacher and just a minor detail, wasn't going to disagree with her that the letter 'Y' was a vowel. I saw her point and didn't want to ruffle her in front of her in class. It was a struggle I could tell. Then they cheerily sang out an uplifting song she had taught them, sung to a steady beat on one repeated note:

"Ber blik ship; ber blik ship; Hiff u nay wull; hiff u nay wull; Yissir, Yissir, Yissir, three bags full! One for my Mother, one for my Dad, and one for the farmer who is asleep on the grass!" Well, it certainly lifted me anyway!

One week in, I get the email which shakes me up.

Titled: The 2012 International Education Conference at Barhir Dar University; speaker Valerie McKee on 'Teaching and Learning'.

Blimey. It is going to happen and *in just over a week's time*.

What to wear? My hair is now quite long so I am wearing it in a side plait, a tidy scarf over the head or shoulders and linen trousers will be ideal: a little Ethio with a western touch!

They cover the cost of the flights and hotel which I sort out, but the add-ons like the Blue Nile Falls, I have to figure out. Oh, *and* the all-important talk of course!

A whole day was spent in the airline office booking flights, finding a reasonable hotel that had space, fetching cash from the bank to return to the travel agent to pay for it all, then waiting for the important receipts. Next task is to sort out slides and learn to use the traditional overhead projector and what I am going to say. I have to have a back-up plan too in case there are technical problems such as no electricity. Better get to it!

Now I may be famous, the finance office guy wants to keep in my good books and is keen to get me my pay from the woman with her briefcase on the other side of town. It's always tricky getting about without a car for the office staff but now the office driver is understandably furious. The boss actually was given a car – an old car, it's true – but he typically smashed it up which isn't hard to do around here and now they are without office wheels for a while. The boss is keeping a low profile! That means we either walk which is fine by me, or we get a taxi at the Education Office expense. The guys here prefer to use a bajaj with doors as even they are afraid of the hyenas so we have to wait longer, but that is also fine by me. Encountering one of those which are actually Rottweiler-sized in reality can be a bit of a shock, to say the least, so doors are essential for me.

Personalising your lovely hand-painted blue three-wheeler taxi is crucial. We have many jokes about the use of a rear-view mirror in England and I suppose here furry dice isn't an issue but having a mirror at all is a bonus. Side view mirrors could also be helpful – but not as comedy fluffy ears however which here, where they exist, are a regular alternative. Flashing indicators are only useful if you have a bride in the back and want to show off, otherwise, they have no purpose. For the passenger however it may mean ducking beneath the dangly tickly bits from the roof, or sliding around on some nasty new Manchester United (!) plastic seating as you hack around a bend, and those 'comfy' beaded seats are the rage now as well. Plus, actually, don't expect to be able to *see* out of the windows. They will be darkened with groovy DIY paint, possibly torn and strangely repaired, or perhaps covered with religious symbols – calling on the deity may be some insurance ploy. The stuff cluttering the front windscreen is crazy and so hard to see beyond. I have noticed sheep from markets often riding in these, chickens tied to roofs by the dozen and goats exiting taxis with their owners. I wonder what their fare was? Much less than mine no doubt: a forenji like me is worth a lot in swindled passenger terms!

I mucked up what should have been a happy visit to Gereb Tsedo school this month as they have expanded to three classes in one grade and I only had two sets of alphabets and posters with me. I promised I would bring another next week, luckily a teacher remembered me and translated to the rest what I was trying to say. For teachers of any subject, it is an uphill struggle, so for English, it's massive. I mention also: 'perhaps they may have handles and locks on the classroom doors soon?' Some hope. Apart from the dust that blows in, they are regularly used for waifs and strays of all kinds. Poor children. The central play area is still head-high with ripening wheat but that should be harvested soon; it is all needed income for the school I suppose. The younger year groups I reported have no teaching materials at all in their rooms and my boss back at base was furious, wanted me to make a fuss and feedback this to the cluster supervisor. However, I know this one and unusually this chap isn't particularly bothered about his set of schools. I did return the next week with more resources and observed the use of the new books which was useful for me. I realised at that point that teachers were cherry-picking chunks they, in reality, understood themselves. A lad asked me about my son Thomas! He remembered me from last year in a younger class; *his* name is Thomas and I recall the hard time that boy had when being made to attempt a spelling on the blackboard – being belittled and forced to tears. Another older teacher seemed to know all about me through his wife from yet another school and was keen I should observe to give feedback on his own lessons also. These new books are setting a range of challenges so it's great some are wanting them to work for them.

Thursday, and my airport day actually arrives. The security is usually huge, so to make it more so a few more soldiers and guns in the waiting rooms is all that is needed now. Extra time is normally needed at check-in anywhere in Ethiopia for all the shoes, belts, x-ray of all things at regular points – even on entry to the airport itself, thus it was lucky I could manage an hour of much-needed sleep using one of their great full reclining beds found in Ethiopian airports. That is if you can sleep after a coffee served from the traditional small open charcoal barbecue on the floor of the departure lounge! (Are there smoke alarms and do they actually work I wonder?) On the plane, the girl next to me was terrified and not for the first time, I needed to explain how the seat belt worked. It is likely she had never encountered one in a car anyway. We touched down in the dark which wasn't great as the Barhir Dar airport is being rebuilt and the car park is just a crummy field dotted with pot-holes, plus piles of rubble and sand. The taxi to the hotel I pre-booked was a waste of time as that hotel was overbooked and after a marathon of a barrage of questions, raised voices suggesting blame, finger-pointing and explanations (not from me I hasten to add), I had to accept a room in a hostel for that night only. Finally, asleep at midnight.

Stuffing my day-ruck-sack with valuables and laptop, locking my bag as best I could, I left my things behind the desk before heading out to the conference.

The university is on a vast impressive site and I did well to keep myself together. Last in the University Conference programme, my speech and Q&A session went well. The OHP worked, I didn't cough, fall off stage or let myself down as I explained both my excitement coupled with concerns over the use of the new English for Ethiopia textbooks and the task I had set myself. That job really amounted to creating a dictionary of phrases linked with each section in the texts for Grade 5 to 8 (secondary years in our world) to present to cluster supervisors for distribution. They were actually – though I say it myself – riveted. The puzzled expressions on some faces told me they were in agreement, and it is possible they themselves couldn't explain some of the phrases I gave as examples. From Grade 5 text 'a gate crasher', 'master of ceremonies', 'to abstain from', are linked with areas of our western world and tricky to grasp in this culture, but 'not all that glitters is gold' is a deeply rooted metaphor way beyond many young people's understanding. Higher up, the schools for Grade 8 it is even more difficult as they try to combine health and life issues through an Ethiopian's English scripted comprehension exercise. Imagine unravelling these: 'life…a bed of roses' (really? Roses anyway and gardens just don't figure here apart from the old phrase itself); 'education is a yardstick' – a yardstick? Do *our* teenagers know what that is anyway? The health chapter contained difficult concepts such as 'emphasis on enhancing the body's own recuperative power'… Oh dear. With the odd error at publishing too, direct translation is pretty hard and trips up the teachers as well as the better able student: here the word 'intensity' is wrong, 'with particular intensity on diction…' Then the expected use of dictionaries. Dictionaries are so rare in Ethiopia and using a bulky one which would be needed for the higher grades could destroy any will or enthusiasm. The questions the delegates asked clearly told me they were interested, had learned from my perspective and understood the difficulties that lay ahead as well as how to begin to help teachers with their uphill task. Phew.

After giving my talk I could relax and enjoy everything about this trip. The other delegates *(I was the only white person and the only woman to speak!)* chatted to me a lot afterwards as we had an expedition seeing the sights together in buses – it didn't matter that the tyre blew, another bus was found really quickly (and I had thought everything here was painfully slow but we were 'important' I suppose). I was asked about volunteering issues both in Ethiopia and other African countries so had to be diplomatic; of course, the Ethiopians enjoy hearing how good they are when compared with Kenya in particular. Having been alongside them as a speaker, they were respectful and fine with me so we had a great time. Boat riding on the huge windy Lake Tana in a tourist boat was terrifying for some; any different mode of transport to these 'untravelled' people only used to a local farming or town life can be extremely scary. There was sea-sickness and plenty of gripping onto the sides of that boat as we bounced over the waves on the vast stretch of water.

However, we saw the source of the Nile from the Lake's perspective along with flocks of pelicans and many other different wading birds which I don't recognise – better get that bird book soon! Fresh fish at every meal was another target for me on the trip which was a fantastic bonus. The Blue Nile is called that because of the type of rock or volcanic elements in it from the source apparently, as opposed to the White Nile from Lake Victoria which *is* actually lighter in colour. Lake Tana was stunning enough and since it was just after the rainy season the hippos were swimming happily below the surface more than above it. (However, not seeing a hippo there I admit was a disappointment for me). Reed beds loaded with incredible African birdlife made the British dawn chorus sound like a lullaby. It was incredibly loud! There were fishermen splashing oars while scooting over the waves in their elegant, narrow, flimsy, papyrus boats; but the echo of the call to prayer from Orthodox Christians far out-sounding the mosque microphones was all part of the cacophony. After a brief tour of the maritime museum, we just had time to dip into one of the monasteries on an island in the middle of the lake before a storm descended. At each stop, we were shepherded around like true VIPs and everyone had a great time seeing their country from a different angle and being rightly proud of it all.

Just occasionally I meet a volunteer who I would rather not have to spend too much time with: they may be too critical, or lack spirit and the one here on my next excursion as a university aid was a depressing moaner which I really would rather have done without, however, travelling anywhere in a group or pair is best. So, negotiating a bus trip the following day knowing she'd be bending my ear on the bus was necessary. After a good night's sleep in the correct hotel, all safe and ready to explore the next day complete with a full breakfast, we met at the stop early in the morning equipped with good footwear, water and lunch. It didn't start too well as the driver got arsey with the group of Israeli girls also booked onto the same trip. In Ethiopia for a couple of months, they were volunteering too bright young things who it seems had been given a cheaper price on the back of us paying more to cover the difference and as bright young things, they had discussed their ticket bargains with us! Ooops!

Together we bounced round to the Nile foothills, passing locals going about their daily tasks in their farming communities. Women lugging huge packs high on their backs, herds controlled by quite small children waving happily at us, men harvesting and organising the threshing in the open fields with their oxen teams. No guides. No tourist paraphernalia. At one brief stop, I did buy a couple of scarves by the roadside and am so happy with seeing how they had been made; every loom size dictates the size that can be woven so I was glad these were from a good-sized loom. The 'road' ended and the bus driver directed us to follow a path upwards which probably took about an hour to climb. We clambered higher and higher giving way at times to farmers with their laden donkeys, or groups of chattering women loaded up with everything including their babies. The sound we could hear was just of the people and perhaps a slight background splashing of streams flowing somewhere just out of sight.

Then, all of a sudden, we rounded a corner and whoosh! There it was laid out below us. Across the gorge, many rivers bubbling over rocks between cliffs driven from behind by such a vast body of water and all of these smashing directly downwards.

That was when I simply had to be separate, on my own and just look, listen and wonder; I'm not sure if I appeared rude but at that point, I didn't care. It was too amazing! The noise was deafening. Brown water gushing and crashing down in the sunlight, creating rainbows arcing over the verdant valleys below. We had to get closer; to get below the falling water if we could. By degrees, we made our way down rough paths and crossed various bridges, following the noise as we rambled round more hills and then across a suspension bridge (intact, thank goodness) to the foot of the biggest waterfall. Conversation was difficult between the few of us that made it there but I gather last week it was impossible to get that close due to the high-water levels. So much history, life, the heart-beat of the continent simply laid out before me; around for centuries past and yet to come. Just incredible.

There were only a few children hassling us in those lower marshy levels with fruit to sell and the Israeli girls bought flutes from them. Although these were just bamboo sticks with holes, I did insist they used my alcohol gel cleaner before they shoved them in their mouths!

Barhir Dar itself is a beautiful town worth a visit, and in spite of the army presence, seems calm, tidy and friendly. Having no idea of the snail-pace bureaucracy or corruption behind the scenes, I felt slightly jealous of any volunteer placed there. Overall winning the trip to Barhir Dar was brilliant and I was totally bowled over by the Blue Nile Falls. OK, I didn't manage to see the hippos, but I loved the town, the Lake Tana, seeing another landscape *and* I have been paid a bit of money on top of expenses for my prize so I can now buy the laminates I wanted to provide for school resources. In addition, I can sponsor myself when I do the Addis run in a few weeks' time. (Gawd. Yes, I am!)

While I was in Barhir Dar, I managed to squeeze in a visit to an ex-volunteer's flat to try to help with her belongings. Salli had been flown home with various sicknesses and some of her private things needed sorting before it looked obvious that the place was vacant and the looters inevitably descended. I took some valuable things including a couple of purses that looked special, promising the other local volunteer friends I would send them on.

The flight back to Mekelle wasn't great as there was a woman occupying my window seat and she wouldn't move across. I know she understood me and the flight attendant perfectly. Hopefully, I annoyed her enough by leaning right over often – my elbows can be pretty sharp especially as I am steadily losing weight over here – to take photographs of the views down below us; sadly, I won't have the opportunity to see that again I am sure.

It has been back to work; my stomach is all over the place again but I have to ignore that and press on – not least with my running schedule. But oops, I am already booked for next weekend in the exclusive Gheralta Lodge with Barbara and John which was intended to be a fun, if not expensive, weekend in the country with other volunteers. It's a place where the rich and famous go for a retreat from the 'real' world. I was told that Will Smith had been there the week before so there's no question about it. I just have to get well enough and go there regardless.

The office is keen to hear about my travels and the Barhir Dar University talk. They are so sweet; never get out of this town and couldn't imagine the sights I was describing. I did enjoy showing them a conference photograph of me sitting on the stage holding the microphone up there in front of the packed hall! Then back at base, since I spoke to the conference about the teachers' struggle to deliver the curriculum, although they were concerned, the VSO office in Addis couldn't really deny me funding for workshops after all. It is an expense and they are really careful with their funding, so I was grateful they changed their mind. However, today it is more form filling, but I am good at that. I became too complaisant and used the office computer with my memory stick and the whole VSO section is corrupted, fortunately, I have a few CDs I can try to load with printable work… So, it is full steam ahead on these, interspersed with my regular school visits of course.

I parcelled up the valuables to send on to volunteer Salli in England so carefully, and fingers crossed, they will arrive intact. Wow, a fantastic visit to the post office to find two parcels from home loaded with such great things like chocolate, paracetamols, packet soup choices… I feel very lucky.

As the weekend drew nearer, I discover there is a huge Tigray People's Liberation Front meeting planned actually in my office. Pictures of the deceased president Meles are refreshed and in place, but now being adorned with flowers and trinkets. There was no reason to worry I should be involved as on the Thursday I was asked to open up and hand over the few chairs I had and lend sticky tape for posters. I was out anyway hassling in the market for leggings for my running in public as I will have to cover up on the Ethiopian Run really and that's hard in this heat – thin cheap ones seem the best option. Police cadets seemed to be learning on every street even directing traffic in the town – such as we have traffic – but amusing for me to watch them being assessed on the job. By Friday, most local schools were closed with meetings so there were no guilt feelings from me whatsoever with my next fun trip away!

My friends had it all organised: pick up at 8.30 exactly, lovely large 'posh' well-equipped four-wheel drive with our regular jolly guide friend, Ghere on board. The plan is to see some hidden rock churches on the way to the Gheralta. We were joined by a couple from Barbara's home town and so were a good group. There are camel trains on the road loaded with sacks which I assume are ready to transport the harvest I suppose, rather than the salt blocks from Danakil. We head off northeast to Wukro then Hawzien to a church there which was easy to access. The entrance you could unusually see from the road was white but the fabric of the church was buried right into the mountain behind. It was decorated with amazing paintings and bright ceremonial umbrellas, and since all are naturally kept away from regular daylight, everything is so very bright and fresh. We were shown some ancient parchment books of scripts written in old Geez language. The script was all red ink while the saint's names are all in black. These are strung together roughly and with their wooden covers are so battered I have no idea how much longer they will last.

After a rough bumpy ride – had to disembark at one point to push the car out of one deep pothole – we were dropped at the foot of a mountain ready to climb up to the next church but were surrounded by children wanting to guide us. Visiting this one is very tricky as it is very high up a steep mountain with very few clues on the outside to show what we were aiming for. We managed to leave most of the children by the roadside thanks to our guide and press on with just a few chattering alongside. Halfway up we had a picnic lunch under a tree, studying this new barren landscape, which apparently was a bit like Arizona but quieter and emptier. We looked across and downwards seeing the little farms where oxen trampled grain in circles, pitchforks, haystacks and single wooden ploughs were in action in the small fields which from here look ridiculously tiny. Very medieval, hands-on, calm. The grain is teff here which is a low-lying crop once cut is dried on raised haystacks or roofs, then all covered with thorns to protect it from animals. It is this grain they rely on for their staple injera and which in times of drought causes Ethiopians to starve. Today I have seen small deer, chipmunk-squirrels jumping about, eagles, vultures, falcons and numerous small birds of all shapes and colour.

Finally clambering up into the circular church tunnel into the mountain was well worth the effort. It really was incredible. Huge, completely decorated high arched chapels and a curtained Holy of Holies within. The wall paintings were beautiful, bright and depicting many Bible stories. The one of the weeping Mary with her Ethiopian style very wide eyes will always be in my memory. We descended steadily without any problems but back at the car, my guide had a lot of hassle from other kids over the tip I had given him! Then goodness knows how we did that three-point-turn to get back on the track. Barbara had requested we see the acclaimed ancient fifteenth-century circular ceremonial fan – for a fee of course – but again stunning. When folded, it was stored in the huge thick wooden handles but the whole thing opened up to make a perfect round fan decorated with painted saints and apostles and was as big as the priest holding it. How long this will last is a guess too as already it was fraying at the edges and clearly a heavy thing to lug around wrapped in its old cloth sheeting.

Our last stops were at a museum which housed a surprisingly well-kept collection of ceremonial clothing, cloaks, a crown, shoes, plus the religious books. Unfortunately, the last church today was not so well maintained but fascinating with its natural spring in the font used for baptisms. Bats were flitting about too which were amazing.

Finally, we pulled into the Gheralta Lodge to be welcomed with cold beers before being shown to our beautiful rooms. Mine was in the old hidmo single room style (but updated with an en suite bathroom here, however), windows were just open spaces to the views of the plains and mountains beyond and the sunset reflecting all warm colours onto the rocks. Still and quiet, I enjoyed watching families walking home after a busy day in their fields. Following a deliciously simple meal cooked by the Italian chef using local produce accompanied by wine – yum – and I confess two helpings of chocolate pudding, I slept very well.

A fabulous breakfast which I ate with gusto was followed by what proved to be the hardest most dangerous climb to a church buried in a mountain. The route was partly between fissures in the mountain, up sheer cliffs clutching onto small outcrops or using tiny footholds, one area was called the chimney for a good reason, and it wasn't surprising not many attempted this one. The chap with us struggled a lot and we flicked away quite a few children wanting to lead us up there but who somehow, once more, in their flip-flop shoes or bare feet, scrambled up much quicker than we did in our strong climbing shoes! Thank

goodness they let us women in this church although it is not on tourist maps –
after quite a two-hour mountaineering thing some using guides over the trickier
parts was an amazing church at the top all concealed for hundreds of years. Such
bright paintings kept dark for so long; mainly blue and yellow pictures of classic
Ethiopian faces with large expressive eyes. Going downhill is also challenging
and took nearly as long as the climb but we saw wildflowers like gentians and
cute shy rock hyrax creatures too, which were a lovely beaver-sized relative of
the elephant apparently. The usual swallows, butterflies, eagles and vultures
were flying around us of course. How I love these animals plus I saw a rare
Abyssinian hare *so* close.

Lunch was held back for us as we had taken so long on this climb and was
well worth the wait. That afternoon we relaxed completely…

The next day was a bit of a contrast. I mistook the time and was ready an
hour too early which was rubbish as my legs were so sore and sleep would have
been a better call! The car took us to Hawzien village where we were to catch
the bus. So now onto public transport again is a jolt back to reality. Waiting
around, sellers of 'chat' to chew again sold as standard by the roadside to numb
the brain I suppose, kids selling us what were actually fossils but they said were
'lucky stones', then to be rammed into the bus after haggling and finding exact
cash to pay for it. Luckily, my small bag squished under my knees as no, I don't
want it on the roof thanks very much. Apart from the goats and chickens up there,
anything could happen to stuff strapped out of sight. We drove past Negash again
on the way and since everyone was throwing money for the church out the bus
windows, I did the same, wrapping coins in small bits of paper or folding one-
birr notes to chuck away!

Finally, I arrive at my flat to find the corridor lined with benches on loan for
a function, ceremonial grass strewn about and an invite to the christening I knew
nothing about just up the way. I had already accepted the offer of a sausage-fest
tea at Barbara and John's so I attended both. I changed and dived out again to
theirs first. We had great times sharing pictures and stories and chorizo and veg
supper which was fabulous. Afterwards, I stumbled back past the usual bus
station hasslers to mine where I had to go to the christening party – it would be
wrong not to go – so joining the queue for a sight of the baby then chilli and
injera plus their 'tej' honey wine of dubious origin, I coped pretty well! Actually,
the uncharacteristic Ethio family story interested me as the mother was a career
woman and Granny told me that the mother had used contraceptives between her

two pregnancies and now, she was on maternity leave all set to stop breastfeeding and employ a childminder as soon as she returned to work. Luckily, the banging tunes stopped at ten pm so not too bad really.

Rest of the month…

Monday

My landlord called for water rates and his tip for whatever I haven't a clue. I gave him 100 birr which is far too much but I was beyond haggling and he left me alone. Early into the office to find Solomon preoccupied with the new volunteer pair from Israel: nice young girls I am told and yes, he promised to tell me when he goes to meet them so I can catch up and we can share valuable insights. Wrong…he forgot and trotted off on his own, obviously he has a new target now! I wrote my latest VSO notes and prepared for a workshop.

In the local street, I dropped a 100 birr note and an amazing honest small boy picked it up and tapped me on my arm to return it to me. I gave him 10 birr to say thank you. Back at mine I am running my circuits and making progress.

Tuesday

Clearly, I will have to make my own arrangements to connect with the new volunteers but today I'm to visit Atse Yohannas school which I enjoy. I observed a fifth-grade lesson and unbelievably they did not have enough of the new books. I was cheesed off with the students at first assuming they hadn't bothered to bring them in until I spoke to the frustrated struggling teacher who explained there weren't enough left for their class in the delivery. The Head Amanir reiterated this and said there were no more to be had. I was SO angry and stormed straight back to the office to find out what was going on. The manager there was a bit surprised at my out-of-character fury and back-pedalled a bit telling me not to spend so much energy on that school and he had gone onto a supplier who was sending more copies. Yeah, I will believe it when I see it.

That afternoon I needed a break and a natter with other volunteers up in the Castle café where I let off steam. My feelings were numbed a bit by the discussion about the problems for disabled Ethiopians and the hospitals. It seemed the new hospital has a shiny smart new lift but hospital beds don't fit in it. Wheelchairs are in short supply here as are crutches, the few I have seen are medieval wooden ones with padded armrests if you're lucky. The volunteers from the Blind School also have harrowing tales about the lack of fencing and safety around their compound, of rape and misuse, or disappearance of their livestock they keep there to farm. Very sobering upsetting stories.

Wednesday

The office manager has looked at my paperwork. Then I wasted time cleaning my memory stick I used in Solomon's work computer. Unfortunately, he was in one of his touchy-feely moods and I squeezed out just in time! The secretary put Teddy Afro modern Ethio music on the memory stick for me which is a result. My lead manager wants another written proposal done for a workshop to be held in the Atse Yohannas school hall which is another turnabout…no pressure! Weird tea today back at mine of unattractive, indescribable tinned meat stuff, cauliflower and sweet potato. It filled a hole.

Giant flags are being flown but nobody can explain to me why this should be so. The women in the streets seem to be lugging even larger loads lately. They carry big urns or those massive plastic containers full of water as they usually carry their babies – high on their backs, on their shoulders really, supported by their folded arms underneath. Had a bit of trouble getting my flights for the run in Addis next month paid for, I am not using my credit card as I need to get rid of all of the cash I am paid here. That evening I went to a Japanese film festival which was an utter waste of time and I struggled not to find the over the top emotion about pets very funny. Two hours of violins and hilarious emotional garbage, after which I ran home for a pasta tea and Teddy Afro music. Goodness knows what he sings about but it feels good!

Thursday

It's the Muslim festival of Eid and the Addis Head VSO office is shut apparently – two days closure, Barbara enlightens me – but they did send me an email requesting another revised budget for my proposed workshop here which hopefully may finally seal the deal? My office, schools and the post office are open though and a letter from Ruth loaded with cute bits, paper cuttings and a flat small purse: perfect for my ruck-sack. I walked on to Kedame Weyane school with some posters and alphabets for the younger classes. The teacher was SO happy to have these I will put more her way as I really believe it is much better to have these resources in the schools than stagnating in boxes in my office. As I walk on to Gereb Tsedo school I pass a rotting dead dog among the piles of dumped rubbish. Surely the school children's parents could get the stuff shifted? Their children pass by that spectacle four times a day.

Back at the office I had a stilted laugh and chat with the other ladies who came to see me in my room and I shared photographs to explain more about me. I also met a proud blind man, they come in sometimes and I help them negotiate the winding paths and steps. This chap wasn't old at all and shook my hand with his left as part of his right was missing. He told me he is a high school teacher of English where conversation is key, that he had not always been blind but had lost his sight as a freedom fighter. I told him I couldn't imagine what it could be like to have once seen colour rather than to never have experienced sight in the first place. Today he needed some paperwork from my boss so he followed him around connecting with his voice and sounds. As if life isn't hard enough for these people. Yippee, by closing time the manager has finally signed my paperwork. Thank goodness as the office is now shut until next Monday.

Friday

Few shops were open due to Eid and some marches happened in the town with the women walking and calling strangely at a respectful distance behind the men. I did my washing and bedding today using all the water in its usual rotation mopping floors with the last rinse! Running training today was tricky as I experienced cramp after five km but in the end, I did manage to struggle round what I believe to be 8 ½ km. My book, 'My Dear I wanted to Tell You' by Louisa Young is incredibly harrowing but addictive.

Saturday

Walked in the hills today with Barbara and John and two of his workpeople, but as we had no guide and they have a pretty poor sense of direction, we got very lost. Eventually, after tramping around a crazy route for miles, we found our way to the Hilltop Hotel where we had a much-needed cold beer.

Watching the struggling donkeys so overloaded is a good diversion. Usually, it is hay piled so high you can't actually see the animal underneath which I still find fascinating. How do they know where to go? Opposite mine now the extension is ready to paint; the scaffolding eucalyptus poles are being taken down and lugged by poor donkeys to the barbecue charcoal site in town.

Now I know why the flags are flying everywhere: it is 'Flag Day'! The stadium just up the road which is only used on special occasions is packed with children chanting and celebrating. The weather has turned and they get pretty soaked in a downpour, but the warm wind prevails drying it all quickly. Heavy intermittent rains mean no electricity for me so I have to plan around that this long weekend.

It has been an up and down month; the end is in sight but there is much to do. The distance from family is huge and there are changes when I eventually return to face them but I am feeling more able to cope and stronger. Using my painting more lately as a release has helped me settle better between each crisis. I'm hoping like crazy I keep well enough from now.

Emails from home: the family home is sold in spite of the predicted cracks on the outside front wall and damp areas inside as spotted by the surveyor, so we can give the tenants notice to leave in two months, what a relief.

This month I am so very happy too for Tom and Marnie back in Canada – they got engaged! He sent a picture of the ring – good choice Tom; you're amazing and I am sure will be incredibly happy together. XXXX

Eleventh Month

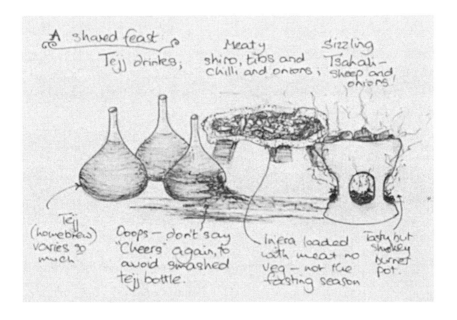

A shaved feast
Tej drinks; Meaty shiro, tibs and Chilli and onions; Sizzling Tsahali – Sheep and onions!

Tej (homebrew) varies so much

Ooops – don't say 'Cheers' again, to avoid smashed tej bottle.

Injera loaded with meat no Veg – not the fasting season

Tasty but shakey turned pot.

Oranges are green and lemons are as well but in Ethiopia they are nothing like limes at all. (Once I had to explain what they were at a vegetable stall to some Chinese people as they were equally confused by the difference in colour.) So that itself has also mucked up organising teaching the 'O' in the English alphabet right from the start! '*I*' is for 'injera' as well in my classes, that big – no, *massive* – round flatbread forever resembling rolled-up pale grey spongey face cloths to me, but there we go. Actually, injera is all right. It tastes a bit sour which is hardly surprising as it takes *three days* to ferment and needs to be cooked in bulk. You see lads delivering this staple food from the central cook-house to the little cafes using the huge baskets balanced on their heads, first thing in the morning. Packed lunches, if they happen, consist of a lot of hand washing before diving into a pot of that day's strange thick sauce using…a wrap of injera! I have been here a while now and still, the office guys check: do I like it? Show us how you eat it, and yes, I use my washed right hand as I should! But they even, after all this time, like to be sure.

This month people are worried about the teff crop for their injera. It grew well enough and was harvested, but during the winnowing process in the fields, it rained. It never rains at this time, not until the April 'small' rains. So, the dried grain got wet and much has been ruined as the correctly timed fermenting process is key. You would think 'well throw a tarpaulin over it then' but there is none of that here, only stones to stop it actually blowing away and thorn branches to stop the animals eating it. It will put the price of food up, the poor will not be able to afford it, 'Food Aid' grain will have to keep coming. (There are other nations involved here for Ethiopian 'development aid' but they have established the growing of *their* crops which are not to serve the needs of these Ethiopians at all, simply their own rice or wheat. It makes me so sad.)

Groups of women walk in from the country to gather by the Mekelle distribution centre to collect their foreign aid sacks of grain: although there is more to eat here than there has been for a long while there is still a need to subsidise some of the staple crops grown in Ethiopia. This they carry back with them to share cooking large quantities in turns in their villages. Kitchens in towns and villages are very spartan rooms with a lot of plastic bowls conserving water, little cooking areas and the communal preparation is done on a central area on the concrete or stone floor. Although modern equipment is becoming more available, local people continue to cook well enough for their needs over a kerosene burner or charcoal fire outside near the house door.

When it isn't the fasting season, butchers kill all their animals early in the morning and hack lumps off by the kilo for the customers from the hanging carcass until there is none left. You could, of course, buy it on the hoof yourself and sort it out back home. I am no vegetarian. I love meat and really miss sausages! But here, I am really put off by the sight and smell of it as I walk by the open shop doors, and knowing that what I would buy is likely needs a gentle long slow cooking for my Western palate – well, meat isn't on my shopping list. Therefore, balancing the pulses, intermittent supplies of other proteins, adding to that dried milk...why does dried milk always taste so strange? My home-cooked diet hasn't been very inspiring. I noted in my diary that I had a great breakfast recently: very weak local hibiscus flower tea bags, plus it took ages to dry-fry the 'toast', then the egg I cooked broke – okay I have to be on the safe side and cook it till hard anyway, but perched on the last scrapings of the Marmite Ruth gave me months ago, it was actually a brilliant start to my day!

Different fresh vegetables from the countryside are brought into Mekelle daily so I am lucky there. However, since the water is particularly unsafe to drink, salads or leafy vegetables and even cleaned fruit can't be eaten unless pealed or thoroughly cooked first. Street food continues to be fresh fruit, nuts, carrots, or sweet-corn which I cannot have unless cooked over a miniature barbecue. Since there *are* cows, sheep and goats, it is a surprise there is little in the way of dairy products. Only one shop in this big town sells a type of Gouda cheese but I feel guilty as I buy imported Dutch margarine, tuna from Thailand and Italian pasta. Cheese triangles have kept pretty well out of the fridge too but again are imported and a rare find. Typical of a developing country, Ethiopia is just beginning to see more of their own packaged foods. These are mainly items in clear plastic pouches and I have purchased local peanut butter and honey, complete with their basic rudimentary labelling, with no bar codes of course. I am now able to be selective about which shop I use for weighing my dry foods, as with experience I have seen whose hands are dipping in, how much dust they are exposed to and how clean the storage area might be from rodents! Then I give it all a thorough wash and looking over before I cook a batch or store it in airtight containers back at mine. Although ground flour is hard to come by don't worry: other types of bread which I have discovered in a few bakers in this large town are delicious and well-cooked I am sure.

One thing I am able to do is collect any packets from my larder and take them to schools where they have nothing for their class 'shop' or maths corner. The small amount of English on the boxes is good for their learning too. Their equivalent of junk food may be a few sweets, and the boys on the street occasionally sell chewing gum pieces, while some shops sell dried breadsticks or crisps – just like those very first plain fried ones we had before the twist of salt was added to the bag! In a country where famine is a reality, it is understandable that the people may be obsessed with eating very quickly and making sure visitors are well fed also at speed. Equally shocking for me, taking a packet of sweets or biscuits from England into the office could lose me my fingers as they rush to snatch and consume them with phenomenal speed. It isn't rude at all; it is linked with life (or death).

Loading up when I go out to eat on either good local meat or forenji luxuries like sausage and mushroom pizza is important. (Mushrooms are not sold here as a rule as they are considered 'dirty' growing below ground.) Regardless of the style of cuisine, it will always come with chillies: dried, powdered, or freshly chopped and their favourite, creamed with horseradish which is seriously powerful stuff. My preferred traditional meat dish is goat or lamb 'tsahali' which is best when it comes in its own little charcoal burning pot. In some more westernised places, it is possible to get chips and they are lovely: freshly cut, nicely cooked, proper chips. The only problem is Ethiopians are not used to preparing them, so if you are lucky and the waitress agrees, there could be a possibility, you have to make allowances when they eventually arrive at the end with the coffee. If I am in family homes visiting, I do my best to struggle through a few injera and try a taste of the four different casseroles on offer but I simply can't eat the quantity I am expected to. Now I have done the rounds a bit where they are familiar with my method and will wait for me to eat as slowly as I do, and that isn't just to remove the fragments of bones in the stews to avoid losing my teeth or worse, but I am in danger of appearing very rude as I avoid being force-fed. Imagine a friendly well-meaning host leaning over trying to push a wrapped morsel into your mouth because this is what they do and think nothing of it. It is hard to say 'no' but they are used to me! When I haven't had the treat of eating in the few places where the food is more my style, I get back to my little electric rings and cook up something from the cupboard to keep me going managing *not* to use the floor for chopping of course.

Overall, this month has been a settled one in schools. The teachers are getting through their curriculum in their chosen ways, struggling with the new English as well as the classroom regular problems: classes of 50-60 are not unusual, lack of equipment around them unless a teacher has made and hung on string paper resources which easily age in the dust and wind; students squashed together onto benches sharing textbooks where possible, struggling to afford a biro, many experiencing shift education with school places at a premium, they just about cope. Many schools lack basic toilet facilities so girls regularly fall behind when their periods begin – but they are often at home anyway when a family member becomes sick which is pretty frequent. Armed with my growing 'dictionaries' of phrases within the new 'English for Ethiopia', I am more able to give practical help to cluster supervisors to hand on. My aim is still to produce one for each level and get them out there with the knowledge now that nearly all supervisors in Mekelle are amazing hard workers, I feel it is worth this effort, writing in a way they will understand, being brief, match the words to the pages exactly so they can find interpretations easily. Then I have to type carefully, get the paper for printing page by page before walking around the city to explain and deliver. I do feel I am getting there.

A typical week this month…

Sunday

I'm laying off oats and porridge this week to see if I can sort out my guts. Oats aren't loose from a sack, but somehow it churns me up I have decided. A supermarket find of pasta which I had for breakfast today and already I feel good. My laps of this tiny flat have now built to 9 km (I'm hoping), which in my terms is ten lots of 450 circuits! Balancing the twists and turns so I vary it on my feet keeps me awake. Thinking ahead, my feet will feel very different as I can stretch my stride on the open path and will not be quite stuck with putting my weight on the front of my foot. Goodness, I hope they don't give out.

Lunch out with Olive, the other 'new' volunteer who still hasn't a flat of her own – I would have gone home by now if that were me still being in lodgings and hotels three months into my stint here. I can't think why there has been this delay as the office is pretty efficient regardless of the problems they face here. The lunch was a bit of a joke, as for a pasta-pizza cafe they had to go out and buy our order of pasta so we were waiting for ages but at least had time for a good natter and made it home eventually before it became dark!

Monday

The office is locked up today. Odd. A cleaner tells me they are out all day. I got into my office and fiddled about then hey presto was invited to the awards ceremony at the Hawelti Monument Hall. I dashed over to the other side of the town and managed to catch three of our office receive awards, so I took pictures. It seemed to relate to civil servants and industrialists, as usual, there were plenty of disabled in the audience. Also, a woman sat on stage signing to the deaf throughout, and there were loads of long speeches microphone-hogging style. As it came to a close, at three o'clock, we all stood holding joined hands high for a stirring patriotic song before we all dived over the road to a hotel for lunch. I was expected to join the group but as the only forenji got shoved to the front in the VIP tent where I surprised them with my eating skills.

I had promised to visit Lemlem school today and managed to whiz over there via the office to collect the new headteacher's stuff. I gave him a special tea towel I had been sent from St Peter's School Sussex, printed with all the children's self-portraits and he was *so* impressed.

Back home, it is the Bonfire Night season. How could I ever explain that here? They would have chopped up Guy Fawkes and fed him to hyenas anyway and certainly would never celebrate as we do in what amounts to burning money every year with fireworks that seem to go off for a long time in November!

Tuesday

In town today I noticed the photoshop people were talking about me and my long linen skirt as I walked by so I popped in and had a fun time chatting while getting my camera pictures printed to give to the office. They persuaded me to try the Ethiopian chewing stick they all traditionally use to whiten their teeth…it is true, they do all have amazingly white teeth. I didn't show my thoughts however when I was disappointed because the stick tasted, well, like a stick!

Had another long parcel ready to post to Canada but again I had to open it up to prove I wasn't enclosing anything weird (like drugs or bombs I suppose), but although sticking it back was tricky, I am used to it now and managed it quickly. With a parcel costing 130 birr when the highest value stamp is 10 birr, it was a lot of stamp sticking: oh, those gazelles jumping across that tube!

However, a lovely parcel from the post office was waiting there for me from an ex-pupil from home today with different food packets and pens which will be great as gifts for my office. A jolly group of men on little stools outside a nearby coffee shop invited me to join them, I declined but they are so generous and giving and I'm sure meant nothing but friendliness by it.

Wednesday

No loo dash on waking today which is a result.

I messaged my programme manager in the Addis VSO office to say following the protocol I would be handing in my notice soon; I think that's the polite way around. Poor chap, he so badly wants me to stay on here.

Fine-tuned my slides for a possible Mekelle Education office workshop.

A teacher called at the office asking for help with what could be a prize-winning project on the new books…sorry mate, that's cheating! I gave him my Bahir Dar paper to read and he left, a bit dejected.

My visit to Mekelle School was very productive. I met the Principal, the local group chap plus the cluster supervisor all together which was a lucky chance. And the library was actually open today so I could see it. Children were in the library for a start, and I arranged with the librarian to call again to help sort it out. There appear to be so many broken shelves, opposite super tidy areas – which to me indicates unused stuff – and heaps stacked up elsewhere on the floor of uncatalogued or dumped books which are a mystery to me.

In the office, the local headteacher Amanir came in asking for more New English books. He had just been sent to their regional office but they sent him back, and all our guys can suggest is he looks again in his storeroom. Such a time-waster which will not help his current mood I am sure.

Thursday

The cleaner lady from the corridor knocked me up for a bucket of water. Luckily, I was dressed, but she took ages pointing at the photographs on my wall trying to grasp who was who in my family. As usual with people who don't know any different, I say my husband is the friend on the pictures and it satisfies them.

Out front, there is a man hacking lumps off trees near the overhead electric wires hanging off a rickety eucalyptus branch sort of ladder. The branches of the beautiful blue flowering tree involved are crashing to the ground so the walkers and bajaj drivers are ducking and swerving to avoid being hit. Flowers here aren't important anyway – unless they're the fake fluorescent variety that look pretty forever and you can dust off.

I have plodded about Atse Yohannas School looking for hidden books, I have now discovered in their original delivery they were about sixty books short, but although the teachers who grabbed their sets first were okay, there were a couple of classes that didn't have nearly enough. As with any resource around here, if you have something, you hang onto it so sharing isn't an option whatsoever, but as I reported this to Amanir he may be able to negotiate a bit of sharing.

Friday

Today I took some of Barbara's visitors to see Lemlem Daero school as they wanted to see a 'typical Ethiopian school'. The guy there never fails: he got the forty to fifty kids up off their benches to do their chanting and staged English dialogue performance, so everyone was happy.

In my visit to another school to observe lessons and give feedback, I discover that they have forty books more than they need and extras for other grades. I returned via the office again to tell the guy who deals with those schools…fingers crossed but they may not agree to hand them over. I gained points however as I gave the office photographs of their award ceremony and they are incredibly pleased. A good result.

I think I may have persuaded the office crew to stop cleaning their ears with their biro tops. That pointy bit is just so dangerous apart from off-putting!

Ayele has replied to my email; so disappointed that I am leaving and telling me he is praying to God I will stay.

My office manager has been off all week now so I haven't been hassled for workshops. Phew.

Celebratory cheese omelette and a doughnut for my tea washed down with gin and lemonade, at room temperature of course!

Saturday

Clothes shopping this morning. I thought I had hassled well for my running leggings but I am told I could have got them so much cheaper. Grrr. Then trying to find Ethiopian sports shirts for gifts back home is so hard. The sizes are very small, nobody here is large! I measured the largest not quite 40" shirt which in their sizes is XXXL and not big enough so got one for myself; XL seems about right for my UK 10.

Sent in my notice to VSO for leaving and booked their leavers workshop in Addis. I'm feeling weird about it but it's done now.

Oh well, press on. I watched BBC's three o'clock football with the three hours difference now it should be a nice early evening relaxation on my novelty fuzzy TV, but again, luckily, the kit colours were clear enough and I got quite animated!

Glad I didn't go to the Hilltop Café last night for drinks with Barbara's group. It is nasty walking back along the road, it's a long way and on a rare occasion, if I am late and alone I simply have to run and hoped for the best. Apparently, their drinks order involved complaints to the manager and a normal late night was very late it seems. Phew.

Ras Tefari's governance of Ethiopia from 1913 has mixed reviews but that name in itself is important around the world. He was the last Emperor, said to descend from Solomon and the Queen of Sheba, but he changed his name at his coronation to 'Haile Selassie', which means 'The Power of The Trinity'. The early part of his reign saw Italy being allowed some foothold in Tigray but their troops moved further south leaving behind stories of mustard gas attacks and horrendous massacres by Black Shirts as far south as Addis Ababa. Since Ethiopia is based around agriculture, the killing of the farmworkers left the countryside in ruins and recovery after the Italians left in 1941 has not been easy. Haile Selassie had been forced into exile for a while but returned to remain in power until 1974, however, a side effect of Selassie's war with a fascist power was to give the Rastafarian movement in West India a cause. Regardless of his lack of understanding of his own people, political troubles and corruption back home, on the flip side Selassie visited Jamaica in 1966 and was treated like a reborn messiah. The Jamaican flag depicts the black-maned Ethiopian Lion of Judah on their red, green, yellow Ethiopian colours. The song by the Wailers gives us some insight: 'Rasta shook them up' for sure at that time! A small village outside Addis Ababa was set up for returning West Indians and African Americans. Bob Marley's widow came on a visit to the capital recently and the trip was celebrated by my office, so happy that a statue in his memory is planned for the city – which will keep the links with Rastafarians alive forever.

Everything is in a rush for the rest of the month. The office managers returning after their unexplained week's absence, plus I am only now hearing that my line manager is retiring in a few days which means a weekend office barbeque. The timing of a barbecue then for me is perfect as I am away in Addis at the run the following weekend. But now suddenly hearing my manager, Gamunzadik is retiring is a shock for me. I tried to talk to him but he is emotional and all I can glean is that it is compulsory to retire at 60, with the average age in Ethiopia being 45, it's a grand old age and the jobs are needed for the young. So, he will be taking all his holiday allowance (such as that is here) and leaving as soon as possible. He's such a lovely hard working, quiet, thoughtful guy; they will miss him here for sure.

After a few days planning visits and workshops (still unfunded and in the air), I hear by chance that the day for the office celebratory lunch meal is not on the Sunday but the Saturday! Luckily, I had bought a contribution of bananas, dates and biscuits which would be usual to eat with the coffee so I took these in when I thought was a reasonable time for lunch. I was too early as the chilli crushing, onion chopping and carcass hacking was still underway on the office floor. There was even a cauldron set up bubbling with stew and a barbecue burning towards one side in there. Thank goodness the usual dust cloths were draped over everything but this time to keep out the smoke rather than the Mekelle dust storms. I watched another pan of entrails, offal and bones being put together and gave myself the job of waving a switch I had sourced from the garden over everything to try to keep the huge number of flies away. When it was all stewed up, everyone gathered to eat including the secretaries, guards and driver, and I made appropriate 'yum' noises as I did my best to gather some food with my injera. I was very good and only had one beer – not the done thing as a woman to be seen to drink alcohol. It was very friendly and a good event finishing after we were well wired with coffees at about three o'clock. The obvious mess bothered me with banana skins chucked under chairs, bones thrown over shoulders, spillages everywhere, I think an event outside the hut would see Ethiopian dogs and hyenas clearing it all up pretty quickly. No doubt the cleaner will have it sorted by Monday afternoon.

I did manage to meet with Gamunzadik as he cleared his desk in a very downhearted mood Monday morning. As I am too petrified to use my kerosene gas burner, it is still in its box, I took it in for a gift for him and he was incredibly happy; kept checking it, making sure I wasn't going to change my mind. Such a gentleman. I really don't care if he sells it on, it is mine to give and the less I have to sort out anyway in the coming month before I downsize all my belongings the better.

The bag is packed for Addis and I have loaded many things I can leave at the VSO head office. The day finally arrived. I shared John's bajaj with its God-fearing driver up the steep hill to the airport, I was sure we wouldn't make the hill, and no, we didn't, not without a lot of pushing and walking alongside, and with a few prayers by the driver of course. Great start. On the plane, the views of the fields below were fantastic so I took some good pictures from my usual window seat. The Addis hotel had no reservation for me. Marvellous. I had booked nice and early so maybe there's a lesson there. Instead of hanging around, I did my offloading at the VSO office and picked up my running t-shirt they had organised for all of us complete with its logo for this year: 'I am Running for a Child', along with our team green cap which could be useful I suppose. The finances by them were all cleared for the medications I still needed and I was able to get a vaccine for Egypt handed over so had that done later at the hospital as well. Brilliant result.

Back at the hotel, I had a brainwave. Here I am generally known as 'Miss Valerie' but perhaps I had been booked under 'McKee' after all. There followed a very odd stilted conversation with the receptionist. At one point she thought I needed ice cubes. Then she said not to worry my friend McKee was already here; sorted! I could relax. I haven't much money left at all so it is really handy having others who are in a similar situation in the same hotel or nearby to chat, walk about or share meals with. At an NGO trade fair, I was able to buy a few scarves for presents and some cute practical carved wooden things or basketry crafts but generally, Ethiopians don't understand souvenirs as we know them. I love my simple mug with its zebra handle and picture of an Ethiopian lion (with its redder mane) made from one small branch. We did go to a jazz club which could have been great if we had been allowed to dance, but we had to sit still and just listen to the great Arabian/Spanish/African mixed sounds.

Sunday morning, I couldn't sleep in, too anxious about the run. Our hotel group left for the VSO office and were first there with the rest arriving at 8.15 for group photos. I did not bring my camera as I am feeling apprehensive about my valuables before I even start. The bus took us all to the edge of the site to begin a few warm-up stretches. There I discover in the conversation that many are not going to rush this one or even run it, so as I am on a mission to do my best, I work my way to the front feeling a bit lonely. The squash was beginning to be annoying and I had to physically shove a kid away from intentionally grappling with my bum-bag hanging on my front and I thought fairly well zipped, flat on my stomach under my shirt with my purse buried in its inside pocket. My hat and flip-flops were safely hanging on either side of my belt and thankful now I have no camera on this trip to worry about. The start wasn't staggered so I jostled away with the hundreds alongside me at a bit of a fast walking pace really, clutching my damp cloth which I usually carry when running to keep cool and the obligatory water bottle of course. The theme colour of green and red this year was everywhere and many groovy young runners had personalised their t-shirts. I was glad I had chopped and shortened the sleeves off my standard medium shirt. After a couple of kilometres, the group spread a little and we were running. Along the way were chanting groups, clown type characters usually found on massive runs like this, great local music, dancing stations, lots of selfie photo stops and at 4 km, a water cannon. My knee went strange at 7 km so I slowed a bit but happy to see the official water station was at 8 km, by then my water all gone and the empty plastic bottle chucked over a bridge in true Ethiopian style.

Three water vans were all parked, handing out drinking water bags, so I fight my way to the first van amid a vast crowd all clamouring for water. I am shoved from all sides and we all have to reach high for these pouches. My head told me to back out NOW and keep safe. It was a terrifying moment and I reversed out as best I could unhurt but shaken. But my bum bag inner zip gaped open and the purse, gone. As a forengi, I am a good target I suppose. Triple bugger.

Feeling incredibly pissed off now, I just want this over with. So, I spurt on and just run pushing myself all the way to the finishing line. The medal is good, but where is everybody? After a while, I spot another volunteer cap and we meet up, I don't know him but I stick to him like glue as still, I feel vulnerable, fragile and exhausted. A pre-planned meeting at a central café turned out to be a good idea and eventually the group all gathered wherein the chatter I realise I have beaten all of them which I suppose is a result. However, I have to scrounge drinks off the others and a bite to eat as now I have no money and Sue, James and I share a taxi back to our hotel – but they pay!

I'm glad I have James there as I feel weak and he takes over the demand for a spare key from the rather too-relaxed receptionist. Typical, my room doesn't have one. He insists they get the manager to sort the lockout and after an hour, he turns up (it is Sunday after all,) so the rest go and get showered assuming it is all okay and there is nothing to worry about. I get teary as it appears the engineer – the guy with a drill – has to be fetched next to drill off the lock and fit another. The receptionist becomes really angry.

"Don't cry!" She's yelling right up close, in my face. "You are not allowed to cry; stop it!"

Blimey, I had better get a grip or she's going to smack me.

The manager is gentle and checked if I was okay; VSO are our family he tells me and there is no charge. I watch out the corner of my eye the receptionist listening behind her desk and feel the prickly growling. The engineer takes another hour to arrive, well it is getting late now. But his drilling skills are dreadful and I would have taken over to fix it quicker myself if I could persuade him to let me. I can't go out until its sorted but have to hang around where the action is as my stuff is in there and these places aren't safe at all. Finally, he fits the new lock and I'm in showering. Finally.

The meal in the Zebra Grill was much needed; the chewy lamb ribs I picked at, nibbling every bit of meat like a starved idiot. But the apple pie and cream afterwards such an unexpected treat and took my mind off the aching knee and events of the day.

The next day, I enjoyed breakfast with Sue as we planned our meet-up for the VSO organised leavers conference weekend. I gave the receptionist my letter of thanks and some money for the lock which, oh dear, made her mad again.

"He said no pay for the lock. You are our family."

But today I feel stronger and insist particularly as I want to stay here again in a few weeks, so Miss Valerie books it there and then to avoid yet another confrontation. The taxi guy felt sorry for me hearing second hand somehow all the hassle and reduced the fare; so cute. These standard Ethiopian Airlines airport lounger beds are a welcome treat as the wait is long for my connecting plane. Back in Mekelle, I am recognised by the taxi drivers now and sharing a taxi with a businessman is easy and so much cheaper.

Retrieving my laptop from under the mattress, I can catch up on emails if the sluggish internet allows, message friends to keep any national newspaper cuttings about the Great Ethiopian Run if they appear there, and feet up, enjoy the original delicious Gouda cheese I bought in Addis for my tea.

Home-wise I have just heard my purchase for number 19 is going through. It has been accepted by the estate agent as they know me and are selling our family home as well…handy link. Poor Jeanne is having to deal with the legal papers as she has power of attorney for that too, fingers crossed it isn't too messy. The old house was sold, then by that afternoon the buyers had changed their minds quickly snatching back a third of their deposit. At least it is rented until the end of the year, but it doesn't release the cash I need to buy no 19.

Managed to get online long enough to sponsor Ella for her 'Movember' challenge! My lovely children, may they always be thinking of others.

Jeanne emailed me this month: Granny is really poorly but recovering in St Neots hospital. Very worrying. Yes, I can stay with them on my return, and yes, they will pick me up from Heathrow. I am so grateful for my amazing friends.

Twelfth Month

Three Two
guineafowl pots

R.I.P☺

First day back after *the* run is an effort but I have to go to the schools I have booked to carry out usual practical help or advice with 'pedagogy' departments (teaching resource stores to you and me), teachers and heads of year groups. I walk very steadily. No rush today. At Mekelle school, even the head Cluster Supervisor is locked out for some exam times the older students are taking, so I take the opportunity to have my impromptu meetings... I have struggled there so don't want to waste my time. They liked my medal as well!

While carefully making my way back, I met a girl from Lemlem Daero school with her mates who was one of the St. Peter's school in Sussex pen-friends I had set up there. On seeing me, she was excitedly telling her gang about my role, very happy. I popped into Barbara's office and glad I did as we are invited to meet the British Ambassador who happens to be in town *the next day*! Sure, I can shuffle my dairy.

In my office, I bumped into another cluster supervisor I know well who was keen to bend my ear on how unhappy he was with the Education system overloaded with bureaucracy, and rather than listen to me, he just needed to sound off. He has 'made plans' but is keeping those under wraps until he is ready to leave apparently. I can now understand the impact of money and donations on how we as volunteers are viewed here. Past volunteers loaded with potential gifts – Band-Aid and so on – have likely had difficult times attempting to avoid corruption or simply being made to hand it over to the loudest or the highest. I am beginning to feel the workshop funding may well be best left at Head Office and my work on a practical level is actually better in the giving and receiving.

Got dressed up the next day for my Ambassador meeting at the Axum hotel, luckily a short walk from mine… I'm still pretty shattered. Ha though I managed a beer in his round. He and his wife were exactly as I would expect and she even wore her pearls! Barbara and I talked a lot describing the education system about which he clearly knows very little at the moment, plus the local life of a child really. As they left, I was handed their bouquet gift as they couldn't take flowers later on the plane: fresh roses sprayed with crazy gold paint that was flaking off in clouds, probably imported from Kenya I thought. I got all glittery just by smelling them! They went off to lunch with the team from Nicholas charity school, but at least we had our say.

Outside in the real Ethiopian world, the weather is unusual right now; rainy when it should be dry and hot. It will ruin the hay and winnowed grain too on the ground. By the time I walked back to my flat, my shoes were completely muddy and needed a scrub, so coupled with no electricity I only had the energy for a snack before bed. However, I did finish the gin, I won't buy any more now as I am counting my weeks left.

One afternoon, I came back to my flat to find my balcony door open and the landlord's son out there fiddling about with the water meter. All the parts were neatly laid out on my table and as it became dark, a relative rang him every few minutes – I am sure he would have finished the job if left to it. He eventually went but as he did so he was telling me a piece was broken and he would fix it 'tomorrow'. Luckily, I had enough water in buckets and pots to last till then. Sure enough, early the next morning he returned and phew, I was washed and dressed. It took an hour to mend and I managed to stop him mopping the floor in the rough vigorous Ethio style – I need that mop to last a few more weeks thanks. Then a worried relative rang my mobile. Strict instructions were given to the effect that what he had done in the flat was not to be spoken about to anyone. If I was asked, pretend I don't understand what they are asking so the less I know, the better, OK? Sure. In a country struck with random water shortages…best not to know I agree.

A Principal from a boarding school for orphans which is out in the wilderness came into my office asking me for help. It is very flattering and I would love to go there so am trying to get the office car to help, but since the office boss smashed up his 'new' car, the only office vehicle is still incredibly busy and there is no way I am going out there alone, even if it is 'only 5 km outside the city' in some taxi or other – much as I would love to see another hyena!

Snippets for this month:

Tuesday

Stuck in my office is a laminator from one volunteer so I have bought laminates for the printed alphabets piled in a cupboard in my office; I intend to give them to schools but they need to be practical. Each sheet costs me a bit but hopefully, I will get some of that back. Think positive: I'm not having to buy the paper piece by piece. There are three large classroom globes stashed too: I have to give these out. Walked to Meiweini and Hadnet schools today who are so grateful for anything. The English teacher in Hadnet is such a gentleman, it is a pity they are not treated with as much respect as they could be in the poorer schools.

Wednesday

Street sellers are now selling what looks like vetch, wild tiny pea pods with only two to three peas in there but they chew on them by the barrow seller and pile the shells in the gutter there, so I tried one today and they're really delicious.

New headteacher at Mailiham school moved there from Kisanet to turn them around. The banter with him is fun and he was made up by the things I gave him. At Alene next door, I gave loads of crayons and a rare find – a pencil sharpener, I know they will be treasured and well used.

Thursday

A booked visit to a school out in the hills can't happen without a lift there plus I don't know how to get there and its exam season about now so could be shut… I overhear the office car is going to the Ayder area which is a way out for me so I get a lift. The old head from Lemlem Daero was so huggy when she saw

I had made the effort to call in! The school is huge with so many children walking for hours to cover the miles every day down from their farms in the hills.

Phone call while there from finance: get to the central office for my pay today, that is *early* this month! I walk back into town to finance to find my mate is with her briefcase of cash. This time she had a cockerel (probably for their next celebration) wedged firmly behind the filing cabinet and the random crowing for 'help' made me jump and laugh in turns.

Next stop was in the bank wanting to check my balance and as usual, here I get shoved to the front being a forenji, but the guy clicks his fingers to get people to move back a little from the counter for me which makes me feel even more embarrassed. It's a bit like when they want to get attention from a waitress for example and they clap their hands, it's uncomfortable for me and rude really.

Back to the office where the secretary Regat invited me to a meal for some saint's day or the other but it is yet another fasting weekend so the biscuits I have are not appropriate. Since she is preparing for her feast and not at her desk, I borrow her computer to type more dictionaries and made great progress as the office was quite empty and peaceful.

Nearly fainted on the way home feeling really unwell yet again. I know the Guardia signs now after three bouts and stopped at the pharmacy, it's easy to buy antibiotics, but four during this year so far is getting serious. I was told I may have to go to an Addis hospital for tests but at this point in my year, that is the last thing I would agree to. I *still* haven't let anyone touch my long hair with scissors or razor!

Friday

Dreadful sleep as my guts are all over the place again. It resembles a sherbet fountain I decided, all night fighting those bugs.

Email from VSO says they have sent the money. Where can it be? I can't find it in my account.

More typing in the morning, a couple of chaps were in there too and at one point we had fun shooing out a pigeon before they locked up, telling me the office is moving on Monday!

Then it was round to the secretary's house. How tiny it is with no space at all to move, there were tents outside and benches where we sat with our platefuls, the whole thing was a bit of a speed-eating event as I discovered a lot were on a food crawl but I tried my best to look as if I was enjoying it and after giving Regat a tea towel as a thank you, I made my way back home.

I left my glasses in the office. They do know they're mine but it's a worry, maybe open tomorrow, you never know.

Saturday

Office locked. Looks abandoned.

Now that I have been paid, I can buy flight tickets with cash which is better although I'm bothered about my Christmas trip to Egypt, the politics and Prime Minister Moursi's problems are getting worse but the tourist coast sounds okay; still, better get insurance to cover myself. Sitting in queues in the Airline office is just fine by me as I am feeling extremely weak.

Following that, I went on to the post office to find two much needed lovely cards from my girls (xx!) plus a note to say I had a parcel to collect. The bitch behind the counter was all smiles telling me to come back Monday as I couldn't have it today…even though I saw the parcel boy who I know well there at his desk. Grrr.

Barbara and John have some lively Australians (oil barons I think) staying as they drive in their beast of a four-wheel-drive round Africa. Their take on different areas is interesting: Egypt = dysfunctional but still good to see; North African countries the best; Ethiopia the worst for begging for money – *in their opinion.*

Sunday

A better night and not quite as weak thank goodness, so I braved leaning over a bowl to wash my hair this morning without falling over.

Marches and flag-waving lads in lorries going by mine, something about Nationalists Day whatever that means, but it is a lot of huge flags.

Managed to climb with Olive propping me up, to the Castle, where we sat talking for hours over a couple of cups of tea and a bowl of chips. The kids hassling us for money got me unusually cross today: I'm just not in the mood. She's off on a trip to the Danakil Depression, we are told not to go there as it is too dangerous but she's still not got her place to live so nothing better to do at the moment.

Monday

No, we haven't moved offices. It doesn't look likely in the near future. Stifled yawn. The office guys are all at a big meeting around the corner which gives me space to do what I want.

My cupboards are still too full of resources. My target this month is just to get distributing as much as I can to schools where I have seen a need and that way downsizing what I have to move too. Perfect. Then I will box all the rest and tape it well just in case they actually do move when I am not here.

Had a productive day at the remote Ayder school too. The meeting went ahead as planned which was great, after which I saw the new Peace Corps volunteer for a while. He needs my help to get started as do all the English teachers. This means now I have met him; I will not have to tramp all that way anymore. Result. But the principal, who I do like, blew it a bit for me by asking me to get her son a laptop! Just like that. Yeah sure, I don't think.

Near Ayder school is a huge orthodox Christian church, where the general public go to kiss the walls and pray. *Poor old woman*, I thought when I saw her shuffling along in a crouching position. I have seen this before where the person just can't stand up due to polio or similar diseases; the shoeshine man near the office is so jolly and happy but is permanently stuck in a squatting position, moving on his feet and knuckles somehow. So, this little old lady wasn't surprising me. What *did* shock me was that she stood up suddenly and I realised was using her long skirts to hide the fact she was having a dump! On my return past the church, I was careful to avoid the pile of poo she had left. Diseases or what?

What a start to the week. A snotty cold has really kicked in today and I feel so dreadful, I just need sleep! Good to feel organised though.

Tuesday

VSO email: a banking error I am told means the money for workshops is in the wrong account – they will correct today; but I calmly sort my response, they had better keep it until a better opportunity presents itself in the new office, I have no time left now.

Went to Mekelle school as arranged and had to be cute and nice when the deputy, who himself chose today for our meeting, had a go at me for not turning up last Wednesday. The next lesson he wanted me to watch was in three hours-time so I had to be creepy-nice, hand him the papers I had prepared for him and simply leave.

Walking the route back to mine via the post office, I collected two lovely presents from friends at home… I will enjoy hanging Sian's bunting in our hotel room in Egypt with my Ella!

The whole month generally has had a pattern, the odd day office closed for no apparent reason, hanging around smiling hoping the manager will sign my 'leaving' forms and purple stamp them, even though I am not doing workshops or getting more funding sent through. One Saturday when the office was properly open, I pretended to be working just so I could keep hinting, then goodness knows why but I actually agreed to attend a meeting, at which I was expected to speak which made them pretty happy. My fame has helped!

I have walked to so many schools which usually are the main ones in their cluster giving my dictionaries when I have managed to print them off, hoping like crazy they will distribute them and not keep them to themselves. I am making a point of telling the cluster supervisors when I have, so at least they know and can keep an eye out for resource sharing which isn't easy here.

Nicholas School was one of my visits too, I have observed a lot of lessons and looked carefully at their library overloaded with a mix of adult fiction and compilations from America. The teachers there are so receptive to ideas and did understand when I showed them some books which personally, I would not want my own children reading; over here some material on sex and drugs is really inappropriate. The compilations are difficult to use if you are learning English but some have lovely illustrations or material which could be useful in other ways. I will get the German volunteer linked with their school on board and I am hoping she can work on that. On my way back, a child walked with me hardly talking but holding my hand all the way into town to the post office. So cute, stuck to me like glue. Jude has sent me a newspaper which is really good to read, but I wish there wasn't so much about how awful Egypt is at the moment, riots in Cairo, all people involved. I just hope my flights are okay. I am scared enough already.

Opposite my flat, the building work has continued and although the shifting of blocks and cement is quiet as they climb ladders in bare feet lugging the stuff they need, suddenly it became been pretty noisy. As the concrete levels are raised to the next floor, they have to knock out the eucalyptus poles and then the metal plates which act as moulds to contain the concrete. The tin plates won't shift without a lot of smashing and bashing, followed by the din of crashing metal on the ground!

The weather here has been cool at night so I have been using both of the itchy VSO blankets, but I need an umbrella against the hot sun in the day. I am on my third umbrella now so there won't be another however bent this one gets in the strong winds. Olive returned safely from the Danakil; the volcanoes didn't go off either so that's good! We have had the odd meal and get together with other volunteers wherever they may come from; there seems a pattern as the younger ones are German. The Peace Corps Americans are all ages and jealous of our VSO pre-placement briefings so they ask us about a lot of small details, although they do seem to have more placement trips and jollies. Some are paid rather well too which to me isn't the point of volunteering but there we go! Meanwhile, there is no sign of Christmas here at all. Ethiopians love twinkly things so any stray found tinsel is up all year round. I have a few things in the flat and am launching into my chocolate advent calendar (thank you, Jeanne, it did arrive in one piece!), but I have to admit I don't mind *not* bumping into the shopping frenzy everywhere as it is in other countries. Paper is scarce so why waste it on cards when you can hug your friends and tell them how you feel?

Back in the office I eventually get my forms for leaving purple stamped plus shock horror, their move could finally be happening. Sorting through it all has been exhausting but at last, my VSO gear is taped and ready. In the central garden, there is a massive bonfire for all the stuff they will not be taking. I just couldn't believe it: Health and Safety eat your heart out! The wind is swirling, as usual, old dusty paper files blowing about, the odd ink cartridge is there, plastic bottles, not a problem. And it's still blazing away as they lock up and leave that evening.

The day to fly to Addis for the 'Leavers Conference' arrives and all goes as it should through the Mekelle airport. I am sure on the plane I didn't mistake the steward saying: "This is how you respond when the oxygen masks drop down from here and here… (Then he demonstrates breathing into the mask.) Please read the card to update yourselves on the rest of the safety procedures."

Blimey! Hope everyone can read! We fly through clear skies past a big wind farm and over the tiny fields complete with clearly marked round shapes where oxen have been going in circles threshing the crops.

The poverty in Addis is again striking, young mothers begging along with many others carrying deformities as I whiz in my bargain blue glossy-painted taxi back to my hotel.

The room they have given me has recently fitted double glazed windows and nobody knows how to close them. As with many new things, they didn't invent them, don't know how they work so they get broken. Luckily, after a lot of pushing and pulling I can get them shut for safety and anti-dust reasons before I lock my bag in a tall cupboard. I can only hope for the best and leave my room to walk to the VSO head office. Jo, the medic, who was supposed to be sharing my most uncomfortable lumpy double bed with me is now lodging with other medics so I am able to select the least lumpy patch of springs to sleep on. Sue is with another group around the corner so that evening after our meal together, I am on my own. I get a taxi the 100 yards back as it is just too scary to walk.

The leaver's workshop was held in the new programme office which was all as plush as it could be, meaty lunch at 'Elsa's' nearby, I have just finished my antibiotics but still have to be off the dairy for a few days to let my stomach have a chance. By all accounts, I seem to be ahead with my paperwork but there is a mountain of it to check over and we need our exit visas – you can't just get on a plane and fly away from Ethiopia. Bank accounts have to be downsized rather than closed, I don't want to leave money behind but only 200 birr is allowed to be carried out the country as well…tricky when a taxi in Addis costs 150, a cheap hotel is 280, so every step needs planning. The course also covered all sorts of different things you wouldn't normally need in addition to a placement debriefing, apparently, a returning volunteer usually finds the culture shock stressful so VSO try hard to make it more bearable.

We are a group of about twenty so pretty much need similar appointments as we go to the Police Station for fingerprinting and criminal checks. By chance, the Dutch couple, Ellie and Rob staying near me are a brilliant force. Some of the group got lost in the maze of offices and we had to find them and get them out! There were four stations, or windows, which we had to visit in turns and Ellie got us through to each with the right paperwork and photographs. Her rottweiler skills got both of them plus Sue and I in and out in ten minutes. Then there was the obligatory fingerprinting, she sneaked a picture of me nearly having my fingers broken by the guard twisting my hands about, but worth it as we could collect our papers *the next day*. WOW! We had been warned that in some cases it could take a few weeks to process everything and a return trip after Egypt could have been very expensive for me.

All the while, the queues were huge of literally hundreds of young girls waiting in lines at each of the four positions aiming to get leave to 'work' in the Middle East. It is so sad and they are mainly Muslim girls who really haven't a clue what awaits them. Their brothers, fathers, pimps were all huddled outside by the walls waiting till they came out holding the correct forms, and l did see many more later at the airport catching flights to the Emirates or Beirut.

At one point, Rob and I had time to have a natter with some shoe-shine boys by the nearby prison, they couldn't believe it that I polished my own shoes! Then they tried to sell us teeth whitening sticks: why do we pay for scrub brushes and foam weird mixtures when a humble stick does the job? On the plus side too, as I had planned in the cost of a couple of extra nights at least while waiting for forms to be authorised, I could now afford to move into a decent hotel for one night and get off to Egypt without any worries about being unable to go home next month. Great! Hot water, a comfy bed with crispy sheets, a decent steak sandwich and a TV that worked.

After a great lazy breakfast, Sue and I met up to catch a taxi for the Police Station one last time to collect our leaver's papers all purple stamped and done. Maybe I will catch up with her in England? Who knows what awaits each of us? Glad I hadn't closed my Ethiopian Bank account as I needed to use their cashpoint and exchange bureau to get US dollars for Egypt.

I didn't have to worry anymore; Cairo airport is out of the city and fine, then on to Sharm el Sheik where I waited in arrivals. I was SO happy to see Ella come through after me. For me, Christmas has always been our traditional family time but I felt I no longer had a family unit, so getting away with Ella was incredibly important. For us both on the plus side the next few days at Sharm would be a mix of beautiful blue skies and seas, diving off boats, swimming in pools and waves, having fun decorating our room Christmas style, gift-giving and great tasty meals, souk shopping and café's with lovely food and drinks – including the 'Hard Rock Café'! On the downside, as tourists, we were fewer in numbers owing to the state of unrest in Egypt, so were hassled like I have never known anywhere in the world before. Some restauranteurs were apologetic realising how difficult it was for us women in their resort, while others and those selling anything were quite rude and very aggressive. It happened absolutely everywhere we went; so tainted going out anywhere really. Women are not seen to be working in-front office so we had to deal with these pushy men and their attitudes all the time. Then there was the final straw of the hotel run taxis back to the airport to depart. Mine was fine. However, Ella's was a nightmare. The driver practically propositioned her, had flowers ready, drove her in a secluded detour. She flipped and managed god knows how to get him to deliver her to the airport where she ran in shouting for help... I have written to the hotel that he works for but I know that is a waste of time. I just am grateful nothing worse happened.

Back in the UK, my friend's cancer has returned with a vengeance. Pat has written to me to tell me herself and I can't stop thinking about it. She has taken the trouble to send me a special book: 'The Man Who Planted Trees' by Jean Giono and in it, she has written a personal note for me about life being a lottery. By all accounts, she may last till I get back but she's really sick. I search for some scarves but they have to be soft and lightweight I think, but bright and fun. Luckily, I got them in the post pretty quickly so hopefully, they don't take too long to arrive. The Christmas post in Europe/the West is likely a problem now whereas here there is simply no change.

Ella sent me a hysterical spoof video of Grandma in her Christmas cracker crown, and Ruth shared the laugh on Facebook which was really funny. I need a lift as I am struggling with an email from HMRC about my tax form, repaying money I apparently owe from the rental income and getting them to understand the old address will not be usable in the new year, and so I am registering a temporary new one, it's a bit of a list for HMRC to get their heads around... I'm hopeful.

Had great Skype sessions this month, including Ella and Ruth, and I am so glad Ethiopia hasn't outlawed this Skype connection as they threatened to earlier this year. Another time I saw Tom too in the Winnipeg deep snow with his dogs. That time he was cheesed off waiting at home for the boiler man to come and although the cat had chewed through the laptop wire his phone was working luckily!

My diary also notes tricky home debates. Grandma's 90th birthday bash is very soon after I get back and apparently, I need to discuss it with her sons. Oh, OK, but not sure how I can make a difference from out here. More importantly, knowing it is going to be a cold winter I don't want the family house left without heating this winter. The letting agents are telling him the tenants are still in there, but Jeanne, who is being an amazing go-between in the village, said the house is unoccupied... What can I do?

Thirteenth Month

Leaving Tigray: hot, dry, dusty farmland, low cloud brown river still flowing...

This will be my last flight back into Ethiopia and that's making me feel weird. As we park at Addis the captain lifts my spirits with: "Well, we've arrived at Addis Ababa where it is currently 25 degrees and if we manage to get some stairs to disembark, you will find that out for yourselves!"

I didn't have to hang around for long before my connecting flight returned me to Mekelle. Landing is pretty routine and all is well at my little flat, so in spite of feeling really rough (probably from aeroplane germs), I force myself to get out to buy my fresh veg and what I *think* is a decent bottle of local red wine – I can't translate this Geez writing at all! – for the volunteer's New Year's Eve celebration. The group for this event is a funny mixed group which includes Katherine, the more recent volunteer. Since she is on her own with little UK support, living in a flat near the town centre, I think she is amazingly brave and does appreciate our teamwork. Out here for the 'Mums for Mums' charity, she has to accomplish lots of hard work supporting the numerous abused young mothers. The girls tend to be very young widows of much older husbands likely from an arranged marriage but who could have died through old age or disease. Since they are not virgins anymore and probably with a baby in tow, they are easy targets for abuse and rape. Incredibly tough. Another American woman I have met here has taken on the role of an Ethiopian woman and traditions, she was a volunteer once but met up with an Ethiopian man and it seems they are getting married soon. Good luck to them both but the culture difference is enormous and I have myself a slight secret doubt about his reasons for making this serious connection…a ticket to the West perhaps? Maybe I am just being mean.

So, we all get together in a house in a part of Mekelle I don't know well at all with the US Peace Corps lot, plus I am meeting up with Olive too who is just around their corner now. The food was great and we had a good lively time. The discussions were particularly interesting too and perhaps in my Mekelle life I have had to be reserved and super-sensitive but I felt that evening I was a bit outspoken – maybe it was the alcohol talking but hey ho.

My theories of teaching art and music went down okay though, few knew it is not on the general school curriculum here at all and I think creative subjects have a vital part to play in education. I know it will not grow food as such, or pump the water from the earth, but we all have different brains and teachers need to find the skills each has to help every child do their best for themselves. Then a big 'oops' as I argued about Ethiopian slum clearance with the architect guy. I believe these people enjoy living in their sturdy one-roomed hidmos which are their traditional houses. Although we wouldn't perhaps choose to live in these ourselves, with no windows, one room, cooking outside, meeting together in groups on the dusty street under the trees, but for us to come into their country and decide they are in need of clearance in order to put the people in one-size-fits-all condominiums, from my perspective it isn't necessarily the right answer. Their houses are really cool (they are beautiful too!), easy to maintain, the cooking outside works well, the clean tidy looking flats I am in don't have constant water, but true the toilets are better than squatting in the storm ditches as others do, but my message is: please be careful. Live with them a bit before you make judgements. Probably wasted my time but I tried.

I did agree and thought more deeply about the Derge regime here as being as horrific as the Khmer Rouge in the Far East: both having fascist rulers and mass killings of their own people. Thank goodness no blood has been shed with the death of the Prime Minister Meles this year. We wrapped it up at 10.00 with Auld Lang Syne using New Delhi time we decided for our midnight!

Great Happy New Year messages from my children: Tom in the morning with one hour to go in Winnipeg and Ruth already there. Ella's was fun too as she is now a godmother to her mate's little girl and was joking about her responsibilities including teaching her how to apply fake tan! XX

As with so many things here, nothing is straight forward for me. The Ethiopian calendar has Christmas (Genna) in early January. It is hot now and we are back to the dry dust-blowing winds of Mekelle. The Western volunteers are still taking their holidays and not always around the town this week but schools and the office all carry on as usual. I am keeping records now of the classrooms, resources given and used, and the libraries where I have had some influence as I am very aware time is running out. Gamunzadik is seeing out his last couple of hours before being forced to retire but happy to share with me this idea he has for a little extra work teaching English to small groups in his village.

The latest forty-day fasting season as a run up to the 7th January celebrations is nearly over and the planning and clear excitement tells me that I have to expect a disrupted school system, random office closures, banks, shops too. In town, I am searching for eggs – true fasting should mean no eggs either – to vary my plain biscuit, bean and lentil diet, while Britain has been feasting: stuffing, cream, wine, puddings, cakes, fridges and freezers rammed (what are those? I have forgotten!).

Christmas here means lots of churches chanting over the loudspeakers, yet another goat or sheep on the BBQ, lots of dancing, plus a weird hockey-style game which they are playing with wooden sticks and a carved roughly circular wooden ball called Yegenna chewata. It is curious to watch and I wish didn't remind me of that Alice in Wonderland crazy game they played with flamingos for hockey sticks. A few imitation Christmas trees are on sale in the few hairdressers' shops. Here they are so out of place nobody would recognise a fir tree anyway and I *have* seen them decorated with large plastic fruits and tinsel – who is Father Christmas anyway? But they twinkle, and they will be up all year round I am sure, gathering dust but looking out of this world!

In this time of preparation, I go to the Atse Yohannas café where I can sit on the balcony overlooking one of the main roundabouts in the town and watch the world go by. I buy their days special: a meaty lunch which anywhere else in Europe I would have sent back but here although it proved very hard to chew, I'm stuck with it. The roundabout has a temperamental fountain in the middle which can actually look good, the traffic such as it is, goes around it in whichever direction that is quickest. By traffic I mean: a few cars, bajaj taxis with animals on the roof or inside, herds of sheep, the odd lorry, bikes ridden with an animal for slaughter on the handlebars or over the shoulder, women lugging stuff on their backs, some men on customised sort of ancient wheelchairs, hand-driven three-wheelers propelled by hand for those with no legs, and the disabled lady I see sometimes crawling along on all fours. The disco opposite my flat is always loud and banging well into the night, so there is no point rushing back for a bit of peace from the balcony with its entertaining views and action below.

On Christmas eve itself, as ever 'family' is really important, so I was invited to my landlord Hailom's family 'do'. Woken early by the irritating 'chop chop chopping' noise on the floor above my head, I was up and ready for the hour's walk across town and I messaged when nearly there for help with locating his house.

"Oh, we've left for my brother's, go there."

Luckily, I know this one as it is near the Nicholas School area, so change direction for yet another three-quarters of an hour walk skirting the northern part of the town, passing at one point over a stinking river where a hyena was sniffing around what looked like a dead dog.

I met the brother and his lovely, ordinary family, ate my meal and the standard three coffees. Hailom then appeared very late, announcing that as soon as I have eaten my cake and puddings, we are off to his house for a meal. Thank goodness the brother vouched for me as I was pretty stuffed. However, at Hailom's I did have to have more coffees and cakes. They all appreciated the little gifts I gave of napkins and pens, I eventually left in a taxi which I abandoned in the town centre to walk the rest of the way as I was completely wired and bloated and needed some fresh air. The street corners are piled high with valuable skins again (complete with skulls and hooves), ready for the skin merchant to buy and take away to be cured. Once the heaps are gone there is no trace at all except blood-stained pavements and a smell that needs another rainy season to shift the evidence.

In the meantime, I have decided to continue with Nicholas School as my main project even though it is a good 50 minute walk, with dipping into my other clusters on the way – if they are open of course since they are all in their 'holiday' mode. Walking about is good now I know I am seeing things with a different eye; will I ever see this again? Photographs are still disrespectful to many. Up near Nicholas was an old woman hand-pressing her cow-pat shapes for drying on the side of the warm stone cow shed wall ready for her fuel supply. She showed me the cow inside, in the darkness, but her daughter went berserk as she rightly thought I was about to take a photograph. Oops. I certainly wouldn't take a picture of the two poor horses shoved into the road nearby, so dreadfully thin, fly-blown and sore.

My meetings with the Nicholas headteacher go well and this month is no different. Tesfagabir is writing a paper apparently on 'time management' and asked my advice on a few points. I began with, "So, where is the clock?"

He is normally very serious but we had a laugh and he writes that down. I agree to give three hours training in their library to their English teachers and any NGO's who can attend – anything to be useful, and they are so receptive plus they do turn up as arranged. It is well worth it. The librarian, bless her, is having to deal with my ideas and she can't be finding it easy. We did have a battle about the shelf of dictionaries. Yes, I admit they are tidy and look organised – *up there*. And they will stay tidy as nobody can reach them. However, she did work hard along with me once I neatened everything up so the overall reorganisation didn't look a mess. I'm knackered but job done!

The two horses are still there in a stinky state of collapse and I pass them carefully to get to the Mercy School, where I spot the two women who have been lugging sacks of gravel on their backs all week to re-surface the road. They have thorn bushes around their schoolyard as well rather than the barbed wire I usually see at entrances, but these thorn spikes I swear are two inches long and I was told they are actually used for stitching! A ten-year-old boy in a novelty high-viz jacket enjoying using his equally rare 'stop' sign is directing traffic to allow students to cross the road but even by Mekelle standards, the traffic is a bit heavy now! That child can barely be seen over the donkeys and their loads!

On the Gereb Tsedo school side of town, there is a clear difference in extreme poverty and all that entails. I wrap my shawl over my nose and feel bad but have to avoid holding hands with a keen child, nor do I cross a field as a short-cut (I have seen what goes on in that), neither do I go on the hedge-side of the path because I know on the other side of that truly is the most disgusting ditch ever. Near the school sits a relatively young guy all bundled in rags, in the middle of the pavement. I have never seen him move and he doesn't actually beg but is always there. Poor bloke. The children have school uniform but it is so incredibly threadbare it is hanging draped somehow over their other clothes underneath. If I can off-load resources there and know they are not wasted, it is a worthwhile trek.

Another contrasting school is Hayelom. It has a shift system so a lunch break for teachers is a change-over. They use 'monitors' but these are just older children with whips. It is so depressing. Threadbare kids anyway being herded by shouting and whipping surely isn't conducive for their learning. The English teachers were pleased to see me and I did what I could in the time spent with them, but it is such a long way across Mekelle for me I simply can't do much there. I feel the need for a lift myself so stop at a bread shop on my way back after that one for a dose of sugar-laden cake.

Barbara and John are away on a holiday so I am able to have their key for fresh garden herbs and a shower there if I need to. John has bequeathed to me his old big sports bag that needed mending and hopefully it is no problem for me to sort. Although it had no handles or shoulder strap, I am using some old belt pieces to fix it as I need it for the journey back to England. The 25-kg bag I came out with is pretty full now! This week I have been dealing with a string of emails and requests from the VSO head office in Addis but well worth the effort as I have tickets back to Heathrow all sorted. Now it feels very real.

Emails from home tell me about the inventory for the final sale of the family home. Yes, I would like the cooker, please. The house still isn't signed over but if everything is in place, I am hoping like crazy it can't be difficult.

Another set of emails tell me the purchase of my little house in the village is nearly finalised: fingers crossed now all goes according to plan. I am very excited about that. Good to have some positivity.

This last month's office work is hit and miss. Open or shut at random times then odd 'important meetings' they pressure me to attend somewhere in Mekelle the next, along with occasional demands from a few chaps there for help with paperwork which is expected to be done in a blink – but my forms to leave, or for my pay, are not so important it seems. I'm having to be incredibly patient and keep my face out there so they don't forget my requests. It involves bursts of sitting about again obviously in the way, and my diary notes that I am often just 'pretending to work out of the packed boxes'. Little extras like trying to sneakily eat chocolate I have been given without being seen is funny and one chap happened to spot me and cheekily demanded it from me. Not likely! But I did go out to get sweets to share with them, but *when I decide!*

Then one day the office is open and I am told, "Wait a minute, the car will take you to the finance office for last month's pay."

Too right. However, bored with waiting for half an hour, I set off on foot and eventually arrived there to find the finance office shut away in their own meeting. More waiting. The queue grew in that time to over fifty workers but luckily when the cashier turned up all grumpy, I was pushed to the front. Was she in need of a calm creepy English face which I decided must be the reason? Possibly, as I was paid ahead of the very long queue. I did feel sorry for the rest but made them laugh as I exited her room, all smiles giving a dramatic thumbs up to the waiting hoard, indicating the delay would be worth it but thinking, *Actually I have just one more of these visits and then I am done.*

Now Olive and I meet up in the afternoons. She also had to rescue me once from a shop all shaken up as I was holed up in there after being followed and hassled badly by a couple of weirdo men. I had dived in the tiny shop for safety, quite shocked and rang Olive to meet me there even though the lads were still hovering about as we left together. It hasn't happened that often but it is pretty scary even after all this time in Africa. Olive is taking over a lot of my kitchen things, plus I can also stay at hers for a few days if needed in between before I fly to Addis which will be perfect. I am giving the lady living with her son in the pile of stones near the bus station some of my clothes. The tricky thing is I can't give her anything too nice, new-looking or colourful as she would be robbed for it – or worse. So it goes here. Kat has some of my clothes she needs now too for her 'Mums-for-Mums' work which is perfect.

Apart from that, all my walking through town helps me buy a few things at the market to take home: woven fans, the odd woven bowl, injera mats. I wondered what they thought of me chasing that amazing iridescent blue starling feather for my collection! Street life goes on regardless of the festivities and the rare, blue, door-less telephone boxes are to be avoided as they are generally toilets although once I did see someone curled up asleep in one! The old man with his switch keeps his two cows neatly near the path but their horns are massive and take up quite a bit of space. Labourers are grading their mountain of stones for a concreting job sieving it through an old bedstead propped up for the purpose. The chat drug-seller is busy as usual, the boxes of fruit are still delivered at the juice bars and the dentist surgery opposite continues to make me laugh as I read the strangely written posters to call in, demonstrating how you could change your nasty brown gappy mouth to the pearly white smile on show, no problem! Pairs of street sweeper women work hard in the absence of actual litter gathering street food remains, twigs and bits from trees, the dustmen all covered head to toe in thick rubberised coats and balaclavas leap out of their carts and pick up the sacks piled up ready. There is just the one set of working traffic lights in this town which holds the bajaj drivers for a few moments and they rev up to compete at such a slow speed, but it's the pride, I think, of getting away first. By the looks of it, this week a couple of zebra crossings have been painted and some yellow lines…what are they for I wonder. Bet you still get run over wherever you cross! Still, they look tidy. I see it now, a couple of women in overalls put rocks around the next patch to be done before getting to work with their little hand brushes and tiny pots of paint to give Mekelle a westernised street look.

Pat has received the soft cotton twinkly scarf and is impressed it covers her radiotherapy hair-loss brightly so wants more…no problem, my friend.

While I am in this dusty heat, the image of Tom in Canada learning to ice-skate is something I find hard to get my head around, it is, however, his local sport and there's plenty of ice, that's for sure.

The African Football cup on TV starts now and my little box has some reception but I'm struggling to get to grips with it all, doesn't seem Ethiopia will do particularly well but they are well supported.

Timket is the next event for Ethiopians to celebrate and feasting happens all over again, lasting three days. The first day's feasting is for one of the three wise men in the New Testament, Balthazar, who was an Abyssinian so the Epiphany time is incredibly special just for starters. Some relate the difference between the Gregorian calendar (set out for the world by Pope Gregory XIII in 1582), and the Ethiopian calendar back to the time it took this wise man to return to Abyssinia with the 'Good News' about Jesus Christ's birth. Others say Abyssinia wouldn't accept the Roman Catholics church decree for the seven years difference on Jesus' birthday. Either way, it is pretty special.

The second day's main event celebrates Christ's baptism in the river Jordon, while day three is the feast of their special saint: St Michael the Archangel. This particular festival is celebrated in the hottest time of the year by the most massive marching through the town I have seen to date. It all seems to start from different local churches gaining crowds as they progress to meet together at the focal point in the town. The throng was actually scary for me that by ten that morning police were stopping all traffic from moving as there were people jostling everywhere. So once again, as there were too many people and I felt vulnerable on my own in that multitude, I got myself up on that café balcony and this time they were better organised with rows of seats facing the roundabout in the centre. For the price of two mango juices, I had a fabulous two-and-a-half-hour show with another great view. It was all white, glitter, gold, fabulous colourful woven umbrellas, red carpets rolled and unrolled for the special priests as the hoards progressed down the street. In the square below somehow, areas opened up to allow circles of men to dance using sticks and drums, and thus take over the entertainment. That in turn then fizzled out early in the afternoon allowing everyone to move off to their different churches.

My last week in Mekelle, and the education office is finally on the move! There is a horse and cart loading the chairs and desks to plod all the way across the town and deliver at the other end so it will take quite a few trips. It all has to go before the office workers relocate there in a couple of weeks. This means some are already setting their work out on the floor and my office floor space has been adopted by a few guys so that's that. I had a visit from a bloke around the corner who wants me to record stuff on his flash-drive – mostly Bible stories which I do not have, so we settle for 'Frozen Planet' which I think should be great for his English language learning. He's far too friendly saying things like 'you are beautiful', yeah right, and I am glad at times like these that I am leaving so I am busy packing in the evenings, sorry chaps. For a few days at work, I have mentioned a Muslim holiday coming up this week and used that to say I need a prompt final salary payment as *I go next week*! I have sorted the figures needed for my final paperwork, written up reports, watched my boxes loaded on that cart for the new office… Then I hear, "Yes, Thursday is a holiday so the office is shut."

The following day I spent standing, waiting, getting my last purple stamp and literally running the distance to finance before the woman closed her briefcase. She was pretty shocked I gave her a little present before staggering back to my office where I am told I simply have to join them for coffee at ten the following day, Saturday. Barbara and John have arranged a Saturday leaver's walk, meal and gift-giving time too. Olive is really unwell right now so I am having to juggle both events and then move out of the flat on the Sunday on my own. No pressure.

Somehow, I had my regular solid fried eggs and dry toast before getting to the office. The bonfire of papers and junk is lit again by the three people there so I mooch about till the coffee is on and more arrive by 11.30. Then SO lovely they had clubbed together to buy me a present of a strange plaster picture of African animals and a painted cloth picture of an Ethiopian woman in full coffee ceremonial costume. Since Ethiopians don't do souvenirs, I wonder where these came from and how much they must have had to put towards it. *So* kind. Another office lady had bought me a locally woven scarf in thick wool which she gave me quietly later, embarrassed, but we had lots of hugs and a few tears. As a freedom-fighter, she had been through so much and I respected her strength too. The manager was pretty emotional and said I was like family to each of them there which means a lot. Goodness, I will remember these lovely people.

Luckily, I had a packed lunch handy as I was late for Barbara and John's and we set off for our last walk together in the hills. Crazy horned cattle, buzzards and vultures all out there along with the beautiful small birds flitting around in the thorn bushes. We followed the walk with a meal at our favourite meaty menu place so enjoyed that washed down with another weird drink, tejj. I really don't want to get to Addis totally sick yet again but had to just get on with it. The event ended with us trying not to find it funny we had smashed the tejj jars together with our 'cheers' and spilt quite a lot through the broken glass. Much bowing and humble nodding as we backed out of that one.

Suddenly, I can't think straight. The house we are selling at home in the below zero temperatures has frozen and suffered a major burst internal pipe. I have been sent reports of ceilings broken down, decorations and walls all soaking. The cooker is swamped. The sale won't be signed over till it is sorted; hopefully, the buyers will not pull out. I can't buy my house now because of this either. My brain is all over the place right now and oops, my language is not great either!

Trying to put my home mad situation to the back of my mind, Sunday saw my last packing and leaving the flat in a well-stuffed taxi to Olive's. We had a gathering at the Castle which luckily wasn't too teary. One volunteer recently arrived has written a poem about me which I will keep forever I am sure. Amazing. I was totally exhausted by the time I crashed on Olive's spare bed trying to ignore the stupid pigeons pecking on the tin roof. The latest presents have had to be packed into hand luggage and fingers crossed they survive.

The flight over very dry golden fields complete with cattle and their dangerously long horns, sheep and goats looking biblical and grubby hiding in any shady tree, sad donkeys, it all was very special this last time. Addis airport was crazy with extra security due to an African conference held in their gorgeous new building aiming to sort out the latest problems in Mali, Kenya and Algeria.

Ayele's meeting was also upsetting and he still is begging me to reconsider and stay longer. In between VSO meetings and final form filling, I am buying scarves for Pat, coping with more power-cuts, ignoring begging texts on this phone which I will shortly dump in the office for the next lucky volunteer winner. Banking means leaving that tiny carefully calculated token amount in my last account here. Then I am trying to get insurance as I discover my insurance runs out at midnight the night before I fly but I am just too late and decide I will just have to risk it and do without. I am exhausted. I simply don't want to hear about the state of the home building insurance as well right now. My cute taxi guy, Tesfai wants to charge me a good price for the airport run so I tip him well, bless him, as I join the queue with the latest mass of Muslim girls bound for the Middle East. Flight instructions: 'Go to Gate 8'…wrong. The lack of the TV screen isn't helping the few who do as we're told to eventually realise we should be at Gate 4. Lots of hanging about and reading 'Wild Swans' yet again, it is a huge book so I leave it in the airport Ethio Book-Bank as I finish it just in time.

Finally:

Landing here in Ethiopia and being whisked away to the Red Cross Centre in Addis Ababa felt as if I was part of a movie and I was in the battered crazy blue taxi seeing the world unfold with the opening credits. There have been plenty of moments when it has been just that, a film rolling with me in it. I have had to pinch myself at times and say: "I am in Africa!"

196

Routines took over, learning to be either incredibly bored or rushed along, trying to fit in but not *so* much I lost my identity, and coping with any weird stuff – from unwanted chat-ups to sickness to water shortages, has pushed me a lot I'll admit. Constant contact and supportive messages from my family and friends have been invaluable. Writing bulletins and my diary too has given me a focus and helped me pull myself together as well.

When I leave this place, it will be with mixed feelings. I still feel very lucky I have been here in Mekelle. It is an ordinary place as far as Ethiopia goes and because of that has been left alone by tourists. People here are open, kind, happy and friendly. OK, I get the odd 'money; money' calls or the 'hey sister…', but if they didn't ask – well they could be missing a chance! It isn't a hassle at all. During the daytime, I am safe and enjoy walking through the cobbled back streets lined with trees and stone houses, seeing real-life horses, carts, men, women and donkeys carrying crazy huge sacks, street cleaner women sweeping the leaves, the old woman in her own stone hut lined with card near the big roundabout draping her washing on the palm tree. There are sheep bleating on their way to someone's back yard, buzzards overhead and chicken sellers. Groups of flip-flopped children play football with stuffed socks, dogs lying about anywhere, tiny shops permanently open waiting for a shout for the woman to serve from the back. Very small children call me 'forenji!' and love it when I shake hands or wave, pool balls click on smart tables hidden away within many houses, men on low stools under the trees enjoying coffee – and the roasted beans-smell filling the air is brilliant. It is in the main areas where there are beggars, taxi buses, bigger carts, a few cars and more bustle. Street sellers fill the pavements with their pitches of neatly arranged fresh foods, unwrapped crucifixes, tooth sticks, chat, watches, electric sockets, socks and underwear; it is all very clean and wares are constantly flicked for dust. Market areas are bright noisy places the world over and Ethiopia is no different. Mekelle's market is relatively new having been recently rebuilt after being bombed but it isn't out of place and has a charm of its own. Town streets have themes: furniture, clothing, sacks or barrows of food supplies and lots of metalwork. Very little is delivered in cars or vans but I have learned to hold my breath when one comes along as the fumes and exhaust clouds are dreadful. Luckily, for the time being anyway, it is all carted or carried around.

I will miss these lovely people. They are living through difficult times and it isn't over yet. Their strength and togetherness will see them through anything I am sure. To us, Ethiopia is a relatively unknown far-away place, mind you, the locals don't know what is really going on either; directives from the Party or Government are obeyed and cover-ups abound, but we don't ask and life in general struggles on. Only the very young families do not fully know the realities of war: division, hardship, disability or death. There is the everyday sadness too which they don't notice at all. For me, it is painfully clear: if it can't be eaten or do a job of work, then it is a waste of space. Development is happening and I really hope Ethiopians keep their character. At the moment there is no litter really – there are bins but having little packaging or goods that aren't functional or edible means there isn't the rubbish to deal with. Bottle tops are counters and phone credit cards play money in schools; everything has its purpose or it simply isn't here. There are no card shops, no post boxes and every precious sheet of paper or envelopes being sold individually. In the Education office, life will go on. Biros and notepads will be kept locked away, computers will still be a novelty but the TV will go on from time to time for the news or traditional very Ethiopian background music. I hope and think I have made a difference and the schools and teachers I have been able to support will remember 'Miss Valerie'. Education here is improving at such a rate that it will continue to be difficult for teachers to keep up with the changes for a while yet. I shall be watching progress with great interest back in England.

The flight back is smooth via the River Nile strip up to flat sandy Cairo. The airport easy, and luckily, I am used to waiting by squatting on marble floors but being unable to recline my seat on the next international night flight isn't a great experience! However, as I am just so excited about being in Great Britain again, as ever, I cope.

Ethiopia is a fantastic mysterious big country with an incredible history. There are African wild beasts and varied landscapes with mountains and lakes and open plains. Everything feels different and the people who make the place are both beautiful and amazing. Although I know Ethiopia has to join the developed world somehow, I hope it does not lose its individuality and uniqueness. When I finally land in my homeland, how I will be feeling? Quite likely very sad, but excited to be 'home' again – which I shall appreciate even more…

Heathrow airport reminds me how far ahead we are technologically and I switch into Western mode, collect my baggage from the correctly designated carousel, walk the long sparkly air-conditioned corridors through customs and out into the grey terminal to be greeted and hugged by my friend Jeanne. *Roll the credits!!!*

Post Script one week on

- I realise I have talked like an express train to everyone, and it took me a few days to calm down.
- There is a big worry I am putting on my friends too much, I am not in good health and clearly thinner than I was. I have to see the doctor.
- I have found the technology all around me from the basic street lights to hospital advances and motorway signage, all taken for granted here and so shockingly different. I marvel at it all as I drive around.
- It is thrilling to see rain, clouds and skies everchanging, catkins on the trees, snowdrops pushing through in gardens. So beautiful.
- There became a need for quiet times to myself to reflect and to try not to be miserable. I have no right to be down. Anyway, there is a job to seek, clothes to buy plus a car and a house!
- I am worried about the many next steps I have to take.

And finally

- The house sale finally went through a year and a day after it was put up for sale, and with the help of my friends, I have managed to buy my little house with its garden.
- Out of retirement, I am a part-time teacher with time to enjoy seeing my families – wherever they are in the world.
- There was thankfully a good hand-over to Hailemariam Desalegn as Prime Minister after Meles Zenawi died in 2012. Then in 2018, Abiy Ahmed was elected and hopefully has made peace with Eritrea for which the Nobel Peace Prize was awarded him in 2019: a fantastic step in the right direction.
- VSO is still active and making amazing progress supporting their countries in need.